The Reference Library
of Jewish Intellectual History

ACADEMIC
STUDIES
PRESS

JEWISH PEOPLEHOOD

Change and Challenge

Editors:
MENACHEM REVIVI, EZRA KOPELOWITZ

Boston
2008—5768

Library of Congress Cataloging-in-Publication Data

Jewish peoplehood : change and challenge / editors, Menachem Revivi, Ezra Kopelowitz.
p. cm.
Includes bibliographical references and index.
ISBN 978-1-934843-24-6
1. Jews—Israel—Identity—Congresses. 2. Jews—United States—Identity—Congresses.
3. Jews—Israel—Politics and government—Congresses. 4. Jews—United States—Politics and
government—Congresses. 5. Israel and the diaspora—Congresses. 6. Judaism—21st century—
Congresses. 7. Israel—Ethnic relations—Congresses. 8. United States—Ethnic relations—
Congresses. I. Revivi, Menachem. II. Kopelowitz, Ezra.

DS143.J458 2008
305.892'4073—dc22
        2008030826

Department for Jewish Zionist Education

www.jewishagency.org

www.ujafedny.org

ISBN 978-1-934843-24-6

Book design by Batsheva Levinson

Published by Academic Studies Press in 2008
28 Montfern Avenue
Brighton, MA 02135, USA
press@academicstudiespress.com
www.academicstudiespress.com

We wish to express our acknowledgement to the following authors for their distinguished contributions to this collection:

Yonatan Ariel
Ami Bouganim
Arnold Eisen
Laura Geller
Michal Govrin
Moshe Halbertal
Ezra Kopelowitz
Riv-Ellen Prell
Michael Rosenak
Shmuel Trigano
Michael Walzer

We wish to acknowledge thank the Partnership that brought them together to deliberate and produce this publication, for their generous assistance:

The Department for Jewish Zionist Education,
The Jewish Agency for Israel, Director General Alan Hoffmann,
and UJA-Federation of New York, John Shapiro, President;
John Ruskay, Executive Vice President and CEO

We also wish to acknowledge the dedicated work of:

Ilana Kurshan, Abstractor and Manuscript Editor
Gila Ansell Brauner, Manuscript and Publishing Editor
Neta Katz, Research & Development Unit Project Director
Sagir Ltd. Translations

Contents

PREFACE

JOHN S. RUSKAY

This volume had its genesis in recent endeavors to create and foster initiatives that strengthen the understanding of collective Jewish identity, in order to address changes that have been in the making for quite some time—at least since the beginning of modernity. As we live today in the most open and accepting period of history in which Jews have ever found themselves, we find we are no longer held together as a people by external forces. The question of how to build and foster a sense of collective identity poses therefore one of our most salient contemporary challenges—one that the Jewish federation system has begun to confront. It is the evolution of our response to this challenge that I will trace here, in an effort to explain just how and why *Jewish Peoplehood* became an explicit part of the mission of UJA-Jewish Federation of New York over the past decade.

In New York, as in virtually all North American Jewish communities, "federations" were the result of a merger between the older long-established Federation—created in the early decades of the 20th century in response to the challenges posed by waves of immigration to the shores of North America—and UJA—which had been created in the mid nineteen thirties to provide essential funds for rescuing Jews from eastern and Central Europe and bring them to Mandate Palestine, as well as to support the pre-state state-building enterprise underway in the small Jewish community of the Yishuv.

The historic challenges that confronted world Jewry after World War II provided the context and the impetus for the emergence of the North American Jewish Federation system as an unparalleled philanthropic and communal enterprise. The challenges facing world Jewry produced an overarching agenda: building and defending the Jewish state; rescuing Jews throughout the world; and combating Anti-Semitism wherever it reared its head. For many Jews in North America, giving to their UJA-Federation campaigns was a natural channel for the expression of their sense of Jewish Peoplehood; it was their best way to become part of the grand plan of building the Jewish future. Following the most devastating era of Jewish history, our continued perception of vulnerability created strong group cohesiveness and a recognition of interdependence which made real the slogan, "We are one."

From the period of the creation of the State of Israel until the early 1990s, the tasks before us as Jews made constant demands on our attention and required massive resources. The fall of the iron curtain in the former Soviet

Union required mobilization and focus, in order to help resettle millions of Jews: Jews from Ethiopia, Syria, Yemen, and other countries who needed help finding their way to successful lives in Israel. Once again, Jews felt a sense of unity through a shared mission.

In the past decade, Jewish demographics have changed dramatically— 85% of all Jews reside in two centers of Jewish life (Israel and the United States). With most Jews living where they want to be, the age of rescue is coming to an end. Now that the external threats to us as a people are on the wane, our gaze shifts inward. Recently, as the existential threats to Israel were perceived to be substantially reduced (a temporary phenomena, to be sure), increasing numbers of observers have begun to raise a series of questions:

- At a time when the external threats to our people appear to have abated, what will ensure a sense of collective solidarity and cohesiveness among and between Jewish communities?
- How will collective Jewish identity and responsibility be strengthened, at a time when the Jewish agenda—certainly in North America—has shifted increasingly towards matters of strengthening individual Jewish identity?

With external threats in decline, heightened divisions along religious and ethnic lines are increasingly challenging the notion of *Am echad*: one people, with a shared history and shared destiny.

It is in this context that UJA-Federation of New York, North American's largest Jewish Federation and the largest community-based philanthropy in the world, undertook a major reorganization in 1999. While the reorganization focused on many dimensions not relevant to this volume, its point of departure is highly germane.

Although UJA-Federation was the product of the merger of UJA and Federation in 1985 (and parallel mergers took place at different times in the various North American communities), vestiges of the pre-merger distinctions still lingered. Specifically related to this volume: prior to 1999, the divide between "*overseas*" and "*domestic*" in terms of assets, allocations, and leaders was clearly discernable. By the last decade of the 20th century, many leaders and observers—certainly in New York—had come increasingly to regard this distinction as anachronistic, reflecting an earlier period of Jewish history. Said differently, in an increasingly global society, they recognized that Jews are part of a global Jewish People and that those who care about Jews and Jewish life in New York are similarly concerned about the health and welfare of Jews and Jewish communities in Tel Aviv, Moscow, and Buenos Aires. Hence, the reorganization mandated that UJA-Federation conceptualize its role in the world and set out to actualize its mission globally.

This reorganization also mandated a reorientation of UJA-Federation planning. We had to redefine our mission: no longer were we concerned about saving Jews from persecution: our mission was now about strengthening Jewish communities by promoting caring, deepening individual Jewish identity, as well as fostering a sense of collective responsibility, and ensuring a safety net, for acting in times of crisis through a network of agencies that span the globe.

This conceptual rethinking necessitated a structural reorganization. We created three mission-based commissions:

One for *Hesed*: the human service and caring agenda—recognizing that in voluntary Jewish communities, acts of *Hesed* have the power to reinforce community.

The second for *Hinuch*: the Jewish identity and Jewish education agenda.

And the third, named aptly, *The Commission on the Jewish People*—was a commission whose mission provides the impetus for the writing of this volume.

Charged to forge an overarching vision and set of strategies to guide the Federation's global planning in several broad areas, this commission was created with a duality in its role and mission, on behalf of all our people, from today into the future. First, it was to provide oversight for UJA-Federation planning related to *aliyah* and *klitah* which, it argued, would only be significant for those with high levels of commitment to *klal Yisrael*. Second, it called for UJA-Federation to enter the "glue" business, developing strategies and supporting initiatives that could reduce division and enhance integration between the prime divisions in Jewish life: geographic, religious (denominational), and ethnic. The commission thus called for strategies to enhance Ethiopian Jewish integration in Israel, Russian Jewish integration in New York and Israel, and towards an increased understanding and appreciation for the rich diversity of our people. Finally, it also developed initiatives designed to strengthen identification with and responsibility for other Jews throughout the world, i.e. collective Jewish identity.

It was this last challenge—to develop initiatives with the purpose of study-ing collective Jewish identity—which led to this volume. In its early years, as it sought to understand what was then a new mandate—Jewish Peoplehood—the leadership of the Commission came to recognize that there was no existing curriculum in the Jewish world, formal or informal, that had the explicit goal of strengthening Jewish Peoplehood, a term used to refer to identification with, commitment to, and responsibility for Jews throughout the world (*aka*, collective Jewish identity).

Thus began a journey which first led to discussions with the Jewish Agency leadership—Sallai Meridor and Alan Hoffmann—and the Ministry of Education in Israel, which led, in turn, to the understanding that if a curriculum were developed, the Minister of Education would agree to have it tested in the Israeli 6th grades; and the Director General of the Education Department of the Jewish Agency would agree to integrate such a curriculum into the preparatory program for the 1,400 *shlichim* who travel each summer to work in Jewish summer camps in North America and the Former Soviet Union.

Far more was needed—further consultations with summer camp directors and those responsible for curriculum in the Israeli public school system. But those heading up this endeavor recognized that the development of pilot curricula required a shared understanding of the elements of Jewish Peoplehood in the first decade of the 21st century. It is this recognition that led to the commissioning of the review on the papers appearing in this volume, and which served as the basis for a consultation in Israel to review and discuss them. Each of the articles here seeks to deepen our understanding of the contemporary understanding of the concept of Jewish Peoplehood during the first decade of the 21st century, so that it can provide a platform for the next stage of this initiative: the development of curriculum.

In conceptualizing curriculum, it is critical to be cognizant that we live in a new global context, both in the Jewish world and beyond. It is precisely in this frame of reference that we have so much to learn together about how to maintain the unique nature of Jewish life and the Jewish People which have, in different contexts: shared history, shared texts, and continue to share destiny. And it is this commitment to deepening our understanding about the challenges and opportunities that face us as a people that led us to reorganize and, as one element of that, brought us to this volume. May it promote reflection, discussion, and debate which will both deepen our understanding of Jewish Peoplehood and enable us together to seize an extraordinary moment in the history of our people.

Dr. John S. Ruskay
Executive Vice President & CEO
UJA-Federation of New York
March 26, 2008

EDITORS' NOTE

MENACHEM REVIVI, EZRA KOPELOWITZ

This book represents a dedicated endeavor to create an in-depth, scholarly response to the question: "*What is Jewish Peoplehood, and how might Jewish organizations consciously promote the connection between individual Jews and the Jewish People?*"

That this collection is a first attempt of its kind by intellectuals to address the question of "Jewish Peoplehood" should be regarded with surprise. After all, "the Jewish People" is an ancient idea and intellectuals have been pondering the nature of Jewish identity and belonging for centuries. However, as we wish to demonstrate in this foreword, the current usage of the term "Jewish Peoplehood" is very recent. This book is part of a wave of interest in the concept that constitutes, in itself, an innovation in both the English and Hebrew languages, as well as in the world of Jewish organizations.

This foreword describes the background story leading up to the publication of this book. We also look at how the particular story of this book falls within the larger story of the Jewish People in contemporary times, one which is generating an evident need to explore and reflect on the concept of Jewish Peoplehood.

Thinking and Doing Jewish Peoplehood

Whereas, prior to 2000, "Jewish Peoplehood," as a term, was rarely employed by Jewish organizations or intellectuals, today it is a central concept in the strategic planning of an increasing number of leading Jewish organizations. Conferences are being held about this concept and books are being written. Funders are allocating increasing sums of money to programs that adopt the Jewish Peoplehood concept, while leading Jewish organizations are drawing on Peoplehood as a central organizing concept.

At the time the chapters of this book were being written there was no serious body of intellectual work to match the increasing interest by Jewish organizations in the Peoplehood concept. Since 2006, two magazines have dedicated issues to the topic of Jewish Peoplehood, a position paper providing an overview of the field has been published, and there is the forthcoming publication of a volume titled, "Conversations about Jewish Peoplehood."[1] The lack of an intellectual body of work, however, has led to growing gap between the applied use of the Peoplehood concept and the philosophical and sociological content of the term. To our dismay, we often hear our colleagues who are Jewish professionals state: "Our organization is committed to promoting Jewish Peoplehood, but we really aren't sure what Peoplehood is, or if the concept is really useful at the level of programming." We hope that after reading this book, you will agree that there is a world of content to the concept of Jewish Peoplehood.

In the ideal, frameworks should exist to bring the practical work of building Jewish Peoplehood into the same enterprise as those intellectuals who are thinking and writing about Jewish Peoplehood. However, to our chagrin, the worlds of "thinkers" and "doers" remain for the most part separate from one another. It is our concern that this book will be read, debated and mulched not only by other intellectuals, but also by those decision-makers and practitioners who are building Jewish Peoplehood on a daily basis in the worlds of culture education, media, politics, religion and elsewhere. Beyond that, we also wish to see a more sustained attempt to initiate discussions about the nature of Jewish Peoplehood, outside of intellectual gatherings and closer to the action of everyday life.

The process leading to the conference at which most of the papers in this book were presented was, in itself, an attempt to combine thinking with doing. The goal of the conference and the resulting book is to map out pathways for building Jewish Peoplehood. Each chapter in this book offers a different entry into the topic, with alternative worlds of content and cultural assumptions about the nature of the beast.

The conference was held at the initiative the *Israeli American Jewish Forum*. The *Forum* was the brain child of Marvin Lender (a prominent American Jewish lay leader) who, with Yossi Beilin (a prominent Israeli politician), created in 2000 a framework to facilitate dialogue between American and Israeli Jewish leaders. The *Forum* aimed to open communication and dialogue among key decision-makers and community leaders, including leading political figures, business people, philanthropists and scholars from Israel and the United States.

In 2003, the Forum initiated "the Jewish Peoplehood Project," with the UJA New York Federation and The Jewish Agency for Israel acting as co-sponsors. Marvin Lender and Dan Meridor were active in the process on behalf of the

---

[1] Beren, Susan. 2006. *Shma* Magazine issue on "Peoplehood and Justice" <http://www.shma.com/oct_06/archive.phtml>. Contact Magazine issue on "Jewish Peoplehood: What Does it Mean?" <http://www.jewishlife.org/pdf/spring_2008.pdf>; Kopelowitz, Ezra and Ari Engelberg. 2007. "A Framework for Strategic Thinking about Jewish Peoplehood," Tel Aviv: The Nadav Foundation; Galperin, Mikhail D. Conversations about Jewish Peoplehood, forthcoming.

Forum; John Ruskay and Alan Hoffmann respectively represented the UJA New York Federation and the Education Department of The Jewish Agency; Menachem Revivi coordinated the project on behalf of the Forum. As described by Ruskay in the Preface and Hoffmann in the Afterword to this book, the Peoplehood project is also situated within the matrix of additional discussions and strategic planning processes taking place in Israel and the United States.

The cornerstone event in the life of the Jewish Peoplehood Project was a conference in July 2005, in Israel, at which most of the authors who appear in this book contributed early versions of what became the book's chapters. Ezra Kopelowitz was charged, with the assistance of Neta Katz, at the Research Unit of the Department for Jewish Zionist Education of the Jewish Agency, to oversee the logistical and intellectual framework required for getting the process and resulting book off the ground.

The *Israeli American Jewish Forum* disbanded in 2006 and, with that, this particular phase of the Peoplehood project came to its conclusion. At this time, the UJA New York Federation and the Jewish Agency continued with the development of the next stages, as described in the Preface and Afterword to this book by John Ruskay and Alan Hoffmann, respectively.

The unique think tank and dialogue that the *Forum* sought to promote are now embodied in this book. In the same way that the various partners sought to bring a broad variety of Jewish leaders to a common table, so the process leading up to this book brought into a common discussion Jews from different backgrounds—Americans, Israelis and a European, from secular, traditionalist and different religious backgrounds. The outcome is Peoplehood in action. In order to think Peoplehood the conference upon which this book is based needed to do Peoplehood. Each author brings to the table a perspective grounded in the national, cultural and ideological background from whence he or she comes. The resulting meeting allows for a much broader intellectual horizon than could otherwise be attained. On one hand, as you read the chapters, a common set of themes emerges. These themes are addressed by Arnold Eisen in his keynote chapter. On the other hand, these common themes are taken in very different directions by each author, creating a intellectual experience of Jewish multi-culturalism par excellence.

A New Concept

We will leave the work of framing the intellectual content of the book to the keynote written by Arnold Eisen. Here, we want to take a step back and look the historical significance of this book. As we stated above, while the idea of "the Jewish People" is ancient, the concept of Jewish Peoplehood is new, both to the English and Hebrew languages. The significance of this book is that it aims to imbue this fledgling concept with intellectual content.

A search of major English language dictionaries conducted by a columnist in the "Jewish Forward" showed that, prior to 1961, the word "Peoplehood" did not appear in any of them.[2] The author shows, for example, that in the 1969 edition of the "American Heritage Dictionary of the English Language," "peoplehood" does not appear—whereas the word does appear in the 1992 edition. There, the concept was defined as follows: "Peoplehood: The state or condition of being a people or one of a people: 'As symbols go, few are as national and sectarian as the menorah. It is the symbol of Jewish Peoplehood'."

The first significant use of the Peoplehood concept that we are aware of was by Mordechai Kaplan (1959). In this volume, Ami Bouganim notes that prior to 1954, Kaplan used the term "nationhood" or "civilization" to describe the Jewish collective.

In 1954, however, Kaplan feels the need to qualify the comments he made in 1935...Kaplan rejects the concept of nationhood, offering in its place the concept of Peoplehood. In the preface to a new edition of his book *Judaism as a Civilization*, he writes: "The concept 'nationhood,' as applied to the Jews, has come to be closely identified with statehood, and was, therefore, in need of being replaced by the concept 'Peoplehood'."[3] In a series of articles written after the establishment of the state, Kaplan frequently used the term Jewish Peoplehood. (Quoted from Bouganim, in this volume, pp. 84–85.)

Like the contemporary intellectual who is interested in the Peoplehood concept, Mordechai Kaplan sought a term that would allow him to describe the complex nature of Jewish belonging as he perceived it in post WWII America. However, it seems that, apart from Kaplan, there was no other sustained intellectual focus on the Jewish Peoplehood concept in the United States until after 2000.

Interest in the Peoplehood concept among Israelis is even more recent. In 2003, a group of Israeli educators requested permission from *The Academy of the Hebrew Language*,[4] to use the term "*amiut.*" They posited that existing Hebrew concepts, such as "*clal yisrael,*" were too closely tied in to the Jewish religion in the minds of non-religious Israelis and that a term was needed that would capture the idea of belonging to the Jewish Peoplehood in a manner transcending religion. A representative of the Academy answered the query of Kopelowitz and Engelberg as follows: "The Academy did not approve the word Amiut. The reason for the negative response: Not every English word should occasion the creation of new words, when there are already existing words in Hebrew that can be used."

---

[2]   Halkin, Hillel. "Peoplehood from the Jews?", in the *Jewish Forward*, June 11, 200 www.forward.com/articles/58274/

[3]   Kaplan, Mordechai. 1967 (1937). *Judaism as Civilization*, New York: Schocken Books., p. IX.

[4]   The official body charged by the State of Israel with creating new words for the Hebrew language.

Only time will tell if a new word to describe Jewish Peoplehood will gain official sanction and/or widespread use in Israel. However, it is clear that, prior to 2003, no one felt the need to create a Hebrew word for Jewish Peoplehood, and that there are those who are now pushing for a change. Why now? Why the need among some Jewish organizations and intellectuals for a new concept to describe the sentiment of belonging to the Jewish People? And what is the significance of the interest in the Peoplehood concept in this first decade of the 21st century?

The Decline of Jewish Ideologies

The intensive use by Jewish organizations of the Peoplehood concept and intellectual interest in the topic in almost all cases began no earlier than 2000. At this point in the paper, it is sufficient to note that major organizations, such as the United Jewish Communities, the UJA New York Federation, the Jewish Agency for Israel, the Israel Ministry of Education, the Diaspora Museum, the Avi Hai Foundation, the American Jewish Committee and many other smaller organizations are either adopting the Peoplehood concept as an organizing principle in their organizations, or initiating high profile programming with an explicit focus on Jewish Peoplehood—all since 2000.

The thesis we wish to develop here is that the sudden take-up of the concept of Jewish Peoplehood by Jewish organizations stems from an ideological vacuum that developed in both the United States and Israel[5], beginning in the 1970s, but whose impact is only now being felt.

"Ideology" denotes "an organized framework for making life meaningful." "Why is it meaningful to live a Jewish life?" *The answer to this question, when it is organized and propagated by organizations, is always ideological.* The question is: <u>which</u> ideology and <u>what</u> are its characteristics? Major Jewish ideologies over the past two hundred years include variants of Zionism, religion, liberal humanism, and socialism, *inter alia*. The answers provided to the questions of Jewish meaning by the 19th and 20th century ideological movements no longer capture the imagination of large segments of Jewry. The outcome has presented a serious problem for the leadership of Jewish organizations. Whether for fundraising, communal, educational or political work, all these organizations need to provide a convincing rationale for their actions or, over time, they will lose members and resources. Within this reality, the idea of Jewish Peoplehood is viewed as a possible avenue for organizations to reach out to their constituents.

---

[5] We are focusing on Israel and the United States, as this is where the Peoplehood discourse has taken off.

Jewish Belonging is No Longer Obvious

Jewish emancipation marks the entrance of Jews into the modern era and is a significant landmark for understanding the significance of the current use of the "Jewish Peoplehood" concept. Emancipation refers to the granting of citizenship rights to Jews—a process that began at the end of the 18th century in France, subsequently spreading across Europe over the course of the 19th century.

The granting of citizenship rights offered Jews the opportunity to leave the organized Jewish community (the *kehillah*) and create alternative communal frameworks, or simply leave Jewish life all together. Most importantly, emancipation created the need for all Jews to ask questions like, "Why is it meaningful to live a Jewish life?" "Why should I remain part of a Jewish community?" Prior to emancipation, most Jews did not think to ask or address these questions, as the State mandated their membership in a Jewish community. Only with the "right to leave" does a Jew need to ask: "Why should I stay?"

Emancipation also brought a shift in the paradigms used by Jews to describe one another. Previously, Jewish belonging was organized by geography (e.g., Litvak vs. Galicianer). In the post-emancipation era, Jews began using labels like "Zionist," "Socialist," and "Religious," as well as variants within each category, to describe themselves and others. Each of these labels drew on an ideological framework for answering the question: "Why is it meaningful to continue to live a Jewish life?"

Despite the need to ask: "Why be a Jew?", for those who opted to remain within the Jewish community, the ideological frameworks provided by the various movements continued to provide compelling answers through the 1960s. Regardless of differences between the ideological movements, their adherents took it for granted that they offered convincing responses on to why they should continue to belong to the Jewish People. Jewish organizations could raise funds or recruit members based on the claim that they presented the best way to live and nurture Jewish life and the good of the Jewish People. Jewish Peoplehood was a taken-for-granted state of belonging to the Jewish People.

Major social changes played out over the second half of the 20th century which are undermining, or have already undermined, many of the moderate or centrist Jewish ideological movements. The nature of these changes are beyond the scope of this foreword,[6] but the end result is the same—large numbers of Jews are no longer strongly attached to meaningful Jewish ideologies. Many are adopting what the sociologist Herbert Gans called "symbolic ethnicity"— a shallow form of belonging that relies on ethnic food and occasional

---

[6]   For an overview of 20th century changes in American and Israeli society and their impact on Jewish identity and belonging see Kopelowitz, Ezra. 2005. "Jewish Identities." In: Modern Judaism: An Oxford Guide, Editors: Nicholas de Lange and Miri Freud-Kandel. Oxford: Oxford University Press, pp. 205–215.

participation in collective ceremonies as the primary markers of Jewish life.[7] Others are looking for serious alternatives, often finding them in either the extremist sectarian ideologies of the Orthodox right that reject the idea that Jews can embrace modern life and remain fully Jewish, or else in assimilatory ideologies produced by the Jewish left.

Despite the decline of centrist Jewish ideology, the vast majority of active and identifying Jews remain in the middle—they embrace life as full citizens of their respective societies and at the same time desire a compelling answer to the question: "Why be a Jew?," if only to answer their children's questions.

Jewish Peoplehood, we propose, is an attempt by the leadership of the major Jewish organizations and movements at the center of the Jewish socio-political and religious spectrum to respond to the loss of a compelling "middle of the road" ideological vision. Jewish leaders and educators seek to provide compelling answers to their constituents about issues of Jewish belonging, and they are looking to the Peoplehood concept as one possibility.

The importance of the book before you is found within this historical setting. An examination of the Peoplehood concept provides insight into the intensive search taking place amongst Jewish moderates for a meaningful and vibrant framework for the organization of Jewish life in the 21st century. Each chapter in this book offers a looking glass into critical issues that face the Jewish center at the turn of the 21st century.

Jerusalem, April 2008

---

[7]   See Gans, Herbert. 1994. "Symbolic Ethnicity and Symbolic Religiosity: Toward a Comparison of Ethnic and Religious Acculturation," Ethnic and Racial Studies, Vol. 17 (October), pp. 577–592; and, Gans, Herbert. 1979. "Symbolic Ethnicity: The Future of Ethnic Groups and Cultures in America," Ethnic and Racial Studies, Vol. 2 (January), pp. I–20.

JEWISH PEOPLEHOOD
Change and Challenge

Introduction
FOUR QUESTIONS CONCERNING PEOPLEHOOD— AND JUST AS MANY ANSWERS

ARNOLD EISEN

Editor's Summary
Arnold Eisen provides an introduction to the concept of peoplehood. He draws on and alludes to the other essays in this volume, all of which are united in their claim that peoplehood is the concept best suited to cope with the quandary of Jewish identity. Eisen shows why the concept of peoplehood has not historically been a coherent one, and how nonetheless its component elements may be identified. He considers the way in which large numbers of Jews might best be persuaded to act upon this self-definition, in a way that ensures a thriving Jewish future. Finally, he argues that conversation is crucial to strengthening the Jewish People in our own time and in the years to come.

My favorite moment in the collection of essays before you comes about halfway through Moshe Halbertal's incisive reflection on the vexed and perplexing situation of contemporary Jewish identity. Jews have had more than two centuries of experience with modernity, Halbertal points out, and half a century of life inside and outside a sovereign Jewish State. The result of all this history is that Jews can no longer agree on who or what they are. Is Jewishness essentially a matter of *religious covenant*, i.e., of faith? Does it consist primarily of *nationality*: membership in the group, participation in its culture, citizenship in its old-new country? Or is there a third basis of self-definition, a resolute *cosmopolitanism*, a heritage of vulnerability, marginality, creativity and dedication to repair of the world? What I admire most in Halbertal's essay is his refusal to pass judgment on, much less to seek harmony among, these disparate trends: "I am incapable of carrying out the dialectic maneuver that would create a pseudo-synthesis between the opposed perceptions of Jewish identity in our time." The remainder of his article is devoted to a candid explanation of why synthesis can only be approximated but never achieved. A pluralistic acceptance of the various modes of being a contemporary Jew, he suggests, is perhaps the best way of ensuring that Jews have the luxury of worrying about the nature of their identity for many years to come.

There is something unsatisfactory in Halbertal's response, to be sure. We are faced with a problem, the awareness of which seems to have grown over the intervening months. "Whatever Happened to the Jewish People?" asks a recent and trenchant article in *Commentary*. Its authors worry, for once, not about the declining numbers (and allegedly imminent disappearance) of the Jews in America and elsewhere. Nor do they fret (at least not directly) about the rising rate of intermarriage and assimilation now evident everywhere in the Diaspora and among all non-Orthodox Jews. Their concern is rather the declining sense on the part of American Jews that they belong to and bear responsibilities toward other Jews. Jews not so long ago took such allegiance and identity for granted. They were Jews, a part of *Am Yisrael* (the people of Israel), caught up in its fate, participants in its collective dream and destiny. Now they are not sure what they owe to whom, or who they are. It is this problem that occasioned the meeting in the Jerusalem hills in July 2005, at which most of the papers in this collection originated.

Consider the evidence: In a recent survey, less than half the American Jewish adults under the age of thirty-five agreed to the statement: "I have a strong sense of belonging to the Jewish people," compared to 75% of those aged sixty-five or older. In contrast, just a decade ago, slightly more than half affirmed that they recognize responsibilities to other Jews above and beyond their obligations to humanity in general. The consciousness of belonging to a group defined by shared history, common family, collective ideals, and distinctive patterns of marriage, residence, occupation and behavior seems not to have survived the new options and divisions created by modernity and Zionism. As sociologists have noted, religion in America is characterized by denominational switching on the part of "sovereign selves." Ethnicity is often merely "symbolic." Hence the felt need on the part of many American Jewish leaders, educators and parents for answers to the question of what can unite Jews despite their divisions and in the face of societal and cultural forces which seem to pull Jews away from Judaism. The head of Hebrew Union College, Julian Morgenstern, put the matter with welcome directness in 1943: "Nation, people, religion—what are we?" Some sixty years later, his question is even more salient. It seems, in fact, inescapable.

The second of Morgenstern's three options—"People"—appears to the contributors to this collection, and to me, to be the concept best suited by far to answer (or at least cope with) the quandary of Jewish identity. Indeed, peoplehood is probably the *only* concept that suits the present situation and meets present needs. "Nation" and "religion" are each in their own way too all-encompassing. They demand more than many Jews are willing to identify with in terms of belief or behavior, and thus render significant portions of the population outsiders to a group which they know belongs to them and which they want very much to claim as their own. On the other hand, ethnicity and heritage are too narrow. They miss out on much of what makes Jewish identity attractive and even compelling to many Jews—a part of the self for which they are profoundly grateful and that many are profoundly disappointed not to transmit to the next generation. Only *peoplehood* seems just right. It betokens an identity in which religious as well as secular Jews, Israeli as well as Diaspora Jews, and traditional as well as liberal Jews (to list only a few of the many dichotomies), can feel equally at home.

But what does peoplehood mean, exactly, and can it work? I approached the task at hand with four questions, which I also posed to the other members of the group.

(1) A philosophical question: Is there a Jewish People?
(2) A sociological question: What must the Jewish People do?
(3) A strategic question: Can the project succeed? That is, can large numbers of Jews be persuaded to adopt and act upon this self-definition, in a way that ensures a thriving Jewish future?
(4) A tactical question: How can we advance the project of Jewish Peoplehood?

Here I shall set forth, revise and expand upon those questions, in part by drawing on the ideas of the other contributors to this volume. Then I shall attempt to answer them. Collectively, I believe, the essays presented in this volume—even if they allow for no definitive answers to our quandary, and certainly propose no synthesis of the various options facing Jews—do point towards work which the Jewish people could profitably undertake.

1. Is There a Jewish People?

If the concept of peoplehood is not coherent, the reason is in part the historical developments charted throughout this volume. But that vagueness has another cause: Jews in the Diaspora and Israel alike have had a vested interest in blurring the bounds of Jewish self-definition.

American Jews since the start of the 20th century have presented themselves as an *ethnic* group in certain contexts and for certain purposes, but as a *religious* group in other contexts and for other purposes. They have had rights to protect and interests to further. Stressing both axes of self-definition was instrumental in that effort. America, the modern society that has arguably been most supportive of Jewish life, has proven uniquely supportive of the blurring of self-definition. In his essay in this volume, Shmuel Trigano, echoing a great deal of scholarly research, argues cogently that Emancipation was not unconditional as far as Jews were concerned. The granting of civil rights, economic opportunities and social acceptance came at the price of rencounciation by Jews of their status as a primordial collective. There would be no room in France or elsewhere for a "nation within the nation." Only

America was different. In this "nation of immigrants" possibilities of communal identity presented themselves which could not have existed in Europe.

It is important to note that history has left its mark on American Jews, nonetheless. Pogroms and persecution are a memory, but they are not all that distant. Anxiety about Anti-Semitism remains widespread, even sixty years after the Holocaust. Jews worry lest they betray a degree or sort of distinctiveness which the larger society—despite social acceptance of minority groups and Constitutional guarantees of religious freedom—will not countenance. Hence the Jewish people's vested interest in both ethnic and religious pluralism, and their persistent habit of defining themselves in both terms depending on the situation. American Jews are pleased when their rabbis alternate with Catholic priests and Protestant ministers at public functions, such as Presidential inaugurations. They seek to be part of "rainbow coalitions" alongside Italian-Americans, Chinese-Americans, African-Americans, etc—are they not Jewish-Americans, after all?

Israelis have engaged in comparable activity. David Ben Gurion, Israel's founding Prime Minister, would often remark in the 1950's and 1960's that he was not interested in nationalism (or Zionism) but only in Judaism. As far as I can tell, Ben Gurion never clarified exactly what the term Judaism meant to him, though it seems to have signified a secular Zionist form of messianism: the eternal mission of the Jewish people, crucial to the redemption of all humanity, which would be possible only when the people was once more ingathered in its homeland. Ben Gurion recognized that Israel needed a civil religion, and he set about fashioning one out of the sources and symbols of Judaism— the menorah, the olive branch, the Bible. He needed to unify his new nation of diverse immigrants, to mobilize their energies for the sacrifices involved in nation-building, and to legitimate State activities which had no precedent in the previous two millennia of Jewish history.

Israel has exacerbated these modern dilemmas in obvious ways, and I think Ami Bouganim is correct in arguing that contemporary Jews cannot resolve the question of who they are without facing up to **theological** and **political** questions occasioned by the existence of a "Jewish State"—questions that many Jews would often rather avoid. Rabbinic Judaism, Bouganim points out, is permeated through and through with Diaspora *political* assumptions. These are made problematic or irrelevant by renewed Statehood. Yeshayahu Leibowitz's early essays made this case brilliantly. Israelis struggle with responsibilities toward Jews and non-Jews for which the Jewish legal and philosophical traditions offer no precedent and little guidance. For them, the theological and political are inextricably intertwined.

Judaism itself has always fostered this sort of boundary-blurring. The covenant at Sinai binds Israelites to one another as well as to God. They are to be a "kingdom of priests and holy nation." Holiness and priesthood reinforced nationality and kingdom, and vice versa. Modern history in some cases split apart what the covenant had joined, allowing for the possibility of Jews who saw themselves and were seen by others as Jews, but who wanted nothing to do with God and religion—as well as Jews who wish to be Germans or Frenchmen or Americans "of the Mosaic persuasion," loyal to their faith and its fellow-adherents, but finding the other constituents of their identity elsewhere. At various points on the modern roads they traveled, large numbers of Jews opted to choose one or another of these alternatives. These same circumstances have led many Jews to detach themselves from Jews and Judaism altogether; most, however, have retained some attachment, however attenuated, and have continued by and large to regard the Jews who have made the opposite choice as Jews nonetheless, members of the same group, rather than ruling them out of Jewish history and destiny. This need not have been the case, and in some cases it is not. Some Jews have established a "wall of separation" between "religious" and "secular." In most cases, however, interest and principle alike have driven Jews to blur the boundaries between nationality and faith. The result is lack of clarity on the part of many Gentiles and even many Jews on just what being Jewish means or entails.

Although the project of defining and fostering a greater sense of Jewish Peoplehood arouses (for good reasons) the suspicion that we are again trying to blur or cover over a crucial distinction that is better kept out of view, I see no other option. It is helpful, I think, not to settle either for a concept of *nationhood* (itself rendered more complex of late by a vast literature) or for *ethnicity* (likewise the subject of much discussion and debate). Israeli Jews might well prefer to think of Jews as a *nation*: a powerful concept over the past two centuries, more powerful in many instances than rival concepts such as religion, socialism or democracy. They are citizens in a state. Almost all serve in its army. Many American Jews would feel more comfortable thinking of Jewishness as *ethnicity*, precisely because, as Herbert Gans argued decades ago, it is a fairly trivial concept in contemporary America, at least among white people. Ethnicity is "symbolic"—a matter of nostalgia, festivals and food. *Peoplehood* stands between the two.

But it is, I believe, more than safe half-way ground. The component elements of peoplehood make it a uniquely useful and authentic way to think about Jewish meaning and Jewish belonging in our generation, in our situation. *Am Yisrael* translates even more exactly to "people" than to "nation" of Israel, given that not all nations today have the familial and tribal basis of the "Children of Israel," and that nation is often associated with statehood, which the Jewish people lacked for most of its history. Peoplehood has other conceptual advantages as well, which become clear when we consider what it comprises.

2. What Must (the) Jewish People Do?

What I have called the **sociological** question—what elements constitute Jewish Peoplehood?—is therefore more than merely sociological. It is constitutive. The Jewish people as a whole cannot exist unless critical masses of Jews engage in all or some of the activities that **constitute, mark and perpetuate** the existence of that people. At present, these elements are lacking for many or most Jews in Israel and Diaspora alike (though the particular elements present or absent might differ in each case). What are the component elements by which peoplehood is constituted and marked?

The conception of "civilization," first developed by Mordechai Kaplan, is instrumental in deconstructing peoplehood, as Bouganim points out. Civilization means peoplehood: a conception capable of including, and holding in tension, differences which should not be dichotomized but cannot be overcome or synthesized. In *Judaism as a Civilization*, Kaplan offers a list of what constitutes a civilization:

> land; language and literature; mores, laws and folkways; folk "sanctions" (i.e. values); folk arts; history; social structure. All are even more difficult to identify in America today than they were in Kaplan's day. Jewish shared values, for one, have been severely weakened with generational distance from immigration, reduced by lack of common daily experience and possibly devastated by inter-marriage. When it comes to shared history, they are equally lacking . . . Americans are notoriously ignorant of their nation's history, and Jews know precious little of theirs. They also lack a shared physical space, i.e. distinctive neighborhoods of their own. Although, admittedly, diaspora Jews in America and elsewhere are concentrated today in a relatively small number of urban areas, they live side-by-side with people of all backgrounds. And finally, although there is a Jewish-American culture popularized, for instance, at Jewish film festivals and on the Arts pages of *The Forward*, it is not clear that a shared possession of particular slices of high and popular American/western culture makes up for the absence of the rich Yiddish, Ladino and Hebrew literary traditions that flourished in decades passed.

The widespread absence of these elements is made vivid by two recent works by prominent Jewish authors, one an Israeli and one an American.

Amos Oz' memoir, *A Tale of Love and Darkness* makes clear what is meant by the term peoplehood. The narrator's family story is so intimately and palpably bound up with the story of his people (especially those newly ingathered to the homeland) that the two stories blend. The personal becomes totally inseparable from the national.

Philip Roth's, *The Plot Against America*, set in 1940's Newark, suggests what American Jews might well need to experience in order to feel solidarity with far-away Jews they do not know: tangible marks of shared suffering that are happening to people recognizably like them in a here and now just like the one they themselves inhabit. Pogroms and blatant discrimination in the America that Roth imagines enable and force the American Jews whom he describes to identify with Jews overseas. Reality imposes historical knowledge that Jewish educators must otherwise struggle to impart through classes or "informal education." Without this sense that individual circumstances, constraints, achievements, tendencies, sensibility, etc are derived from the past one shares with other Jews, choosing to make common cause with Jews is unlikely. The more that being Jewish seems to be a matter of choice rather than fate, we might say, the less significant it is to be chosen, and the less likely that Jews will choose.

Roth's novel clarifies several other ingredients necessary for cultivating a sense of peoplehood, including distinctive neighborhoods, shared occupational niches, friendship circles, in-marriage, and the constant presence of "others" who are not like them. These comprise what American sociologists call "structural ethnicity." As a result, Roth writes, "There were Jews who needed no large terms of reference, no profession of faith or doctrinal creed, in order to be Jews...Neither was their being a mishap or misfortune or an achievement to be 'proud' of. What they were was what they couldn't get rid of—what they wouldn't even begin to want to get rid of. Their being Jews issued from their being themselves, as did their being American." (p. 220)

As Roth demonstrates, America does *not* promote among Jews the sense of shared fate and common enemies in this way. Indeed, it impels Jews to reflect on how much they share with members of other groups—and to believe that they belong to more groups than one. Hyphenated identity requires the presupposition that harmony if not actual synthesis between the two sides of the hyphen is possible and even desirable. In contrast, life in Israel promotes this realization of shared fate among the Jews who live there or visit; it can similarly affect Jews who read about attacks and defense in the "Holy Land" without keeping a safe distance from the disturbing facts on the ground.

Joseph Soloveitchik, an Orthodox thinker, argued for two elements that are necessary for binding Jews to one another: A covenant of fate and a covenant of destiny. The former refers to a sense of a shared collective situation, and particularly of common enemies.

Soloveitchik had no hesitation in speaking normatively about what Jews must do in order to be Jews. He knew what covenant demanded. History, as he recounted it, bore inescapable normative lessons; indeed one could trace in it the presence (or temporary absence) of God. Michael Walzer and Moshe Halbertal, among others in this volume, explain why any such statement concerning Jewish "destiny" will inevitably alienate many Jews. Both writers advocate a pluralistic acceptance of difference as the prerequisite to Jewish peoplehood. They oppose what they consider to be vain attempts to overcome difference by excluding some Jews from the collective or trying to absorb one definition of Jewishness (e.g. covenant) into another (e.g. nation). Riv Ellen Prell notes perceptively along the same lines that "Peoplehood is a project rather than a thing in and of itself." It cannot but hold universal and particular in tension. The question, then, is how one can advance that project, while not allowing the inherent tensions to break the conception of peoplehood (much less the people itself) apart.

The key move in this respect, suggested by several contributors, seems to me best captured by the notion of **conversation**. Not education, the imparting of skills and information, but **dialogue** among various sorts of Jews. This discussion takes place inside particular Jewish communities linked through overlapping networks to other communities or across the boundaries of such sub-communities. It involves encounters between individual Jews and Jewish history, texts and rituals; meetings with near or distant members of one's own family; meetings with those who are not Jews. The upshot of this call for multiple forms of conversation is that the third question I posed at the outset—strategy; whether Jews can be brought to consensus of action if not consciousness—is premature. It should probably be put off until one has probed the fourth question: tactics, what can be done to engage Jews in the conversations that *may* well result in a shared sense of Jewish culture and so, of peoplehood. Indeed, as I have suggested, the conversation might **constitute** a significant portion of that culture. Let me explain.

3. How Can We Advance the Project of Peoplehood?

The literary critic R.W.B. Lewis wrote that, "every culture seems, as it advances toward maturity, to produce its own determining debate over the ideas that preoccupy it...The development of [a] culture...resembles a protracted and broadly ranging conversation: at best a dialogue—a dialogue which at times moves very close to drama." Mere talk won't do. Nor will mere ritual: scripted behavior enacted unthinkingly, out of habit (though as we know such behavior leaves its lifelong cultural mark, for good and for bad, on those subjected to it at an early age). The point, rather, is structured, learned discussion prompted by a set of (largely traditional) symbols, rituals, activities, texts and ideas. These, working as a whole, create the sense of overarching coherence amidst a diverse set of participants ranging across geography and generations.

They compose a sort of manual for building peoplehood, one that overlaps to a great extent with the set of instructions one would follow in order to foster intentional community. Laura Geller lists several tools which have proven valuable in Los Angeles and elsewhere. Ezra Kopelowitz offers still other detailed suggestions by way of analysis of camps, synagogues, and other sites where peoplehood in his view is either engendered or hindered. Michael Walzer writes that if Jews are to respect each other in their differences, as they must if peoplehood is to exist and thrive, they "must learn that our national history is also a religious history...[and] that our religious history is also a national history." The key here, of course, is that Jews must learn and study, not only so as to master what they study, but so as to accept the fact that members of their group hold radically different notions of religion and nationality and that, "though the memberships coincide, nation and religion are not the same thing Bouganim, alert to the same requirements, calls for "new political and theological midrash," a new attitude to God and Torah study, a new attitude to repairing the world.

The commonalities in all these approaches are readily apparent. Any program for the nurturing of peoplehood will partake of most elements on any one contributor's list: encounter, study, ritual, joint social/political action, experiences of face-to-face Jewish community. It is no less important to note, however, that no one set of tools will suffice for every Jewish individual, group or situation. Prell argues convincingly, if the case still needs making, that **gender** is crucial to personhood, Jewish or otherwise, and therefore is essential to Jewish peoplehood. Michal Govrin, in her autobiographical essay, demonstrates this claim: "Writing in the first person feminine," says Govrin, "drove home for me the magnitude of the challenge posed by the introduction of women into the canon, by the opportunity of formulating—out of the fullness of the feminine experience and consciousness—the feminism and the masculinie attributes of humankind and of the world." Govrin explains that, "Jewish selves who identify as active members of the Jewish people are fashioned by the encounter of Jewish selves in formation with Jewish rituals, texts, communities, history." There seems to be no shortcut to the realizations arrived at through such personal experiences and first-hand encounters, whether with war or anti-Semitism or piety or ritual or love. These experiences can only be undergone by individuals, one at a time, taking uncharted routes leading to unpredictable outcomes. Even in collective settings, different individuals will come away with different experiences and outcomes. They are the stuff of art, not of science, whether or not the Jew concerned is an artist, such as Govrin. They involve passion and, frequently, pain.

The same could be said of fashioning peoplehood, I think. The project depends upon countless individual realizations, decisions, forebodings and plans. It can be inspired, but rarely directed. And yet we know what is required if inspiration is to take place.

4. Can the Project Succeed? How to Measure Success?

There is no doubt that some Jews—large numbers of Jews, in fact—will continue to reach maturity in the decades to come bearing a robust conviction that they are part of the Jewish people. Israelis will have this consciousness inculcated through calendar, language, landscape, rituals, education, and the ever-present danger of a collective enemy. Religious Jews too (and not all of them Orthodox) will have this consciousness, whether in Israel or in the Diaspora, because they believe themselves obligated by covenant to all other, whether or not these other Jews recognize that covenant as binding upon them as well. Cosmopolitan Jews may well feel some attachment to Jews who, like them, take on universalist causes, and reject particularist ("tribal" attachments)—in the name of *tikkun olam*, or some related Jewish ideal. Weaker forms of recognition and attachment may well be evident among Jews who identify subjectively with one or another organized body of Jews but refuse every offer of actual membership. Still other Jews spend their years rejecting this or that form of Judaism, and are therefore defined in part by what they feel impelled repeatedly and passionately to oppose. At worst, then, we are likely to see an attenuation of the sense of peoplehood; but its actual disappearance would be unlikely.

Many Jews have been fortunate to have moments when the idea of people-hood suddenly took hold. For me, the moment was particularly poignant...

For whatever reason, I found meeting Argentinian relatives with whom the American side of the family had lost touch for sixty years, strikingly powerful. To meet in Jerusalem, and converse easily in Hebrew, with a professor whose grandmother was sister to my grandmother; to talk in shorthand born of shared experience (we work in closely related fields) within five minutes of meeting for the very first time—this is precious experience of peoplehood indeed, powerful testimony to links binding Jews to one another. To meet others of the family in Buenos Aires, and feel no less a bond despite the inadequacy of communication in variously mangled bits of English, Spanish and Yiddish—in a richly cosmopolitan city where Jews cannot entirely feel at home—this too bore witness to connectedness and bore deep into the soul.

Federation slogans used to highlight the fact of *mishpokhe*, of family ties among Jews, but it dawns on one after an experience of this sort that Jews really are connected by multiple family links. Jews are often not that far removed from one another, if only they knew, or cared, or cared enough to know and explore the connection. Intermarriage will immensely complicate this sense of family, to be sure but will not eliminate it. Disputes over who counts as Jewish may add strain to family connections but these are never free from strain, in the nature of the case. (Some of my new-found relatives are not on speaking terms with others. They are family, after all.)

The advantage of the personal familial relation as a means to heightened consciousness of peoplehood is the same as the richness revealed in Govrin's autobiography. This is the way we all experience and fashion identity nowadays. We put pieces side by side, and perhaps join them together. The arrangement changes as we do—and yet much of its remains in place. Our families take this sort of form these days: children of one marriage playing with half-siblings of another, spouses lined up in the front row for a *bar* or *bat mitzvah* alongside ex-spouses and their spouses, individuals of complex familial connection comforting one another at *shiva* or dancing *hora* together at a wedding—perhaps only males with males, females with females, but joined by family ties in *simcha* or mourning, nonetheless.

I admit that it is not immediately obvious why these bonds should hold. It is no more obvious than why a religious Jew should decide that he or she shares identity and responsibility with Jews who believe that there is no truth to religious faith and no authority to the *mitzvot*, but who have decided that Jewish Peoplehood is a good for its own sake, or that strengthening the Jewish people is its own justification. And it is no more obvious why a non-religious Jew should decide that he or she shares identity and responsibility with Jews who believe that they and they alone possess the truth where important matters are concerned; that they enjoy God's blessing because they obey God's will; that non-religious Jews are only a means to be used for ends that religious Jews alone are qualified to determine. It is no more clear, and perhaps less so, that Diaspora Jews will continue to make common cause with Israelis who believe and proclaim that Diaspora existence is illegitimate and rightfully doomed to disappear. Or that Israeli Jews will make common cause with Diaspora Jews—increasingly, a minority of world Jewry—who see no obligation to share the burden for which Israelis are spending so much of their resources and all too many of their lives.

Yet these Jews do make common cause with one another, and I expect that they will continue to do so in significant numbers for the reasons of shared history, situation, concern, activity, experience, values—and shared hope—that I have set forth. Facilitating the entry of Jews into common conversation will increase the chances that this bonding will occur and that it will survive the divisions which so beset it. The conversation takes place one encounter at a time, each experience building on the next. Taken as a whole, they constitute, mark, and perpetuate Jewish Peoplehood—a never-ending project as each generation, community and Jew resolves, in turn, to make it last.

THE PROBLEM OF JEWISH PEOPLEHOOD

MICHAEL ROSENAK

Editor's summary
Michael Rosenak argues that "Peoplehood" is a meaningful, but problematic, operative concept to describe what draws Jews to one another. This term may be either descriptive (describing what is "out there" and researchable), or prescriptive (reflecting a more abstract vision of life and humanity.) The former corresponds to what Soloveitchik terms the "covenant of fate"; the latter to the "covenant of destiny." Today, Jewish leaders are committed to a formula of Jewish unity based on a covenant of fate. Rosenak demonstrates that this commitment rests on several overly narrow and hence problematic assumptions, as the Biblical prophets themselves would have understood. Instead, he offers evidence for the vitality and stamina of a Jewish People bound by a covenant of destiny, and concludes with his sense of the tasks facing Jewish leaders today.

In Search of Commonalities

I shall open my discussion of "Jewish Peoplehood," with several related pre-senting problems:

- Does this term, which refers to that which draws Jews to one another, describe something essential about Jewish existence?
- How does it point to some vision of Jewish life?
- How, in general, is this notion useful?
- What are we really looking for, and why?

After all, have not the close-knit communities of "the people," *amcha*, to whom the concept accorded a sense of identity and a focus of identification, virtually disappeared?

- How is it, then, despite the difficulties it raises, that the notion of Peoplehood still seems so rich and promising to wide circles of Jewish leadership?

Let us consider some other terms that we might use to describe our commonalities. *Nationality* is certainly not appropriate today, when the Jews are being reconstituted in Israel as a nation, while Diaspora Jews remain by choice citizen-members of other nations. As for the term *religion*—while appropriate in the Diaspora for members of various denominations within which most engaged Diaspora Jews find their Jewish identities, it leaves out the secular Israeli almost in principle, as well as many Jewish secular humanists worldwide.

The term *Peoplehood*, then, seems apt and useful. As a concept, it seeks to promote Jewish self-identification without requiring shared religiosity, or a cultivation of national culture, or large stores of national fervor, although all of these are cultural and existential options. On the religious plane, it does not mandate faith or even interest in God, nor traditional commandments or institutional belonging. On the cultural plane, it does not even require a common language; and it does not insist that all Jews come on Aliyah, although many Israeli Jews might insist that the battles of the covenant of fate are fought on higher ground in Israel.

Furthermore, *Peoplehood* remains helpful in enhancing Jewish life, because it points to a paradigm that can blur the great differences among Jews and still somehow hold them together—despite the variety of ways in which Jews discern themselves as Jews, despite the different degrees and kinds of their commitment, and despite the varied ways Jews see "the other," both Jew and Gentile. Perhaps Peoplehood provides a prism through which we can acknowledge the differences between Jews without abandoning loyalty to them and self-identification with them. The concept of Peoplehood, then, may enable us to become more fully aware of how these other Jews are different from ourselves, even while we continue to search for commonalities between "them," (whoever "they" are) and ourselves, (whoever "we" are). Obviously, if there were no such commonalities among Jews, *Peoplehood* would lose all present-day meaning and all normative force, even if it remained useful in describing or imagining the Jewish past, and nostalgically depicting "life with the people."

To come to grips with these questions and problems, we shall identify some concepts that may clarify matters and then examine some underlying issues in contemporary Jewish life.

Descriptive and Prescriptive Commonalities

The common ground we seek, and hope to find among Jews, may be either descriptive or prescriptive, or both. In the first, *descriptive,* mode, we ask: what is there "out there" that draws Jews together and how this Jewish "togetherness" expresses itself in the public (researchable) domain. In the second, prescriptive, mode we ask: what do we see Jews doing, as visible manifestations of their diverse conceptions and assumptions about *what it means to be a Jew* and: *what should be done by Jews* who perceive it as significant and hence, obligating.

Looking at matters through the first of these prisms, the descriptive one, we see Jews living in certain historical and existential situations that are clearly recognizable and seemingly inescapable, and which elicit the type of behavior patterns we would expect. For example, on Yom HaShoah we may expect Jews to have a heightened awareness of what we remember together and what bonds of kinship we share; what horrific animosities we have suffered, and how we have responded to them. On the descriptive level, Jews continue to see themselves suffering from a mysterious bias directed against them and they remain aware of the untold aggression that has been directed against them, simply because they were Jews. These phenomena are still "out there," in the media and on college campuses, as in the Purim memories of the wicked Haman, that hateful "adversary of the Jews." These memories and fears, as well as narratives of victory and vindication, still bring Jews together. The concept of Peoplehood can help delineate what Jews endure and how they respond—together.

However, we cannot assume that such "tribal" loyalties and bonds and responses will automatically and perennially protect the identity of Jews. We well know that there are increasing numbers of Jews who question the legitimacy of this deterministic "situation" of (alleged) commonalities. In their view, presenting descriptive phenomena as though they were automatically prescriptive testifies to an ideological agenda of "Jewish identity" that is parochial and manipulative. They point out that if we are alarmed by the statistics of assimilation, then we, too, apparently believe that Jews—at least in today's world—do have the choice to leave all that. Indeed, if Jewish culture and spirit are of negligible interest to them, then why not get away from it? If there is nothing inherently valuable or interesting left as an existential ground for Peoplehood, why stick with it?

As said, a second option in the search for commonalities is prescriptive. For those seeking Jews and Judaism in the prescriptive domain, it matters not how gloomy the descriptive dimension of Jewish life, and for that matter, how gloomy human existence is, as such. They see themselves bound, as Jews, to a specific vision of life and humanity, bearing the imprint of some collective cultural or religious experience, intimating social order and fellowship, or holiness and compelling commitment. They seek to initiate their children into the life of a covenanted or, at least, distinctive historical people. They feel that they are called to an individual and even a "national" life of commandment, or simply—and in a somewhat less theological vein—that Judaism demands that they be both decent and devoted.

This prescriptive view, of what the Jews ought to be, rests on some descriptive foundations: after all, there do exist, in significant numbers and in rich variety, Jews who hold to such a prescriptive outlook, and they can be described. But alas, research into such prescriptive Jews and types of Judaism suggests that the contemporary forms of "prescriptive" Judaism do not seem to point to commonalities. After all, what is common in the life and beliefs of Meah Shearim ultra-Orthodox Yeshiva students and American Reform rabbis? What do dedicated Israeli Generals share in the realm of culture and of spirit with Jewish feminists in Manhattan? It would seem that the greater the prescriptive commitments of contemporary Jews, the more prescription, as such, moves engaged Jews away from commonality.

Covenant of Fate, Covenant of Destiny

The descriptive commonalities remaining after the virtual collapse of spiritual communion and consensus among Jews have been described by Rabbi Joseph Soloveitchik as reflecting what he calls a "covenant of fate"; the prescriptive ones refer to what he terms a "covenant of destiny" [J.B. Soloveitchik: "*Kol Dodi Dofek*" ("The Voice of my Beloved Knocks") in *Ish Ha'emunah* (*The Man of Faith*), Jerusalem: Mossad HaRav Kook, 5731, pp. 86–99) (Hebrew).] It is noteworthy that Soloveitchik describes both in terms of a Jewish-divine relationship: they are both covenants; both involve commanded action and both intimate significance.

We shall return to "the covenant of destiny," but here it may be said that, despite the doubters, the covenant of fate is still really there for most Jews. It is what makes many Jews look for news about Israel first when they peruse the morning newspaper, and what makes them oddly uneasy at charges of undue Jewish influence in government and the arts. This all seems somewhat tragic but, as noted, Soloveitchik does not perceive the covenant of fate in this way. For him, it is part and parcel of the God-Israel relationship. Hence, it demands a willingness to remain distinctive in attitude and action, and to foster unity in the face of persecution or vilification, and formulate an effective response. And the demand Jews see as directed to them—to empathize with Jewish misfortune and to act in unison in the face of danger—is still commonly "explained" by the simple statement that: "We are one people": in our common memories of sorrows endured, in our stubborn survival, in a perilous existence, ennobled by courageous response. Would another people have recreated its commonwealth after nineteen hundred years of exile, three years after the murder of one third of its members? Was this project of restoring the Jewish commonwealth not perceived by Jews as both commanded and redemptive—in whatever religious or secular ways they understood the concepts of commandment and redemption?

So, Peoplehood still seems appropriate to describe the "fate" dimension of Jewish life. But if that were all remaining to engage our energies and to unite us, the ramifications would be deeply disturbing. If the most general aspect of being different is related to being acted upon, to being suspect and strange, then we must ask:

- Do we have "a stake" in continued persecution and insecurity?
- What educational options are presented by an identity based on anti-Semitism?
- Is "fighting Anti-Semitism proudly" an ideal and perennial educational goal? Does it not, if viewed as the be-all and end-all of "Peoplehood," contain the seeds of closed-mindedness, generated by a tragic awareness of living in an unfriendly world?

And, by the same token:

- Can Peoplehood be constructed on the denial of a fundamental tenet of Jewish faith, namely, that in "times to come" (b'acharit hayamim), universal peace will be realized: that "Nation shall not lift up sword against nation" and that the "kingdom of God" will be established and universally accepted?

These are, of course, rhetorical questions. They are meant to suggest that we should not evade a search for a prescriptive formulation of Peoplehood that points to an educational ideal and community-wide vision. We wish to educate towards the idea that what unites us is more than what divides us, that beyond Anti-Semitism there is culture, however conceived. Yet, given the ruptures in the fabric of Jewish life, the questions arise:

- How can this culture be presented and implemented in a manner that does not itself divide religious Jews from secular ones, Diaspora Jews from Israeli ones?
- How can we break away from an obsession with consensus that, all too often, produces vacuous sloganizing, rather than educated discourse?

One course of action that may "move" Jewish Peoplehood, and its implied vision of Jewish unity, into the realm of some prescriptive Jewishness that is not banal involves fostering a community identity that leaves questions of belief, behavior and commitment as open, yet important issues. The identity sought in this approach is one that demonstrates a readiness to be informed by the past, but leaves the present and the future open, "even" to traditional paradigms. This proposed course of action suggests that we explore the past without prejudice, willing to learn from it and studying the Great Jewish Books in order to discover and clarify previous models of Jewish distinctiveness. Then—whether through cursory acquaintance with "the Jewish book-case," or the profound study of it—we may discover that Jewish identity and the uniqueness of the Jews as a group, have taken on many forms: monarchy, a culture of Torah, a dispersed people settled around Jewish religious law, mystic communities and "learning" ones, pioneering kibbutzim, and others. On the basis of the dynamics of Jewish history and culture as we find them on "the Jewish bookcase," we may find today's inner struggles for more—or less—change to be not so uncomfortable, and not so threatening in our search for commonalities. Why shouldn't Jewish distinctiveness be characterized, among other things, by disagreement and diversity? Hasn't this always been the case—is not our whole Talmud built on the concept of argumentation?

(Not So) Hidden Assumptions

So why is there an adherence to a formula of "Jewish unity," based upon a "covenant of fate"? It seems to me that the leadership that is so "taken" with the concept of Peoplehood is, consciously or unconsciously, basing itself on specific assumptions as to what is "out there," and hence, a certain (gloomy) view of what can be salvaged. Yet these assumptions, if they are indeed central to the thinking of contemporary Jewish leadership, may turn out to be unduly narrow, limiting our ability to think of alternative solutions to the sundry problems of Jewish continuity—and possibilities.

What are these assumptions?

Assumption One:
That unless "something is done" to revitalize the Jewish People, the demise of the Jews as an historic community is virtually assured, even if some ultra-Orthodox groups will remain as a sectarian remnant. (Strangely, those who profess not to have fears for their survival—the Haredim—appear, on the basis of this assumption, as part of the problem, rather than as a kind of solution, no matter how unpalatable to most other Jews.)

Assumption Two:
That while Jewish civilization has been predominantly religious, attempts to make religious faith and practice the foundations for Jewish existence in our time are unrealistic and intellectually unacceptable. We all, Jews and non-Jews, live in a secular, pluralistic world, increasingly globalized and "post-modern."

Assumption Three:
That while we are loving children of the enlightenment, it must be admitted that all interesting or important things that have happened to Jews since the dawn of enlightenment have been ultimately corrosive and have contributed to the demise of tradition and Jewish community.

Each of these assumptions exposes different problems to address, and each leads to particular types of action, often positive:

The first assumption requires drawing wider circles of Jews into activities that will create identification and positive Jewish experience. A notable example of solving the problem of the disappearance of the Jews is in "Israel experiences" and, at the other end of the continuum, Holocaust curricula.

17

The second and third assumptions have led policy makers in the direction of Zionism, Jewish Community Centers, camping (for all age groups and for families), and intellectually oriented educational programs for European Jewish leadership. They also suggest expanding on programs and university studies exploring the relationship between Jews and modernity, and encouraging frameworks for Jewish experience.

While these assumptions have proven their value in the policies and programs they have fostered, they are not the only ones by which to understand the Jewish situation. Let us take another look at them:

(a) *The Jews are disappearing; they are a threatened species:*
The fear that the Jews are about to vanish from the face of the earth is not new and has, at least from the days of the Destruction of the Second Commonwealth and the fall of Massada and Betar, always been with us. Articulations of this fear are well documented by Simon Rawidowicz [S. Rawidowicz: "Israel: The Ever Dying People," Rawidowicz, *Studies in Jewish Thought*, ed. Nahum Glatzer (Philadelphia: The Jewish Publication Society of America, 1974), pp. 51–63,] who argues that this mindset of "being the last ones" has accompanied Jews from time immemorial. For Rawidowicz, the flip side of this consciousness of "the ever dying people" *is the never-dying people.* In this context, we may note one of the amazing facts to emerge from research on post-World War II European Jewish survivors: In the years after the Shoah, the *she'arit haplitah,* Jews in displaced persons camps, had one of the highest birth rates in the world [Zeev W. Mankowitz, *Life Between Memory and Hope; The Survivors of the Holocaust in Occupied Germany* (Cambridge University Press, 2002), p. 131.] This chapter of post-Holocaust history may surely stand alongside the establishment of Israel, a mere three years after the Shoah! Both events take place, without a doubt, within the parameters of the "covenant of fate." Both are readily conceptualized by way of *Peoplehood.* But the energies they generated seem to point beyond that.

(b) *Religion can no longer serve as a basis for Jewish life; the People rather than God must be placed at the center of Jewish consciousness*:
Is this really so? What is the role of religion in maintaining the Jews, in the past and at present? What do we know about it?

It can be argued that the world has not become more irreligious at all! True, there has been an increase of secular consciousness, even to an extent among Jewish and other fundamentalists, and this consciousness gives rise to new religious thinking. The fact is that many scholars who research religion have indeed moved away from it and have tended to project their (secular) ideologies onto the subjects of their inquiries. Religion, then, may have changed, even radically, but that was in large measure to maintain its relevance! As the theologian Mordechai Kaplan put it:

Ever since the Enlightenment, Jews have been acted upon by the outside world and its enlightened philosophies in variegated ways which all impact negatively on Jewish identity, faith and culture. Jews, like almost all others, have become modern, to the detriment of the tradition that kept Jewish civilization alive and made it the instrument of salvation [Mordecai M. Kaplan, *Judaism as a Civilization* (New York: Schocken Books, 1967).]

Yet, we may ask: Would there have been such fascinating Jewish movements as modern Orthodoxy and post-modern Reform, Zionism, or "Jewish Studies," without the Enlightenment? Would there have been significant quasi-prophetic figures like Kafka, traditionalist innovators such as Eliezer Berkovits? Statesmen, like Ben Gurion, scholars like Gershom Scholem, sage mystics like Rabbi Avraham Hacohen Kook, creative theologians like Franz Rosenzweig and Emmanuel Levinas? Would all but ultra-Orthodox Jews wish to live without the insights, possibilities and challenges that characterize their lives as modern?

Certainly, the way we cut the cake makes a difference in the ways we discuss *Peoplehood* issues. For example: Shall we provide more funding and channel energies in educating the committed, or should we foster outreach? To paraphrase British Chief Rabbi Jonathan Sacks: Must we tell the sparsely committed and virtually unconnected that without them the Jews will vanish? Or, that they are likely to miss out on the adventure of the Jewish future?

Two Ways of Cutting the Cake

One of my teachers, the late Professor Rotenstreich of the Hebrew University, once presented me with two ways of conceptualizing and reading modern Jewish history, and two ways of teaching it.

Way One: "The Jewish problem" and the Jewish Reaction
In the first of the two readings of history, Jews are acted upon by others and then react in turn. One can, said Rotenstreich, "open" the annals of modernity with the French Revolution, moving then to the rise of the nation-state with its demand, addressed to all citizens, for loyalty. This will bring us to the Emancipation, the apparent acceptance of Jews as equal citizens, and the subsequent growth of Anti-Semitism. In this particular Jewish history syllabus, attention would be paid to European socialist movements and to their Jewish counterparts, the Bund, and to socialist Zionism. There would be a study of European nationalism and of Jewish nationalism as a response—especially, to those national movements that depicted the Jews as "a problem." This course in modern Jewish history would suggest seeing the Holocaust as proof that Jewish "normalization" was an illusion, vindicating the auto-Emancipation of the Jews though political Zionism. Paradoxically, in the lands of liberalism, there would also be a fear for Jewish survival despite the embrace of normalizing societies

of freedom. Here, Jewish experience would not generally include being acted upon in a negative fashion but, rather, of being granted rights, hence too, of "enjoying" the option to assimilate. In combating this challenge, responses such as "never again" and the creation of the State of Israel out of the ashes of the Holocaust are the ground on which Jews build institutions and movements designed to counter the forces of cultural assimilation.

Way Two: Jewish Cultural Distinctiveness and Ingenuity
Rotenstreich's second way of reading modern Jewish history emphasizes internal experience and self-expression. The focus is on cultural initiatives that are indelibly Jewish, and on the distinctive qualities of Jewish culture. In this second scheme, we begin modern Jewish history with the messianic movement of Shabbetai Zvi, and trace the development of the Hasidic and even the Reform movements as post-Shabbetarian developments. Hasidim would be studied, not only for its innovative spiritual modes and messages but also, in the context of the threat it posed to the scholarly and halachically normative traditions of traditional rabbinic leadership. The ensuing polemic would also be examined through non-Hasidic teachings, as these developed within the Lithuanian "Yeshiva world," with its study of Talmudic literature, its adherence to ever more strict Halachic standards, and its moral fervor as found in the "Mussar" movement. Units of study would be devoted to the polemics surrounding the issue of modernity that undermined the Lithuanian and Hasidic worlds alike.

In this second type of Jewish history syllabus, students would learn about radically traditional rabbis who denounced everything new as forbidden by the Torah, (R. Moses Sofer, the Hatam Sofer) and would also explore ultra-Reform and secular faiths, as well as new forms of Jewish life such as: the kibbutz, and modern expressions in Yiddish and Hebrew literature and Jewish music. The debate in modern Jewry about "religion" and tradition would be perceived as having engendered Jewish "movements" that fought over the essence of Judaism. In this syllabus too, Anti-Semitism would be present as an issue, but it would appear as an ideological challenge, or a theological one. As for Zionism, in this scheme of things, students would learn more about such cultural figures as Ahad Ha'am, Brenner and Rabbi A.I. Kook, the first Chief Rabbi of Mandate Palestine, than about politically oriented persons, like Theodor Herzl and Max Nordau—for what stands at the center of its concern is not the "problem of the Jews" but, rather, "the problem of Judaism."

Jews and their *Peoplehood*—and Beyond That

The relationship of Jews to their sense of being one people—to the totality of their complex identities—is a puzzling one, and to the nations of the world it appears often exasperating. It can, however, be clarified by way of various historical perspectives. Let us briefly explore the issue on the basis of some early records of Jewish self-awareness, by way of a few Biblical narratives.

> After the Israelites left Egypt, they remembered the cucumbers they had eaten there and some wished to return on their account to Egypt, as though being an enslaved or a free people was of minor matter, less momentous than cucumbers (Numbers 11:5).

Later, when settled in their land under the rule of Judges, they demanded a king like the other nations, ignoring the pleas of Judges like Gideon (Judges 8:22–23) and Samuel (I Samuel 8) to forego mortal kings, for "God will rule over you."

When the monarchy split into two, after a rather brief period of unified existence, the kings and princes of the time hardly created a feeling of Peoplehood, nor did they even feel bound by such a notion. The two "countries" were frequently at war with one another, and made alliances with foreign powers to better defeat the "other" (Israelite or Judaean) kingdom. We have no evidence that the destruction of the Northern Kingdom in 719 B.C.E left the citizens of the Southern Kingdom of Judaea in deep mourning. The historian Heinrich Graetz states unequivocally what he saw as the prophetic message of that time: "So estranged was that kingdom from those who recorded the memorials of the Israelitish nation, that they devoted but few words to its decline."

As for the Destruction itself, as Graetz would have it: "...the diseased limb that had infected the entire body of the nation, was cut off and rendered harmless." [Heinrich Graetz, *History of the Jews I*, (Philadelphia: The Jewish Publication Society of America, 5717–1956), p. 265.] And while the destruction of Judaea itself, in 586 BCE, together with Solomon's Temple, was an occasion for liturgies and lamentations, it too was, inexplicably, not "the end." After all, it had all been foretold by the Prophets who spoke in God's name. These Prophets, clearly men of prescription, were unique *national* figures, belonging to Israel and Judaea together, towering over kings and unimpressed by the twin kingdoms that were like all the nations in their corruption and unique in their "faithlessness" to the God who had covenanted them to Himself. They were the spokesmen of destiny and they had a working concept of Peoplehood, of a people that was Judaea and Israel alike. How many now remember that Elijah and Amos and Hosea were "northerners," and that Isaiah, who prophesized in the name of *Kadosh Yisrael*, the Holy One of Israel, was a Judaean?

The thoughtful Judaean of the time probably "knew" that there was a reason for the destruction and the suffering. And the Prophets constantly asserted what the authors of the Books of Kings and earlier Biblical books had previously asserted: namely, that the only important "national" issue for both kingdoms was: Would they and their "kings" be faithful to their covenant with

God, recognizing Him as their king? Would they be "wholehearted" with Him? This covenant was eternal. So, when it was all over with these kingdoms, it was not all over, after all. And since the Destruction was not the end of the matter, the Prophets, after their threats had been borne out, became the comforters. Did not even Jeremiah, most melancholy of Judaea's prophets promise, in the name of God, that His people would yet: "buy houses and fields and vineyards in this land"? (Jeremiah 32:15)

But the people of that time, and commentators on the annals of our early history to this day, found other signs of continued life of "the ever-dying" people, as well. To bring one astounding example: The Book of II Kings ends with a description of the courteous manner with which the Babylonian King, Evil-Marduk, treated the prisoner King of Judah, Yehoyachim, last monarch of Judaea. Scripture relates that he released him from prison, "spoke kindly to him, had him eat at his table and provided him with an allowance. Why, after the total destruction of Judaea and Jerusalem, end the Book of Kings with such a jarring anti-climax, with the good manners of a pagan king to the hapless representative of the Davidic line, of a far and distant Jewish glory? It seems a pathetic scene: yet note how one popular twentieth century English commentator on II Kings (25:28–30) views the situation:

> The Book of Kings in its last four verses *concludes on a bright note*. [Italics mine—MR.] The last surviving sovereign of Judah is set free from the rigours of his Babylonian prison. He is shown honour, kindness and good will. In this early period of the captivity, the historian detects an incident which is a hopeful augury for the future of his people, *a sign of the end of the exile and the restoration of the Davidic monarch* [italics mine—M.R.]
>
> [Rev. Dr. I.W. Slotki, Kings, Soncino Press, 1950]

Truly, however much it seems to be over, the reader of the Bible knows this is not so.

This approach to viewing events is not idiosyncratic in Jewish history. Some time after the return from Babylon of a Judaean remnant, following his arrival from Babylon, Ezra, a leader of the fledgling community of Jerusalem, initiates a fierce polemic. He demands that the foreign ("Samaritan") wives be expelled: he foresees that these women will corrupt the Judaeans ("Jews"), inducing them to idolatrous practices (Ezra 9). It has been argued that the Book of Ruth was written in that same period. If so, it is apparent there were others who disagreed with Ezra and who argued, through the prism of an ancient tale, that even a daughter of the despised Moabite nation like Ruth, a contemporary of the ancient Judges, could become a mother of royalty and forbear of the Messiah. Should such a devoted woman, whose archetypical story became a separate biblical book in its own right, be expelled? And what is to be said for a culture that argues about such matters, when it seems to be all over?

Whistling in the Dark?

When scholars like Rawidowicz declare that the Jews will never cease, they claim to be basing themselves on evidence—for they are scholars. However, like all scholars, they work on certain assumptions that underlie their scholarship. When they make statements of hope and faith, are they whistling in the dark—or, perhaps, pointing to intimations of the covenant of destiny that are "out there," waiting to be examined, waiting to be used?

This question arose in my mind during a study session some forty years ago at Jerusalem's Institute for Youth Leaders from Abroad, a Jewish Agency-W.Z.O. institution generally referred to, simply and endearingly, as "the Machon." On the occasion I have in mind, the Machon was being addressed by Professor Marshall Sklare, the noted American Jewish sociologist. Sklare brought many talents to his work, and great honesty. As early as 1964 he had warned his readers, in an article in *Commentary* [(37.4, April 1964); reprinted in Marshall Sklare, "Intermarriage and the Jewish Future," *Observing American Jews*" (Hanover, N.H. Brandeis University Press, 1993), pp. 234–247,] that the statistics presented by alleged experts on intermarriage in the United States were vastly misleading and that American Jews would inevitably have to decide whether they wished simply to be members of American society, or to maintain their own identities as somewhat, and significantly, different—a decision that he considered fateful for Jewish survival in America. In his talk at the Machon, he touched on diverse signposts of decline: in demography, in what he called Jewish "cultural compulsions"—that is, in the ability of Jews to connect Jewish artifacts and experiences with others undergone and experienced—and in the shrinking size of Jewish families.

Looking around the classroom with the practiced eye of a teacher, I saw that all our young "Machonnikim," Jewish leaders-to-be, were crestfallen. Finally, one took the initiative: "But Professor Sklare, everything you say points to the demise of the Jewish People." Sklare somberly admitted this to be so. "But then," said the unhappy Machon-nik, "there is no future for us." Sklare became vehement. "God forbid." "But on the basis of what you have taught us..." Sklare cut him off: "All I said, I said as a sociologist. What I am telling you now, namely that the future of the Jews is assured, I say as a believing Jew." The Orthodox youth leaders in the audience were elated, while the Hashomer Hatzair leaders wondered what he meant by "belief" and whether he was a fundamentalist in disguise, and the Conservative Sklare just smiled.

* * *

All of us have seen and been touched by substantial evidence of the sometimes absurd manifestations of Jewish vitality. And yet, because we often espouse a "covenant of fate" conception of Jewish Peoplehood, for the reasons already discussed, we may sometimes miss them. Among these manifestations:

- The music of Shlomo Carlebach and his many associates and disciples, that has been introduced into every liturgy—Reform, Conservative and Orthodox—and now sung enthusiastically by thousands, in synagogues of all denominations;
- The renaissance of Jewish learning and the revolution in Torah study among women;
- The rebirth of the Hebrew language and the flowering of Hebrew literature;
- The great increase in the numbers of Jews who wear kippot in public, certainly on the streets of Israel, and the various kinds of skullcaps, each testifying to a different theology and sociology: the large knitted skullcaps of the "*Eretz Yisrael*" stalwarts', the "peaceniks" with their smaller, usually black knitted kippot; *haredim*, with black silky or velvet kippot—and more besides;
- The abundance of Israel experience programs and their continued growth.

From whence the energies, the stamina and the hope? I shall return to this question below. But first, I shall speak briefly of what counts as evidence for the future of the Jews, through the prism of a story told to me by a Polish born friend, a Holocaust survivor, a rational and unsentimental man. My friend, having escaped from the Warsaw Ghetto, went on to become a senior Jewish educator in the United States, and eventually came on *Aliyah*, to Jerusalem and the Hebrew University. On his return from a visit to his native Poland, he had a strange and moving experience. Arriving at the Warsaw airport for the return trip to Tel Aviv, he discovered that his flight was slightly delayed. Some passengers, he saw, were visibly delighted at the delay for it gave them time to organize a minyan to recite the afternoon prayer, to "*daven minchah*"—which they would otherwise have had to do, in some discomfort, on the plane. A *minyan* of some tens of Jews was rapidly convened and the "*davening*" commenced. My friend, though not particularly pious, found himself joining the worshippers.

Some days later, in Jerusalem, I found him ironic yet astounded. "Do you know what this means?" declared my soft-spoken friend after he had told me his story. "That is amazing! Think for a moment. Once there were three million Jews there and *then* it could never have happened. Unthinkable: for Jews to make a minyan, to perform a collective Jewish act in a public place in Poland! So why is that now possible?" His voice rose in excitement as he answered his own question. "Only one reason! The existence of the State of Israel! We [Jews] now have a state! So we can pray together, right in front of the Poles!"

My friend had a true "Peoplehood experience." But the essential root of the story did not come up in our conversation which was, indeed, about *Peoplehood* and the covenant of fate. For what led to this experience, and without which it couldn't have happened was actually about destiny, namely:

that these Jews *had to daven minchah*. They belonged to that sector of Jewry that considered itself bound to an idiosyncratic action, behind which stood God's commandment to be a holy people. It is unlikely that most of the *"daveners"* in question particularly reflect on that most of the time—and some of them may not have known how to do that; in a sense, the paucity of their systematic reflection was part of the strength of their behavior. But that "covenant of destiny" was, nonetheless, the reason for which they had been educated to pray. It was, after all, this destiny and this experience of Jewish norms dwelling within transcendence that lay behind the whole story, and made the event possible to begin with.

The covenant of destiny, as reflecting Peoplehood, gives rise to rich questions, but these can be explosive. For example:

- When these Jews recited the *Ashrei* prayer that opens the *Minchah* service, what were they doing?
- How, in post-Holocaust Poland, could they repeat the verses of the *Ashrei*, "God is good to all and His tender mercies are upon all His creatures" and "God is righteous in all His deeds and gracious in all His works"?

The *daveners* may consider the articulation of these questions as betraying the status of the questioner as an outsider, in which case the *minyan* at the airport, a prescriptive act, may once again demonstrate how commitment may unravel Peoplehood.

But there is another possibility: that such questions draw even those who don't pray regularly into the realm of the covenant of destiny that prayer signifies. For here are questions raised for everyone viewing that airport scene:

- What are the meanings behind Jewish Peoplehood that are accessible to us?
- What are the meanings that engendered Jewish feminism, more philosophy of Judaism, more Jewish schools, more Jewish study vigils throughout the night of Shavuot and more "Israel experiences" for Jewish youth?
- What does the evidence say?

* * *

Some years ago, a young man from the former Soviet Union applied to a prestigious teacher training institute in Jerusalem, wishing to spend two years of study, as a Fellow, at that institute.[1] As I was a faculty member of

---

1   I refrain from mentioning the names of Jewish frameworks currently functioning, in order not to presume to judge the importance of any of them. I make one "Haredi" exception that is not, by most of the others, considered to be quite "in the same ballpark."

the Institute, it was decided that I would interview him at a camp site not far from Moscow, formerly belonging to the Young Communist League. This site was hosting a ten-day seminar in Judaism and Jewish leadership and I had been invited to teach within this framework. The young man, after a long journey by rail, came into the seminar camp hesitantly, as though not trusting his eyes, not certain he was in the right place. Standing at the gate to the complex, he asked a young participant: "Is this the place? Is this the seminar for studying Judaism?" He was happily reassured; he had come to the right place. As he came into the grounds of the seminar center, my mind turned from the textual lesson I was presenting, for I could not help but think how many new things, amazing things, were going on around me: a young man who walks in out of nowhere, in search of Jewish study *that is actually available*—the pilgrim's question whether he is embarked on the right road, the tiring trip from Odessa to the hinterland of Moscow that leads to *Yerushalayim Habenuyah,* to a rebuilt Jerusalem. Does that count as evidence for the strength of Peoplehood?

Laying the Cards on the Table

In the covenant of faith, Peoplehood enjoys a richer content, yet is less visible and persuasive—for in our present situation, concepts of destiny are often divisive. At times, they are even imbued with the consciousness of "a righteous remnant"—which alienates most Jews and makes meaningful uses of "Peoplehood" unattainable. How then to make "Peoplehood" a significant platform for living Jewish lives and for planning the Jewish future?

Eliezer Goldman, the late Israeli thinker, has pointed pithily to the core of the dilemmas which we have to address, when we try to make Jewish Peoplehood an outcome of the covenant of destiny. [Goldman, "Values and Decisions" *Forum 4 for the problems of Zionism, Jewry and the State of Israel— Proceedings of the Jerusalem Ideological Conference* (Jerusalem: WZO, 1959), pp. 372–376.] Goldman was an active participant in the historic *Jerusalem Ideological Conference* convened by David Ben Gurion in August 1957, to which the leading thinkers, statesmen and leaders of mid-century Jewry were invited to discuss the central issues of the day. Their task was to articulate diverse positions on the continuum of Jewish life, to make recommendations about the Jewish situation, to discuss the place of religion and Zionism in present-day Jewish life, and to express their views on the effect of Israel on Jewish communities and Jewish consciousness.

Goldman, an analytic philosopher, commented bitingly on a thesis proposed by several other participants, who had urged strengthening the consciousness of Peoplehood as a primary educational goal. Goldman insisted that the historical facts of Jewish existence—"the Jewish heritage" as described by historians and other scholars—were, by their very nature, non-obligatory. They were, after all, only "descriptive." Hence:

> There is no question here concerning the obligation towards the cultural heritage [i.e., there is no such obligation]. The heritage is a historical channel through which the sentiment of obligation, among other things, reaches us [though they come from outside the "heritage"]. The heritage [is the "channel" that bring into view]...obligations to God and to man. It [the cultural heritage] is in itself not the object of obligation. Even the people as an historical entity are not the object of obligations, [though the heritage and the People make these obligations accessible]. (p. 373)

Goldman then suggests two roads toward a significant Jewish life for our times. One is in line with Rotenstreich's experience of being acted upon. On this level, the question of national belonging is not one that is subject to the decision of the will, but is determined by objective causes: persecution, economic separations, common identifying characteristics, etc. As a result of these causes, Goldman maintains, "no man can escape his Jewishness" and the existence of a, "national sentiment can be taken for granted...and can be made the basis for further development." This is the realm of "fate," as we have discussed it.

But there is also a second way. It is "to attempt to extract from the Jewish heritage those values that we acknowledge as obligatory and then try to bend our national attitude towards them." National life then becomes an attempt to embody these values and the obligations which eventually flow from the values.

In the address being cited here, Goldman makes four points: First, that national belonging can arise from objective causes, what we have called "fate." (Note that we have questioned whether what he terms the "irrational element" of that belonging is still as overpowering in the present generation as it was in the past, even in Goldman's generation.) Second, he is saying that descriptions of Jewish life, of historical developments and even of the former experience of "Jewish Peoplehood," in themselves, make no claims for allegiance to the data they are describing. Why indeed should past facts, however enthusiastically researched, and even descriptions of past beliefs, however moving, have the power to coerce to normative allegiance? (Yet we should recognize that many enter descriptive research into Jewish fields of study because they themselves are prescriptively endowed, and think, correctly or incorrectly, that they will infect others with their enthusiasms.) Third, that loyalty to the Jewish People or, for that matter, to any social or institutional framework arises out of that institution's clear usefulness, its demonstrated power to serve human needs, and, often even the need for a sense of historical continuity *for those who need it.*

Finally, Goldman is claiming that only the values we view as obligatory can protect and foster what we are calling Jewish Peoplehood, if we experience these values as embedded in the life of our people, its history and its faith. The educational upshot is that these values must be transmitted to us through the channels of our national culture. Once we have received these values through the channels of our culture, the values must "re-make" the nation and the culture in their own image. These values must interpret "and bend" the facts of Peoplehood to its evaluative or, if you will, its commanded, life. Goldman's perspective is an Orthodox one; for him "the People" exist for the sake of the covenant of Judaism "that make our collective lives an occasion of destiny." True, Goldman declares that he feels a sense of deep kinship with Jews who do not perceive Jewish Peoplehood as inherently "bringing to them" a demand that they observe the laws of the Torah, but this sense of kinship is itself derived and nourished from Jewish norms and values: "If such Jews [as myself] encourage others who are far from Judaism to cultivate what is close to their hearts and regard them as their brothers, it is not because we recognize their right to free themselves [from the *mitzvot*] but because we understand the concept of *Am Yisrael* as including those who do not observe the norm." (pp. 375–76) For Goldman, it is the prescriptive *Halachah* that determines the value of Jewish Peoplehood; non-observant Jews are a part of the Jewish People because that is how "we" (i.e., the Halachic Jews) understand the norm of fraternity with *Am Yisrael,* as a requirement of the *Halachah* itself.

Martin Buber addresses the issue from a non-Orthodox perspective. [Martin Buber: "The Jew in the World," Buber, *Israel and the World; essays in a time of crisis* (New York, Schocken Books, 1963), pp. 167–172.] His national-religious thesis is that the Jewish People, in its formative years, underwent an overpowering experience that it interpreted as a revelation of God. The People understood this experience of encounter to constitute them as both a community of faith and as a nation, a unique occurrence in human history.

> Only in one instance do [religion and nation] coincide. Israel receives its decisive experience *as a people;* it is not the prophet alone but the community as such that is involved. The community of Israel experiences history [i.e., its "national life] and revelation [its religious life] as one phenomenon, history as revelation and revelation as history. In the hour of its experience of faith the group becomes a people. Only as a people can it hear what it is destined to hear. (p. 169)

According to Buber, Zionism in its national-political aspects is, at best, an attempt to provide a ground for the Jews to be themselves; in its social, cultural and spiritual aspects, Zionism ideally seeks to "hear" what is now being "said" to Jews: not simply a religion (of "religious experience") undergone by individual believers, nor by a nation (of memories and as the aspirations of a historical collective.) Israel's task is, "to assume the yoke of the kingdom of God." However the first, political dimension should not be cast aside.

> Since this [the life of dialogical faith] can be accomplished only in the rounded life of a community, we must reassemble, we must again gain root in the soil, we must govern ourselves. But these are mere *pre-requisites!* Only when the community recognizes and realizes them as such in its own life, will they serve as the cornerstones of its salvation. (p. 172)

Buber is not pleading for a "return to tradition," or for observance of the commandments. Indeed, he himself was not traditional and did not observe the traditional commandments. For him, "revelation" is a product of dialogue, a conversation between friends and fellows—an encounter with a Presence that energizes even as it makes ever-new demands of people. Buber cannot share Goldman's, to him, doctrinaire, view of what is prescriptive in Jewish life. He will insist that we never know what God is demanding, until we are open to the religious experience of this moment, rooted in "the life of the nation."

Yet Buber will agree with Goldman that Peoplehood is a requirement of the uniquely Jewish spiritual life, and that it may under no circumstances be confused with it. Should the "yoke of Heaven" be forgotten or neglected, and all that remains is "the People" or, alternately, if there is no more than Jewish religious tradition, a "faith" that makes do without existential ties to the Jewish People, the Jews are doomed, at best, to a sterile existence:

> ...If we want to be nothing but normal we shall soon cease to be at all.
> ...The great values we have produced issued from the marriage of a people and a faith. We cannot substitute a technical association of nation and religion for this original marriage, without incurring barrenness. ("Hebrew Humanism" *Israel and the World* (p. 252)

The thesis I have been presenting, which is indebted to Goldman and Buber, is that Peoplehood is a meaningful and operative concept. But Peoplehood alone, as a term that can point to the need to solve Jewish problems and one that can build on experience of unity in the midst of diversity, will become archaic as Jews have the heady experience of not being excluded and dehumanized, of not having to consider particular "Jewish problems" as their problems, because they can be fully absorbed in non-Jewish societies, Then, it is not the descriptive conception of "Peoplehood," but the intent of Jews to find ultimate meaning in the prescriptions that "arise out of" Jewish life, and that are actually lived out by the Jewish People in a framework of evaluative obligation, which will take center stage. Then (or, rather, now) Sklare's warning, that Jews need to retain cultural distinctiveness even in the open societies in which they live, constitutes a central challenge. If we cannot move towards a destiny that has common elements, however variegated, everything about "Jewish Peoplehood" will come to depend on "fate." This scenario may at times be heroic, but it is profoundly cheerless.

Towards an Agenda

Clearly, my paper is not meant to set an agenda but, rather, to raise questions, hopefully helpful, for those who do. Yet a few remarks that move us in the direction of policies and programs may be useful. It appears, on the basis of the conceptions I have presented, that the tasks facing Jews in general and Jewish leaders, in particular, can be envisioned as threefold:

(1) In terms of the covenant of fate: Jewish leaders must continue to refine the ways in which to identify the specific challenges and dangers facing the Jewish People and the means that assure optimal safety and equity for Jews. These challenges are legitimately and productively seen within the conceptual prism of Peoplehood. They involve recognizing threats to Jewish welfare as ultimately affecting all Jews, working together on the basis of careful deliberation and acting effectively. But neither these problems nor their solutions should become the be-all and end-all of Jewish life, or of Jewish Peoplehood.

(2) Second, Jewish leaders, community workers and scholars need to identify the institutions, guiding spirits, and scope of various prescriptive phenomena developing and intact within world Jewry. The widespread assumptions I noted above—assumptions that largely inform our vision of what can or cannot be done—may blind us to various interpretations of "the covenant of destiny" that are indeed "out there," presenting various options for Jewish life. Foci of Jewish life that expand horizons of Jews who wish to be Jews, such as large-scale informal educational programs, should not be allowed to go under for lack of funds, but neither should the support they are given be uncritical.

To bring a specific and important example: The leaders of the various ultra-Orthodox communities around the world do not doubt that their publics are the wave of the future. Nonetheless, wherever Jewish educational questions are discussed and policies decided, there appears to be an assumption that there is nothing to learn from the educational enterprises of *Haredi* Jewry. Yet it should be noted that there is no lack of teachers in the ultra-Orthodox *Beth Ya'akov* school and seminary system for girls—as distinct from the situation in non-*Haredi* institutions: this is because teaching is held in high esteem as a profession for women, albeit as a pale reflection of the reverence accorded Yeshiva rabbi-educators in the Yeshiva world. The successes of haredi education are blatant—as are its deficiencies and failures. Yet two facts are clear about the subject of haredi education: First, that it has a vision, a conception of Jewish destiny; Second, that it lives increasingly—at least at a technological level, albeit in a peculiarly truncated fashion—in the midst of the modern world. Despite this, strikingly few educational deliberations convened to address the crisis of Jewish education wish to learn from the Haredi experience—although learning from it might also open doors to changing its orientation to such matters as: professional training; expansion of the curriculum; and a more open approach to other Jews. In any case, the principle of Peoplehood applies to the relationship of Jews to other Jews—even when the others do not show much evidence of genuine reciprocity. At least, not at present . . .

(3) A great deal of thought has to be given to ways of *making the existing "visions of destiny" accessible to greater publics.* The various shapes and forms of "The Israel Experience," are examples both of the potential and the difficulties in readying an educational vision for use within different groups and contexts. There is certainly more going on than a generation ago. Leaders need to study these phenomena, analyze their significance, nurture them and help make them more widely accessible, as enterprises of the never-dying people at this stage of its history.

(4) Jewish leadership, in addition to leading the search for Jewish security, must serve the Jews in their search for the meaning of Jewish existence. Here, there will be no blurring of distinctions but, rather, increased efforts of dialogue; pluralism without loss of conviction; learning to see the Jewish sense in the story of a Yehoyachim, restored to a semblance of hope and respect—yet all this without sentimentality, or over-spiritualized mystifications.

In Summation

The concept of Peoplehood, as we have seen, is a foundation stone of deliberations regarding a viable, vital and creative Jewish life. It allows the blurring of distinctions when blurring is called for by the common tasks at hand and when there is a need to organize collective energies for response to problems, challenges and dangers. It clearly delineates the covenant of fate and it builds the context for the variegated *covenants* of destiny in our time.

Yet, Peoplehood as a guiding concept can be problematic in the realm of "destiny" and vision. It can overlook the fact that the existence of the Jews reaches beyond ethnicity, by building contexts and "channels" for the variegated *covenants* of destiny in our time. The Prophets, we have suggested, understood the Peoplehood of Israel has ultimately been nourished and even legitimated by the values that make the Jews both a faith community as well as a people. To cite Buber again, the Jews are a nation because a national existence is required to live by the specific religious vision; the Jews are a nation, or, if you will, a people, because the specific religious task of the people of Israel cannot be implemented except by a people. The religious demand is not made to provide the nation with a culture; rather, the nation exists in order to further the vision that the culture makes accessible. Jewish life, annoyingly, thus always has to explain itself. But this is its claim to eternity, and the locale of its vision: the rationale for not simply being like everyone else, not disappearing.

In reflecting on these issues, I recall a feature that used to appear in the weekly magazine *The Jerusalem Report*: "Shabbat Around the World." This section provided times for the advent and conclusion of the Sabbath in all major centers of Jewish life. Can there be a more pithy metaphor for Jewish Peoplehood than that feature which, in bare names and numbers, hinted at the drama of the Friday sun, hurtling through space, bringing light to zone after zone, and then, moving away into dusk? This is a sundown greeted by innumerable Sabbath lights, as though to banish the approaching darkness or, if you will, to greet the Sabbath. The Sabbath lights are lit together in Tel Aviv and Eilat, sequentially in Jerusalem and Paris—as the Sabbath, together with the ever setting sun, moves to cover the face of the Earth. The associations of Shabbat times touch on Jewish Peoplehood at its core. Is there a better way to point to the drama of Jewish Peoplehood, and the Sabbath entrusted to it, as "a perpetual sign," than the celebration of "Shabbat Around the World"?

THE ANOMALIES OF
JEWISH POLITICAL IDENTITY

MICHAEL WALZER

Editor's Summary

Michael Walzer argues that Jews are anomalous in that they are both a religion and a nation. For other peoples in the world, these categories do not coincide—for Jews, they overlap completely. He contends that although we may wish to overcome these anomalies in order to be like everyone else, there is really no good grounds for doing so. Instead, we should embrace and educate ourselves about both our religious and our national heritages, and demand that others respect us for the way in which we are different.

I am going to begin this essay by reciting what we all know. I hope this will prove a useful exercise, in that making explicit what is mostly informal knowledge, common sense, or intuitive understanding, can often help us think about things more clearly.

We all know how anomalous Jewish identity is, and we all know the reasons. The Jews are a people as well as a nation (albeit for a long time a stateless one), and as such, they are a collective of a familiar kind. There are many nations, and we are one among them. At the same time, the Jews are a religious community, a community of faith, as we say in the United States— which is another collective of a familiar kind. There are many religions, and ours is one among them. The anomaly is that these two collectives are not of the same kind, and, except in the Jewish case, they don't ordinarily coincide. Other peoples or nations include members of different religious communities. Other religious communities extend across national boundaries and include members of different peoples or nations. For us alone do the concepts of nation and religion overlap completely.

Consider first how we differ from other peoples. The French people, for example, includes Catholics and Protestants and now Muslims—and Jews too, who would certainly resent being denied membership. But the Jewish People does not include Christians or Muslims. It does indeed include secular Jews and also distinct denominations of religious Jews, and so one can say that there exists among the Jewish People a range of religious sensibilities (and insensibilities). But it is commonly understood, and it is established law in the State of Israel, that formal conversion to another religion excludes the convert from membership in the Jewish People.

You may ask: But aren't there Jewish Buddhists nowadays? And what about Jews for Jesus—aren't they still Jews? Maybe so, but these identities appear to involve something considerably short of formal conversion: their status is up in the air. What is clear is that there are no Jewish Catholics, Baptists, Methodists, or Presbyterians. However pro-Israel American Pentacostals may be, they can't join the Jewish People without giving up their Christianity—which they don't need to do, in order to join any other people. So the Jews are not a "people" like the others. Zionism aimed to produce a "normal" people and, given the conditions of our exile, that project was certainly a healthy one; the Zionist passion for normalcy has real achievements to its credit. But it hasn't made us like everyone else.

Nor is our religion like all the other religions. The Catholic Church, for example, is a universal, religious community that includes men and women who are members of the French, Italian, Irish, Nigerian, and Korean peoples, and many others, too. The Jewish religious community isn't like that, even though it does include men and women who are French, English, Russian, and so on—because Jews are French, English, and Russian with a difference. The pre-Zionist and then anti-Zionist campaign to create a normal religious community, consisting of say, Frenchmen, or Germans, of the "Mosaic faith," seems to me less healthy than Zionism as it developed, but it was still an understandable response to the conditions of our exile. And it, too, has proven futile: French Jews continue to be Jewish, in both the religious and the national sense. However "French" they are or believe themselves to be, they are as anomalous as ever.

In the United States, it was Jewish advocates of cultural pluralism, most notably Horace Kallen, who invented the idea of hyphenated Americans, thereby enabling us to add "American" to our identity, without giving up "Jewish." Thanks to Kallen, we are not Americans who happen to be of the Jewish religion; we are both American Jews (religiously) and Jewish-Americans (nationally). We pretend that we are like American Catholics, on the one hand, and like Italian-Americans, on the other. But the analogy doesn't work in either case. Many American Catholics, for example, are not Italian, and some Italian-Americans are not Catholic, while our religious and national identities continue, anomalously, to coincide. Even those of us who aren't personally religious, are Jewish in both these senses.

The existence of the State of Israel makes things even more complicated. Here is a Jewish state that has a large and growing number of non-Jewish citizens. Some Jews inside and outside of Israel claim that the state doesn't belong just to its citizens, the way all other states do, but to the Jewish People as a whole, including Jews who are citizens of other states. This would be a greater anomaly than any of ones I have discussed so far, but it isn't true, except in a very limited sense of "belonging." Normally I have decision-making authority over things that belong to me, but the Jewish People as a whole doesn't have decision-making authority over the State of Israel. The state is a democracy, and democracies belong, in the normal sense of that word, to their citizens. So, strictly speaking, Israel belongs to its citizens, including its non-Jewish citizens.

Perhaps Zionist normalcy would be realized if and when "Israeli" became a nationality—for this nationality would extend to members of different religious communities, most notably Jewish, Muslim, and Christian. Doesn't it do that already? But it also extends to members of different national communities, Arabs and Jews, and it doesn't yet offer a superseding nationality. One day, being an Israeli might be more important than being an Arab or a Jew, and then there would be a normal Israeli nation, with a state of its own. But this state would not "belong" to the Jewish People in any sense of the word—that's precisely what would make it normal. We might need, maybe we already need, a new hyphenated identity, Jewish-Israeli, to designate those citizens of the Jewish state (in a national sense) who are also Jews (in a religious sense).

So far, the normalizing projects have failed to overcome the weight of history and tradition. But they haven't failed definitively; they might one day be revived with greater success. And I can see the point of experimenting right now with what might be termed bits and pieces of normalcy. Consider the question of how one joins the Jewish People/religion. Right now there is only a religious way in. But why shouldn't it be possible for prospective Jews to say, "Your people shall be my people" without saying, "Your God shall be my God"? Why do they have to say both together, even in cases where one (or, as is also possible, the other) isn't what they really mean? The search for a naturalization process that might sit alongside the conversion process seems to me entirely legitimate, even sensible, although it is unlikely to succeed in the near future.

But there are motives for normalization that should make us uneasy—the hope, for example, that other people might like us better if we were more like them. Anomaly (OR: Being anomalous) isn't popular. People find us hard to understand. Because neither our national nor our religious community is inclusive in the standard way, we are accused of being parochial, hostile to outsiders, exclusionary, chauvinist, and, in any group except our own, disloyal and subversive. Indeed, we have all heard accusations of these kinds, and sometimes, since we are very good at self-criticism, we are driven to ask ourselves whether, or to what extent, they might be true. Still, we should not have to assume responsibility for the hatred we inspire among (some of) our neighbors. We need not make excuses to the people who accuse us. We have a simple position to defend, before we move on to self-criticism: it really isn't all that hard for our neighbors to live with our anomalies, if they are minded to do so, and they should be so minded. In a world where there are many ways of being different, and an extraordinary diversity of customs and beliefs, what justice requires (from us, in the Diaspora and in Israel, and from everyone else too) is respect for difference—and our own differences are among those that demand respect.

To render that demand effective, we must respect ourselves, and that means, right now, to embrace the anomalies. This doesn't seem to me to be the right time for any large-scale revival of the normalizing projects. We are what we are, and we need to make a secure place for ourselves in the world—a place for ourselves, as we are. If we do that, one or another kind of normalcy might follow in time (or it might not).

What would it mean to embrace the anomalies? We are a single religious community, many of whose members are irreligious, and all of whose members constitute a single people. We belong in two places at once (leaving geography aside). We have a cultural heritage that—as Ahad Ha'am, founder of Cultural Zionism, wrote in his controversy with Joseph Haim Brenner, a founder of Socialist Zionism—"is filled with the religious spirit, which free-thinkers cannot embrace"—but which many free-thinkers do embrace. I mean, they recognize the value of that heritage, even if their engagement with it is critical or oppositionist. Similarly, to quote Ahad Ha'am again, they recognize the God of Israel, "as a historical force that gave vitality to our people and influenced . . . the progress of its life over millennia," even if they deny that the God of Israel exists in any other sense. It is possible or, at least, among Jews it is possible, to stand within the community of faith without sharing the faith—another example of our anomalies. I suspect that more Jews have found themselves in that position over the centuries, than the faithful today will acknowledge. Freethinking Jews have a religious identity because we inherit a religiously inspired culture—in which we find much to admire and appropriate. We can't convert to another religion and remain members of the Jewish nation, but (for the most part) we don't want to do so.

And, similarly, religious Jews have a secular/national identity, because they live as members of a people that is organized and whose affairs are administered, in both the Diaspora and in Israel, by "lay leaders" chosen through political processes—which is to say, not chosen either directly or indirectly by God. And they accept and enjoy the benefits of this identity. They can't leave the people without giving up their religion, but (mostly) they don't want to leave. As a free-thinking reader of the Bible, I would say that something like this was also true in ancient times. The ancient Israelite kingdoms were "like the other nations," exactly as the elders who came to Samuel asking for a king intended them to be. Remember how the Prophets complained about the political prudence of kings like Hezekiah, who lacked, they said, faith in God. Yet Prophets and kings were members of the same nation and the same religious community. Then, as now, the national and religious communities coincided in membership, even though they were different in kind. And then, as now, the political community included people with different (non-Israelite/non-Jewish) national and religious identities. The biblical writers either denied or tried to eliminate these differences, but we cannot do so today. This commitment is crucial to our political rebirth: that the members of other nations and religions, citizens of the modern Jewish state, must not suffer because of our anomalies.

The constant mixing of incongruous elements is our history, and this is what I would teach to our children. They must learn that our national history is also a religious history, which has its beginning in a Covenant with God, which was regularly violated by the people who made it. And they must learn that our religious history is also a national history, driven by political and economic forces, subject to environmental and demographic constraints, exactly like all the other nations. Religious children must study secular texts; secular children must study religious texts. They must all be taught that although the memberships coincide, nation and religion are not the same thing (or else there would be no anomalies). We live differently in each. In the religious community, we associate with Reform, Conservative, Orthodox, and ultra-Orthodox Jews, and also with skeptics and free-thinkers—and then with Christians, Muslims, and so on, outside the community. In the nation, we associate with Jewish-Americans, and Jewish-Italians, and Jewish-Russians, and Jewish-Israelis—and then with Americans, Italians, Russians, and Israelis outside the nation.

Moving among these different associations requires constant changes of style and sensibility. Jews have gotten pretty good at making these changes, and I believe we should celebrate this ancestral talent, rather than trying to reject and replace it—as if it would be better to be always the same, to possess a singular identity, to overcome the anomalies. Of course, we should insist that the world allow us to be what we are; we should act honestly in front of others. But first we must accept ourselves as we are—anomalies and all.

ON MODERN JEWISH IDENTITIES

MOSHE HALBERTAL

Editor's Summary

In the modern world, we have been forced to confront the issue of Peoplehood—of what it means to be part of the Jewish People—with the introduction of the concept of "Jew" into the Law of Return. The Knesset and Israeli courts have become focal points in the struggle over the establishment of modern Jewish identity, a struggle that revolves around the question of whether a commitment to *Halachah* is a necessary prerequisite for conversion to Judaism. This question has faced rabbinic authorities for centuries, as seen, for instance, in the responsa collection *Helkat Yaakov* by Rabbi Yaakov Breish. However, the radical historic change that has taken place in the character of the Jewish collective poses a difficulty to the conventional legal method involving inference from the precedents found in the halachic jurisprudence to resolve the current struggle. The traditional concept of Jewish identity has been replaced by a plurality of incommensurable notions which render the attempt to subordinate the definition of Jewish nationalism to the halachic framework both problematic and mistaken. Instead, we must affirm and embrace the modern Jewish condition as pluralistic, and revise our understanding of Jewish identity and Peoplehood accordingly.

In the modern world, we have been forced to confront the issue of Peoplehood— of what it means to be part of the Jewish People—with the introduction of the concept of "Jew" into the Law of Return. This law, which guarantees citizenship to all Jews in the State of Israel, also grants citizenship to the non-Jewish relatives of Jews, and rightly so. As long as the State of Israel is a relatively desirable immigration destination, and Jews married to non-Jews continue to throng to it, a certain gap will continue to exist between the broad definition of the Law of Return and the interest to maintain a Jewish majority in the country, which is itself the very interest that lies at the foundation of the Law of Return. The state expects the halachic authorities to close this gap by means of the conversion process, in order to enable non-Jewish immigrants that have been naturalized in Israel by virtue of the Law of Return to join the Jewish national collective. However, conversion is only possible if these authorities surrender the requirement of an a priori commitment to the observance of the commitments, which, as we shall see, is no simple matter.

In this essay, I will begin by looking at how the subject of conversion has led to some of the most telling moments in the shattering of Jewish identity and its radical plurality, as seen both in earlier halachic responsa literature and in the contemporary discourse surrounding the Law of Return. I will contend that in our own day, the traditional concept of Jewish identity has been replaced by a plurality of incommensurable notions which render the attempt to subordinate the definition of Jewish nationalism to the halachic framework both problematic and mistaken. Instead, I will argue, we must affirm and embrace the modern Jewish condition as pluralistic, and revise our understanding of Jewish identity and Peoplehood accordingly.

I. Conversion in the Responsa Literature

It is no wonder that a discussion of conversion highlights complex tensions in the self-definition of the group, since the manner in which a community establishes the identity of its members is expressed in the ways it constructs the rules that govern how members are admitted into and removed from that community. The concepts of a community's identity are honed at its edges, in its rites of passage and exclusion ceremonies, its admission demands and exclusion procedures.

In *Helkat Yaakov*, Rabbi Breish, one of the few and most important European Halachic authorities to have survived the destruction of the Jews, discusses the increasing number of cases involving converts whose motivation for conversion is their desire to marry a Jew. According to the *Halachah*, as set down in the *Mishneh Torah* and the *Shulkhan Aruch*, a rabbinical court may not convert people who seek to convert for that reason; however, if they did convert, their conversion would be considered valid after the fact.

Despite this *halachah*, certain rabbinical authorities believed that the new historic circumstances in which the *Halachah* found itself permitted, and even required, that such converts be accepted by the rabbinical court. As an example of support for this contention, Rabbi Breish quotes from a book by Rabbi Menahem Kirschenbaum, the Rabbi of Frankfurt:

> ...Because if they are not accepted, they will go to Reform rabbis, who are not strict about immersion in a ritual bath and they will not be converts according to the law at all, as explained in the Gemarah and in Maimonides and the Shulchan Aruch, that one must examine to see if the prospective convert has come because of a women; but in any case, after the fact, he is a convert. [...] For if this is not done, he will live with her despite the prohibition or by means of a Reform conversion, and they will be considered to be part of the Jewish community and become assimilated into it. (*Helkat Yaakov*, Section 13)

Although Rabbi Kirschenbaum was aware of the traditional prohibition against accepting converts who are motivated by the desire to marry a Jew, he points out two substantive elements of the new historical situation of modern Jewry. In order to address them, a fundamental change in the approach to conversion is required. The first is that an alternative to Orthodox conversion had developed—Reform conversion—and the loss of the monopoly of the Orthodox rabbinical courts on conversion required that they accept a convert of this type, lest the convert undergo a halachically invalid Reform conversion instead. The first element in the fracture in modern Jewish condition is reflected here in the fact that there is no shared agreement concerning the procedure of entry to the community, and no single denomination of Judaism managed to maintain a monopoly over entry.

The second change, which has also been present since the nineteenth century, involves the fact that the couple also has the option of sanctioning their union with a civil marriage outside the Jewish or Christian community, even without conversion. In the view of Rabbi Kirschenbaum and other rabbinical authorities, the presence of other conversion or marriage options required the rabbinical courts to deviate from the accepted normative *Halachah*, because refusal to do so would lead to intermarriage and to the assimilation of non-Jews into the Jewish community. Jews since the Emancipation have entered neutral modern space. They became participants in the civic realm, which allowed them to form a family—the most central human bond—with non Jews and with themselves, outside the church or the synagogue. They have acquired a new identity, neither Jewish nor Christian. They have become citizens of the modern centralized state. Spinoza's bold choice to live neither as a Jew nor as a Christian, but to reside in the neutral civic space has become a possible norm for modern Jews at large. Inhabiting this neutral realm fostered the creation of the hyphenated new identity German-Jewish French-Jewish etc. It added an immense complexity and richness to Jewish identity, and naturally it left its marks on the establishment of entry procedure into this new identity.

Rabbi Breish, who vehemently opposes this approach, adds a third and more central element in the historic changes in modern Jewish identity, the element that in his view tips the scale in the opposite direction:

> "And I am very amazed at the sight—because the rabbis living in the promiscuous cities of Western Europe must not delude themselves, because they know full well that the vast majority of converts are those who have joined their fate to that of the Jewish people in order to marry, and most of these Jews are transgressors who do not want to know about Judaism.—Kashrut, Shabbat, the laws of family purity—all the commandments are an unnecessary burden to them, and they are merely Jews of nationality. They know very well that the non-Jewish woman who is ostensibly converting will not behave in accordance with Jewish law, because her Jewish-national husband does not know anything about Jewish law either, and if this is the case, the matter is simple enough for me, that even after the fact, this conversion should not be considered valid, because the acceptance of the commitment to observe the commandments is one of the matters that can impede conversion, even after the fact. (*Helkat Yaakov*, Section 13),

Rabbi Breish underscores another modern turning point in the meaning of conversion in light of a deep transformation in the modern Jew. The collective that the convert is joining is not the same Jewish collective as it was known throughout Jewish history. The convert is joining a new national Jewish identity that has nothing to do with the Torah or the commandments. While the rite of passage resembles the traditional ceremony at least externally—there is a proper circumcision and immersion in the ritual bath—this convert is joining a community that *Halachah* does not view as the normative continuation of the Jewish People. Rabbi Breish is fully aware that this convert will not observe the commandments, not only as an assumption based on the motivation for conversion, but also because of his or her frank assessment of the national and secular nature of the community that the convert is joining. The option for a new national Jewish identity created in the nineteenth century, which does not view the Torah and its commandments as the formative component of Jewish collective identity, radically changes the perception of conversion and, in Rabbi Breish's view, moves it in the direction of greater rather than lesser stringency. From this time on, rabbis must investigate the nature of the Jewish collective that the prospective convert plans to join through the conversion rite of passage.

Rabbi Breish bases his forceful opposition to this type of conversion on the argument that the commitment to observe commandments is a necessary condition of conversion. However, despite the authoritative and confident tone that accompanies Rabbi Breish's arguments throughout his response, we know that this issue was the subject of intense controversy that began even during the Middle Ages and has continued up until the modern rabbinical rulings. Rabbi Uziel, for example, ruled that the lack of commitment to the observance of the commandments is not an impediment to conversion, and that converts should be accepted even if the rabbinical court is convinced that they will not in fact be observant. As he put it in the following extended discussion on the subject:

> "From everything that has been stated, we learn that the condition of observance of the commandments does not impede conversion, even before the fact."

And, further on, he writes:

> "We are commanded to accept all male and female converts, even if we know that they will not observe all the commandments, because ultimately they may come to observe them and we are commanded to open such a window for them, and if they do not observe the commandments, they are responsible for their sins, and we are innocent" (*Piskei Uziel Bish'elot Hazman*, Section 68).

As Zvi Zohar and Avi Sagi have demonstrated extensively in their book about conversion, this question was the subject of controversy among Halachic authorities in the Middle Ages, and the position that the lack of commitment to observance should be an impediment to conversion is a minority opinion that developed in Ashkenaz.[1]

The conceptual significance of this controversy over the nature of conversion and its implications for the perception of Jewish identity has been formulated by a contemporary Halachic authority, Rabbi Jacob Fink, in the following manner: Those who maintain that the commitment to observance is not a necessary component of conversion view the conversion ceremony as a ritual of rebirth into the Jewish ethnic community. The obligation of the convert to observe the commandments is derived from the fact of his joining the Jewish People. Those who maintain that the commitment to observance is an essential component of conversion hold just the opposite: The commitment to the commandments is not the result of the convert becoming Jewish, but rather it is that which turns him into a Jew. The convert joins the Jewish People because he or she has accepted the commitment to observance of the Torah as part of the conversion process itself. In fact, this perception of conversion is based on the fact that the Jewish People itself became a unique community not because it ethnically belonged to the Jewish race. Rather, the Jewish People was constituted by virtue of its entrance into the covenant at Sinai, which involves the acceptance of the commandments. Conversion is no more than a ritual reenactment of the giving of the Torah at Sinai. Thus, the dispute over the question of the formative status of the acceptance of the commandments makes it possible to identify the inner tension regarding the relations between the Jewish collective and the acceptance of the Torah.[2]

II. The Modern Controversy: Who Is A Jew

Must someone take on all the commandments in order to be considered a Jew? At stake is the very concept of "Jewishness" and the meaning of belonging to the Jewish people, as our modern reality has made all too apparent. The introduction of the concept of "Jew" into the Law of Return and the citizen-registration ordinance has forced the Israeli court in a number of cases to confront the definition of Jewishness, thereby turning the Knesset and the Israeli courts into focal points in the struggle over the establishment of modern Jewish identity. A new border control point has been added to the existing border stations of *Halachah* and the rabbinical courts on the line between the Jew and the non-Jew—the Knesset and the Israeli Supreme Court.

---

[1]   Zvi Zohar and Avi Sagi, *Conversion and Jewish Identity*, Jerusalem, 1995.
[2]   Yaakov Fink, Yahadut veGerut (Judaism and Conversion) in *Noam*, 14, 1971, p. 17. See also Zvi Zohar and Avi Sagi, op. cit., Chapter 13.

Each of the joining contexts—conversion and Israeli naturalization— presents intrinsic difficulties of its own. Conversion is a complex halachic category, the clarification of which underscores deep-rooted internal tensions within Halachah itself concerning the perception of Jewish identity. Receiving citizenship as a Jew by virtue of the Law of Return is also a way of joining, and it too can involve considerable difficulty for the definition of national belonging and immigration policies. However, beyond the intrinsic difficulties posed by each of these two contexts, the attempt to create an overlap between them in the wake of ideological or political pressure has brought to the surface the crisis of identity of the modern Jew, the internal contradictions in that identity and the convoluted relations between religion and nationality and subsequently between religion and state that arose in the late nineteenth century.

This crisis of identity was manifested in a few of the court's decisions concerning who is a Jew, the most visible of which was the Shalit case. Binyamin Shalit, who married a non-Jewish woman, demanded that the state register his children as Jews in the nationality section of their identity cards. The strength of Shalit's argument did not stem only from his subjective consciousness, but also from the story of his life and that of his wife and the expected fate of his children: they joined their fate to that of the Jewish collective, and they raised and educated their children among Jews.

The case of Shalit, like so many others, demonstrates that the alternative nationalist definition of the concept of halachic belonging is not the subjective consciousness of the individual, but rather the individual's willingness to participate in the fate of the community while viewing himself as a member of that community. It is a conception based on the idea of solidarity with the nation's predicament as the constitutive element of its identity. Nationalism is an extension of the concept of fraternity for the members of a single group, whether the empiric source of the group is shared or not. The place of consciousness comes to replace a shared ethnicity, which usually does not exist. But consciousness is not enough. An awareness of fraternity is not fraternity; fraternity is a way of behaving.

Despite the overlap that indeed exists between the two joining tracks, the most outstanding sign of the crisis in defining identity is reflected in the fact that in the most prominent case brought before the Israeli court, The Shalit case, The court ruled in a manner that was different from what it believed *Halachah* would have decided. According to the court's ruling, Shalit's children were to be registered as Jews, notwithstanding the *Halachah* that would define them as non-Jews. An examination of these judgments reflects the rise of a new category of identity, and a radical historic change in the character of Jewish collective identity.

The tendency of halachic authorities when dealing with modern problems such as the case of Shalit is to refer to the precedents that appear in the rabbinic literature and rulings of the Middle Ages. Rabbi Breish and his opponent on this matter, Rabbi Uziel, like many other halachic authorities that debated the issue, use their extensive erudition to find evidence and proof for their opposing positions from the ramified halachic literature at their disposal, most of which predates the nineteenth century. That is also the tendency exhibited by Zvi Zohar and Avi Sagi, who systematically explored the various schools of thought. Zohar and Sagi concluded that the golden mean in conversion does not require a priori commitment to the observance of commandments on the part of the convert as a necessary component of conversion, and that the obligation to observe the commandments is the result of having joined the Jewish People, rather than its formative element.

However, it appears to me that on this question, the radical historic change that took place in the character of the Jewish collective poses a difficulty to the conventional legal method, involving the use of inference from the precedents found in the halachic jurisprudence to resolve a current problem. The profound change that occurred with the rise of the national-identity alternative presented the traditional conversion ceremony with a serious problem, especially concerning the importance of the commitment to observance of the commandments. After all, just as Rabbi Breish contended, the collective that the convert is joining is fundamentally different from everything *Halachah* had known before in the normative Jewish community.

By analogy from the philosophy of science, contemporary halachic authorities are working within a situation of a paradigm shift. The proper halachic procedure to deal with a new problem must be based on the understanding that the relevant components that justify the application of the precedential norms are still present. However, if the paradigm has changed, the very same components that once seemed relevant now take on a completely different meaning.

The clearest sign that a paradigm shift has taken place on the issue of conversion is that each of the positions of the Middle Ages regarding whether a commitment to the commandments is a necessary component of conversion can be applied in the opposite sense in the modern situation. The halachic authorities of the Middle Ages who held that the lack acceptance of commandments does not impede conversion believed this because in the historical conditions in which they lived and worked, joining the Jewish community automatically implied the acceptance of a commitment to observance. In the modern conditions of the growth of a national identity, which offers those joining the option of an alternative Jewish identity that is not dependent on the observance of the Torah, the willingness to convert does not necessarily imply a commitment to observance, and therefore, these authorities would likely also take the position that an *a priori* commitment to observance is required.

A similar claim may be made in the opposite direction. The medieval halachic authorities who held that lack of an *a priori* commitment to the commandments impedes conversion took this view because in the historical conditions in which they lived and worked, a convert that did not fully commit to the observance of the Torah could not in fact be a part of the Jewish community—because there was no Jewish community whose way of life was not lived in accordance with the Torah and its commandments. On the other hand, the modern situation makes it possible to join a concrete Jewish community without acceptance of the commandments. Therefore, it is entirely possible that the very same authority that held in the Middle Ages that the lack of commitment to the Torah was an impediment to conversion would exempt today's converts from this condition, in the context of the Jewish reality after the rise of nationalism.

The modern crisis on the question of Jewish identity, as it is reflected in the conversion rite of passage, puts *Halachah* into a position in which its standard tool—inference from halachic precedent—is no longer applicable. The attempt to bring evidence from precedents from the Middle Ages is problematic because it assumes a continuity that does not in effect exist. The rise of Jewish nationalism brought in its wake a different perception of the identity of the members of the Jewish community, and accordingly, a new approach to the manner in which members may join and leave the Jewish collective. We will not be able to begin to solve the modern crisis unless we inquire deeper into the nature of the plurality of modern Jewish identity and its meaning.

III. A New Jewish Identity

An examination of the complex issue of membership reveals two conceptions of identity which can be termed as the covenantal and the national: one bases identity on a life of standing before God as obligated, and the other bases such identity on solidarity. Yet, analysis of the modern Jewish condition reveals a third conception, no less powerful then the others, which resonates very deeply in modern Jewish life. I refer to the cosmopolitan identity of being a Jew. To be a Jew in this approach is to emphasize the power of particular identity in shaping moral rules and political privileges. A Jew exhibits his or her own Jewishness in his compassion towards the vulnerable, and in its principle stance for universal political and moral values. This form of being a Jew, expressed in the notion of *tikkun olam*, is rooted in the Jewish historical condition of vulnerability and marginality. The capacity to adopt the cosmopolitan point of view stems from that unique stance of the Jew in the margins of society occupying simultaneously the position of an insider and an outsider. The particular moral and intellectual sensibility that informs Jewishness is rooted as well in this approach in a religious tradition that has to be abandoned, given the cosmopolitan stance, and yet it plays a nourishing role for this modern form of identity. Freud, one of the greatest voices of such an approach, expressed this view of the Jews in the following manner:

"In a new transport of moral asceticism the Jews imposed on themselves constantly increasing instinctual renunciation, and thereby reached—at least in doctrine and precepts—ethical heights that had remained inaccessible to the other peoples of antiquity. Many Jews regard these aspirations as the second main characteristic, and the second great achievement, of their religion." (*Moses and Monotheism*, page 173)

The cosmopolitan identity is in itself paradoxical: to be a Jew is to stand against the discriminating force of particular identities, among them the particular identity of being a Jew. It is a concept of identity that questions in an ongoing way its own identity. For its own continuity it therefore needs the other parties of Jewish identity, which are committed to reproduce Jewish particularism to the next generation in different forms. Yet it is important to stress that the cosmopolitan Jew is not one who, assimilated and happened to adopt universal values and a cosmopolitan identity. The cosmopolitan Jew assumes this moral and political position as a *Jew* and that particular stance creates the tension we are highlighting. And so, in light of the fact that for many modern Jews the expression of being Jewish is to adopt the universal standpoint, such a stance should be taken as a third powerful option of modern Jewish identity.

Traditionally the cosmopolitan element was connected to the left, from the Jewish Bund to the contemporary American Jew who, "earns like an Episcopalian and votes like a Porto Rican." Yet the universal calling is not limited to such political conviction. One of the most interesting and intriguing shifts in contemporary Jewish life is the impact and presence of such sensibility in right-wing politics, through the work of Leo Strauss and the place of Jews in the Neo-Conservative ideology and movement. The Jewish cosmopolitan elite is therefore diverse in its stance; nevertheless, it engages its different cosmopolitan universal vocation as a deep expression of being a Jew.

In its questioning particular identities, there is no wonder that the cosmopolitan Jewish identity altogether rejected Jewish Nationalism as a movement that would harm the most cherished and valuable aspect of being a Jew. Such a point of view is expressed in the positions of George Steiner, the most eloquent spokesman for such a stance in contemporary Jewish life. Though the cosmopolitan identity is not in the main stream of Jewish life itself, it produced figures who had an immense impact on general Western culture outside of Jewish life, from Freud to Derrida and to Woody Allen. These figures saw their Jewishness expressed in that sensibility and stance.

The plurality of modern Jewish identity is thus deep and radical, and its basic structure provides three different orientations of what it is to be a Jew. It also, provides a thoroughly diverse reading of the Jewish past. The covenantal identity interprets Jewish history as a stage in which the covenantal relational drama is played out. Israel, which bears witness to God's presence in the world, is driven between the poles of exile and return. Jewish Nationalism sees that same past in completely different terms, analyzing exile as a state of dependency and political and spiritual disaster, and viewing attachment to that past as the hallmark of solidarity and identity. Jewish cosmopolitanism interprets the history of exile as the tragic condition that inspires Jewish political sensibility. Exile is the breeding ground for the Jew as a social critic, occupying the condition of the one who is not imbedded within the order; yet it is close enough to recognize it for what it is, and to impact its direction through moral and political ideals.

We do have what can be called pure samples of these options among leading individuals and some communities. A. B. Yehoshua exhibits in his ideological writings a pure sample of the national identity; R. Joel Moshe Taitelboum witnessed in his life the pure covenantal identity; and George Steiner expresses a pure cosmopolitan Jew. Each rejects the other's alternative as a kind of a looming threat to what Jewishness ought to be, and each is personally alienated from the identity options posed by his rivals. Yet, many modern Jews do not reside in purity in either of these alternatives. For these Jews, the condition of pluralism is not merely a description of the radical diversity of Jewish modern identity in its modern historical form. The plurality resides in their own soul. They, as Jews, are a complex hybrid of identities. They carry in their own soul the fractures of modern Jewish identity and its burdens.

The following introspective thought experiment can be offered to clarify that peculiar condition of hybridity. I see myself as a covenantal religious Jew, and I wonder what will happen to my identity as a Jew if "God forbid" I were to lose all my faith in the religion of Israel. Even more so I will grow hostile to it and perceive it to be a distorted and perverse form of life. I don't think that coming to that understanding would put an end to my affiliation as a Jew. I am a product of modern Jewish nationalism, and my political and historical solidarity with the Jewish People is not solely dependent upon my covenantal convictions.

The same would be true the other way around. I imagine a case in which I came to realize that the project of modern Jewish nationalism reached a dead end—that this modern project actually endangers the Jewish People by gathering them into a fragile and sieged nation state. Even more, I might come to believe that Jewish nationalism distorted the valuable aspects of being a Jew and that it brought upon the Jewish People a moral catastrophe. I don't think that in, such a case, I would lose my identification as a Jew. My Jewish identity is not exclusively channeled through Jewish nationalism; I can rely solely on *Torah* and *Mitzvot* for being a Jew.

I will go further with such a scenario. I imagine a situation in which both of these options—the covenantal and the national—crumble ideologically and personally for me. I cut my bond with both covenantal and National Jewish identity and I adopt an alienated view from them. I can still find myself identifying as a Jew within the cosmopolitan calling. It is independent of the other alternatives, and can stand for me as a rich and powerful conception of being a Jew that resonates and continues in its own manner the Jewish past. This thought experiment is not a wild counterfactual; it might as well reflect actual steps in a complicated personal biography. I know some people who have gone through such a journey of shifting Jewish identities, though each of them did it in different sequence. Such a thought experiment points to the following implication: the radical plurality of modern Jewish identities might reside simultaneously in a one individual when such an individual finds himself to be a product of the complex strands of Jewish modern identity. We as Jews are not only parties to this or that version of the modern Jewish identity; some of us carry this struggle inwardly.

My argument concerning modern Jewish identity is that it reached a condition of incommensurability, in the sense that this term was introduced by Isaiah Berlin in his work on pluralism. Incommensurability implies two features. The first emerges in cases when options are incommensurate and therefore there is no shared scale in which we can measure and create a hierarchy of values among them. The second feature of incommensurability is the assertion that in conditions of pluralism of this sort there is no way to integrate and synthesized the conflicted options in one form of life. We can either fulfill one of them or compromise between them; we cannot fully materialize both of them simultaneously.

In the case of modern Jewish identity, both features apply.

Each of the modern Jewish alternatives cannot be assessed or valued against the other on a shared scale. All of them established convincing realities into their own and they produced and their best a challenging models. I can say even more so, that our Jewish world on the whole will be diminished without these options. The second feature is more important for the purpose of our discussion. There is no way in which all of them can be fully materialize in one system. It is far better to stay in such condition of partial and conflicting plurality then to attempt to achieve a higher all encompassing illusionary synthesis. Such attempts do not reach genuine synthesis; what they actually perform is merely a distorted reduction of one world to the other. In order to highlight the point let us go back to the membership and then to its larger identity and ideological concerns.

IV. Confronting the Crisis

For complex and comprehensible reasons, there has been a systematic attempt to create an overlap between the different methods of joining the Jewish community. On the one hand, the Jewish nation-state wants to use and adapt traditional conversion to make it into a rite of passage into Jewish nationalism; and on the other, heavy pressure is exerted on the state from the religious establishment to make the demands for citizenship by virtue of the Law of Return compatible with the halachic conditions of belonging to and joining the Jewish People. I believe that, given the rift, the continuing attempt by both sides of this dispute to place the two joining tracks on an even footing may have even more serious repercussions than the rift itself.

In the wake of the judgment in the case of Shalit, the Knesset passed an amendment to the Law of Return that provides a detailed explanation of the term 'Jew.' A Jew as defined by the Knesset is someone who is born to a Jewish mother or who has converted. This amendment, which brought the halachic definition of membership closer to the civil manner of joining by virtue of the Law of Return, did not completely close the gap because the nature of the conversion process still remained open. Cases involving Reform and Conservative conversions, to which the Orthodox objected, regularly appeared before the court and the court accepted them as valid, based on the fact that the legislature had not narrowly defined the meaning of conversion. In response to the court's rulings, additional pressure was brought to bear on the Israeli political system to define the conversion process by law in accordance with halachah, and thereby complete the identification between Jewishness for the purpose of the Law of Return and the halachic definition of Jewishness as it is understood by Orthodoxy.

I believe that the attempt to subordinate the definition of Jewish nationalism to the halachic framework is problematic and mistaken. There are two reasons for my objection to this tendency. One is related to the broader relations between religion and state, and the second relates to the perception of belonging that is derived from Jewish nationalism and the role of the State of Israel.

Given the profound disagreements between the Jewish communities and movements concerning the nature and character of Jewish culture, the role of the state is not to adjudicate among them, but rather to enable all forms of Jewish culture to flourish and thrive alongside one another, as long as each grants the others a similar right. In this respect, the State of Israel is a national home because it enables Jews to live as free people in their land and express their culture in both the private and public realm. Any attempt to "Judaize" the country by means of religious legislation would undermine that feeling of a home and the sense of belonging felt by Jews that take a different and opposing view.

This is especially true for the Law of Return, which is the most outstanding expression of the fact that Israel is the state of the Jewish People. Israel cannot at the same time and with the same law tell Jews of the Diaspora, on the one hand, that Israel is their home, and on the other hand determine that it denies the legitimacy of the spiritual leadership of the Reform and Conservative communities. I view this as the clear interest not only of the state but also of *Halachah*. A commandment that is carried out because the legislator compels people to do so lacks any religious significance, and it is not the role of the legislator to determine what *Halachah* is and who has converted in accordance with *Halachah*. It could be stated this way: *In the increasingly intense conditions of the dispute over Jewish culture, the State of Israel cannot simultaneously be a state of the Jews and a Jewish state.*

As stated earlier, the legislator and the court should not have to be the ones to decide on the abstract question of "Who is a Jew." It would in any case be too pretentious, highly charged, and impossible to do so. In my view, the most incisive comments on this subject were made by Justice Zussman in the Shalit judgment: "It is a mistake to ask: Who is a Jew? The multiplicity of meanings of the term makes it impossible to answer this question. One may ask: Who is a Jew for the purpose of a particular law" (*ibid.*, page 512.)

The State and its authorities deal with the question of who is a Jew for the purpose of the Law of Return, the context of which is citizenship in a nation state. Israeli citizenship is not identical to Jewishness. Israel is required as a democratic country to grant the status of full and equal citizenship to non-Jews living and born in it. The advantage granted to Jews in the Law of Return, which defines the State of Israel as the state of the Jewish People, is not intended to create a complete and overlapping identity between Jewishness according to the halachic definition and Jewishness for the purpose of the Law of Return.

Jewishness for the Law of Return is related to the definition of the State of Israel as a nation-state—that is, in its solidarity with Jews and Jews with it. Shared fate is not determined in accordance with halachic definitions of Jewishness. Among other things, it is dependent on the way in which the surrounding society relates to a particular individual. That is why a person who is persecuted as a Jew, even if he or she is not halachically Jewish, should be viewed as a Jew for the purpose of the Law of Return—because the very essence of this law is that the State of Israel is also a place of refuge and asylum. If the State of Israel had existed during the time of the Nazi regime in Germany, the definition of the Jewishness of those entitled to citizenship according to the Law of Return would have had to be identical to the definition of Jewishness according to the Nuremberg race laws. The same goes for joining, the test of which is not subjective in my opinion, and should consist of the willingness to share the fate of the Jewish People and to belong to one of the existing Jewish cultures.[3] I similarly object to the attempt to reduce the traditional conversion ceremony to a rite marking the joining of a modern national collective, and I object to the attempt to characterize the joining of the Jewish nationality by virtue of the Law of Return in terms that are identical to *Halachah*. The former approach will ultimately undermine *Halachah* and the latter, the State.

---

[3]   If the use of the appellation 'Jew' for those joining that are not viewed as Jews by halachic authorities proves problematic, they may be called 'members of the Jewish People', in accordance with the proposal made by Ruth Gavison and Yaakov Meidan.

As I see it, the value of the institution of conversion lies in the very fact that it undermines the perception of membership in the Jewish community as based on ethnic affiliation. Instead of trying to imbue conversion with the character of a ritualistic rebirth into the Jewish ethnos, the institution of conversion must confer a different meaning to membership in the Jewish community. The convert shares the status of a born Jew because, as Maimonides explained, he or she has undergone the same path taken by Abraham, the first convert, and because by committing himself to the commandments, he or she is reenacting the collective ritual of entering into the Sinai covenant.[4] From the fact that conversion is possible, we learn that the entire Jewish People is in fact a community of converts. The descendants of Jews, including those of converts, are viewed as Jews not because of their ethnic affiliation, but because of the obligation their forefathers accepted to enter into the covenant at Sinai, which in the eyes of the *Halachah*, binds them as well. Insisting on a component of acceptance of *Mitzvot* as constitutive to conversion is open to diverse interpretations and it is therefore flexible. In its most stringent form it demand acceptance to live according to the *Shulchan Aruch*, and yet a converting court can insist on the acceptance of one central *Mitzvah* in which the convert obligates himself to perform as a Jew such as *Shabbat* or *Tzedakah*. The debate concerning conversion ought to concentrate on the adequate concept of *kabbalat mitzvot* from a broader notion to a narrow one, rather than succumb to the pressure of the secular government to give it up altogether.

The case of membership is a sample of a larger issue of identity. Accepting the incommensurable condition of Jewish plurality of notions of identity means an attempt to overcome two common responses to this condition. The first is rejection, in which the different parties to the dispute reject the legitimacy of the other. Affirming the modern Jewish condition as pluralistic implies a sense of humility in regard to this problem. No side in the debate is in a position to invalidate the legitimacy and genuineness of each of these modern Jewish identities. The adoption of the pluralistic stance is magnified when we realize that the crisis in modern Jewish identity does not merely mark the partitions between communities. Sometimes they are currents flowing within the same individual.

The second response to the modern rift is the attempt to create a supra-synthesis in which each position reduces the other as part of its overall scheme. Such attempts were made by devotees of each of the three modern Jewish identities. In the covenantal stream the most clear and influential scheme was offered by Rabbi Kook, who viewed nationalism as a component of the great historic movement of Messianic advancement. The same reductive project

---

4   See Yitzhak Sheilat, *Iggrot HaRambam* (Maimonides' Responsa), Responsum to Ovadia the Convert, Mossad Harav Kook, 1987, Vol. 1, pp. 233–235.

THE JEWISH PEOPLE
AND THE ISRAELI NATION

SHMUEL TRIGANO

Editor's summary

Shmuel Trigano examines the tensions between Jewish Peoplehood and Jewish nationhood through a historical overview, from the Emancipation to the creation and development of the modern State of Israel. He demonstrates that the Emancipation was never unconditional where Jews were concerned — the acceptance of Jews into the body politic was contingent upon their renunciation of their status as a collective. Zionism, the only Jewish movement to claim political sovereignty for all Jews, represents an attempt to mend this fault and to incorporate into political modernity the Jewish People who were not accepted as part of their nations of origin. Yet, today, the State is gripped by tensions between the Jewish People and the Israeli nation, categories which do not overlap easily with one another. As more of the Jewish world continues to be concentrated in Israel, we are faced with the ever-more pressing question of the continuity of the Jewish People within the State of Israel, where Jews are still accompanied by the conscience of Exile that characterized their long history of dispersal. If *Golah* may finish, *Galut* as a mood of relationship to wordliness cannot end.

European Jewry, and in particular present-day French Jewry, of whom three-quarters are Jews from North Africa, know, perhaps better than anywhere else and with an instinctive knowledge, what is implied in the present concept of "Jewish People." Indeed, they live in a political framework that still bears the mark of the "Emancipation." Extensively studied by American Jewish historians, the political "contract" that it involves still remains largely misunderstood. And yet it is this **contract** that is significant as far as the "Jewish People" is concerned, an entity that certainly is the product of social imagination, but also, *and more significantly*, of history and politics. The status of a people is necessarily political, which means that it stands at the level of the relations with other peoples and communities. Accordingly, the attainment of civil rights by Jews in the 18th and 19th centuries in Western Europe, at the dawn of democracy, was based on a separation between the individuals from Jewish origin and their Jewish political and *cultural* identity.

As such, as this chapter will demonstrate, the experience of Emancipation is instructive in terms of our understanding of the tensions between peoplehood and nationhood in the modern State of Israel.

The Ambiguity of Emancipation

To use a Freudian notion, the syndrome we intend to analyze stems from the "primal scene" of the process defined as "Emancipation", namely: the French Revolution. The Emancipators accepted Jews in the body politic only as individuals, who should in no respect be distinguishable from other citizens. This condition was admittedly shared with every French individual (with the exception of women and Antillean Blacks who were not acknowledged as citizens) but it carried an additional meaning for Jews, bearers of a specific culture, who were for centuries excluded from Christian society. They *had* to reform themselves more than anyone else. In the spirit of the French Revolution, it is clear that they were expected to relinquish their specific Jewish attributes and put an end to their community-based life. Abbé Grégoire, the foremost champion of Jewish emancipation, declared: "No deputy to manage the civil affairs of the Jewish community; no Jewish communities," as a part of an approach in which Judaism appears as, "Talmudic daydreams . . . a cesspool of human delirium . . . a rabbinic jumble."

The demand to renounce so much of what had hitherto characterized Judaism was actually viewed as a benevolent discourse toward the Jewish fate, for the Emancipators considered Jewish identity a corruption of humanity. Two centuries before Sartre, they accused Europe of having made human beings as Jews, i.e. as pariahs, cast out from humanity. According to them, the "Jewish People" was a remnant of gentile hatred that compelled Jews to closet themselves away from the rest of the world. The same Grégoire asserted that, *"the height of injustice is to accuse Jews for the crime that we have forced them to commit . . ."* One could not therefore imagine, at that time, that there *was* anything positive in the identity of these outcasts. It can only be the result of oppression. As opposed to this corrupted identity, the Emancipators wished to affirm the humanity of the Jews. As Grégoire put it, "Jews are humans, just like us, they are so before being Jews" (Abbé Grégoire). But at the same time, it was clear that in order to be acknowledged as human, they had to no longer be Jewish. The same view is conveyed in the concept of the "regeneration of the Jews" (i.e. their re-creation), which was a corollary of Emancipation.

The problem is that this intellectual and political blindness toward the Jewish People was accompanied by a political and ideological practice that continued to consider Jews, directly or indirectly, as a reality. From the perspective of the State, just a few years after the Emancipation, Napoleon's administration reorganized the Jews as a ***denominational*** community (the "*Consistoire*") to which they were automatically assigned. Almost simultaneously, in civil society, outside the authority of the state or the Enlightenment, a new kind of hatred towards the Jews emerged: anti-Semitism aimed at a people supposedly hidden in the individual Jewish citizen and, from now on, perceived through the prism of conspiracy. The Jewish People was still a haunting reality, present but without being recognized.

The gap between individuals and collective in fact fitted into a wider development, a structural failure of political modernity. Originally, the Nation had been considered, according to the perspective of the human rights' ideology, as a community of citizens, derived from a contract between individuals, as described in Jean Jacques Rousseau's *The Social Contract*. Historical experience has showed that this model remained theoretical. Although designed within a democratic and constitutional framework, the nation-state could not do without a specific, clear and complete historical identity. On this subject, the nationalist phenomenon that spread throughout Europe after the French Revolution and its monstrous outcome, Napoleon's empire, should not be considered a random development, but rather the scales and counterweight—albeit dialectical—of a human rights democracy focused on individuals. The failure to introduce a dimension of national identity into the Human Rights Charter resulted in a kind of massive and violent "return of the repressed."

The Declaration of the Rights of Man, pronounced in French, was addressed to the whole of humanity, and supposed that any person in the world could become French—yet, it rapidly became evident that only Frenchmen could claim citizenship. Napoleon's conquest, viewed through the eyes of the defeated European nations, was in no way universal: it was a war of conquest serving the interests of French domination. *The Jews*, however, were rejected when the nation-state discovered that it possessed, in practice and beyond issues of human rights, an inherent identity that was not solely rooted in its constitutional basis. Thus, the "Spring of Nations" and the 1848 Revolutions—the landmark events in this process—were marked by anti-Semitism.

The Continuity of the People in Spite of Emancipation

The French brand of Emancipation became the key figure of Jewish modernity. Although anchored in a specific context, it eventually addressed geographical areas in which the democratic nation-state had not been established and in which the ideological, political and legal negation of a *Jewish People* had not yet made its mark: Central and Eastern Europe, North Africa, and the Middle East. Napoleon's conquests, from Russia to Egypt, contributed more than anything else to such an expansion. His consistorial model was eventually adopted in all the countries of Western Europe. At the beginning of the 19th century, the condition of the Jews could be seen as follows: wherever Jews were granted equality and emerged from their status as outcasts, they had to renounce their Jewish Peoplehood; *on the other hand*, wherever they were persecuted and singled out, they could retain the collective dimension of their life.

Widespread emigration of Central European Jews to the United States, during the 19th and 20th centuries, or — in lower numbers — to the future State of Israel, is very significant in this respect. Jews were leaving Europe where, for as a people they no longer had a place. Their departure symbolically expressed a survival instinct in the face of a deadlock that extended far beyond their individual condition, itself heavy to bear, especially in light of their impoverishment. They immigrated to the United States, a country which, while modern and democratic, had never experienced the Emancipation. For this reason today, American Jewry finds it difficult to understand the price of the political dimension of Emancipation: they passed from the old régime to modern times without going through the emancipatory experience, and as a result never had to openly renounce the status of a people. In this country of mass immigration, the national population was not an authentic population. The state was federal and not centralized. It was the size of a continent and its western border was open. There was enough room for everybody. In addition, the One God was mentioned in the state's founding charter, without endorsing a particular religion, so that, for Jews, acquiring citizenship no longer meant a radical severance from the most important (religious) symbols of their continuity. In Old Europe, it was exactly the opposite.

Jews from Eastern and Central Europe who chose Israel also tried to ensure their collective status. The *Yishuv* assembled a Jewish collective, by its very formation and in contrast to the surroundings. The objective was to create a state and to establish a Jewish Sovereignty. As for the Jews from North Africa and the Middle East, who currently comprise a near-majority of the Israeli population and a majority of the French Jewish community, they were able, for various reasons, to preserve their bond with a Jewish People well into the 20th century. The colonial power had transferred into these geographical areas the same political concepts as in Western Europe and Jews were the first beneficiaries. A few decades after the Emancipation promoted by the French Revolution, Algerian Jews also became citizens, and then almost all Jews in colonial countries (under the French or English flag) were granted European states' *citizenship*, opening for them the gates of freedom. They emerged from a condition of debasement that branded them collectively as "subjugated people" (*dhimmis*), in accordance with the rules of the Koran, in those countries where Islam was the law. The framework of their citizenship was nevertheless extra-metropolitan, extra-European. Its ascendency on them was less total. In addition, it was in line with the fragmented and disintegrated social web comprising colonial society. The renouncement of the Jewish People implied by citizenship was therefore manifestly less sharp, especially since, with the exception of Algeria, Jews passed from the old regime to modernity without going through Emancipation. Indeed, before the European colonization, they could retain their status as a people despite their very low status, and because of it, since the rank of *dhimmi* applied to a collective unit: it applies to a people or, more precisely, to a minority. The rules governing the subjugated minority were admittedly different from those ruling the "Jewish corporation" of the old regime in Western Europe, but the two situations were comparable. This is not surprising, since it appears that the rank of *dhimmi* was originally copied from the legal systems of the Byzantine Christian Empire toward (and against) Jews, to whom Roman citizenship had been denied by the victorious Church.

Note that these two Jewish population groups—those from Eastern and Central Europe and the Sephardi countries—have a common characteristic: they retained their status as a people until quite late. For European Jews, the Polish experience of Jewish autonomy, as devised by the Bund, was the last hold-out, annihilated by the Nazi Holocaust. The Bund's experience was, in any case, directed towards the agnostic Jewish working class, excluding, at the time, all the rest of the Jewish People—and primarily *other* Polish Jews. For the Sephardic Jews in colonial countries, their time was also over by the end of the Second World War. As soon as the colonial authorities left and nation-states were established in their place, it became clear that, as individuals as well as communities, the Jews couldn't endure. In nearly all of the Middle East where Arab nationalist movements had sympathized with the Nazis during the war, Jews were expelled and robbed of their property. In North Africa, they were driven out, even formally excluded. The fact that the majority of Jews in these countries chose Israel is also a sign of the continuity of their identification with the Jewish People. That a smaller number chose to immigrate to the United States and Canada, countries where the status of people is accepted, conforms to the same logic.

However, France—the second most popular destination after Israel, for Sephardic Jews—is more problematic: the identity of community which developed and is typical of the Sephardi world (the former "Naçao" of those exiled from the Iberian Peninsula, who later dispersed throughout the entire world), comes up against political principles inherited from the Emancipation, which may not acknowledge its legitimacy. The crisis of the beginning of the 2000s, with the development of a new anti-Semitism and the accusation of **communautarisme** (a specifically French notion which signifies that you are disloyal to the Republic) hit it with full force, pointing to a highly uncertain future for French Jewry. We cannot exclude the possibility that an emigration to Israel (and in smaller numbers to the Americas) will take place. The "Jewish People" has always been a problem in France. In a certain way, the survival of Jewish communities in Europe could be considered an anachronism, without any future.

In Europe, the Shoah sounded the death knell for the Emancipation; it meant an end to the individual status of the *Jews as citizens, separate from the Jewish People*. They were indeed destroyed as a people, beyond their many nationalities as individuals. The communities that were rebuilt afterwards entered a post-Emancipation age. The best proof of this is their identification with Zionism. It became the carrier of a Jewish collective identification *within* their former citizenship that had emerged in ruins from the war and the destruction of the Jews. The recent wave of anti-Semitism, in its anti-Zionist raiment, has directly attacked this complex need for identification. It demonstrates that the cycle of anti-Semitism that has hit Europe approximately every forty years since the Emancipation is not over. Europe did *not* change, as one would have anticipated after the Shoah.

From Citizenship to the Nation

The Emancipation paradox (whereby Jews receiving individual citizenship were denied freedom and legitimacy as a collective) is not limited to the discrepancy between the fate of individuals and of the Jewish People. The Emancipation opened the way to a development that had not been foreseen but was, in effect, its dialectic result. Along with the status of individual citizens in democratic nations, a Jewish nationalism, Zionism, suddenly appeared. This movement did not reject the logic of the Emancipation, but proposed an amendment, an adjustment to include the Jewish People. In Herzl's original idea, the Zionist solution should apply *only to those Jews* who failed to integrate as citizens and therefore had to confront anti-Semitism. The hatred of Jews, in his view as well as in Leo Pinsker's, the author of *Auto-Emancipation*, could only be the result of the Jews' failure to integrate and not the failure of the integration process. Herzl aimed only for the return of Jews — collectively, as a nation — to the Western European stage that had excluded and rejected them. Zionism offered a counter-model of individual Emancipation while still retaining a collective system of values. Therefore, the nation that Zionism strived for was *intended* to gather individuals for whom individual citizenship proved to be impossible in Europe and who, through the Zionist movement could return to the Jewish collective and belong.

This solution proved to be so effective that, at the beginning of the 21st century, almost all the Jewish populations that were still removed from the Emancipation process — with the exception of American Jewry — rallied to Zionism, with their descendants gathered in the State of Israel. *The success of Zionism was paradoxical: although it was born in Western Europe, in Paris, in the very heart of Emancipation and its contradictions, it became the overall strategic solution for the continuity of those Jewries, outside Western Europe.*

And yet, this continuity remains ambiguous. Herzl was seeking a haven for individuals crippled by the Emancipation, not directly for the "Jewish People." This fundamental ambiguity was highlighted during the 1950s–1970s, with the immigration to the State of Israel, which had meanwhile been created, of Jews from the colonial countries, the Jews of Islamic Arab countries. The difficulties that this wave of immigration faced were considerable. Subjected to rejection, denigration and discrimination, Sephardi Jews sensed that they were not coming back to the "Jewish People."

The ambiguous return of the Sephardim was a dramatic experience, and is significant for our argument. The terminology that was created in Israel to designate Sephardi Jews as a constitutive entity (related to their existence in their countries of origin) is illuminating. Although they rapidly became the majority, they were identified by the terms "Eastern ethnic communities" (*edot haMizrakh*), and therefore considered outside the "Nation": *deficient according to its criteria, because ethnicity is supposed to be a rank lower than nation.* This hierarchical denomination was indeed reserved exclusively for them since, to this day, there is no such equivalent expression as "Western ethnic communities" (and North Africa is certainly not East of Israel...). One clear fact emerged: if the creation of the Israeli nation assured collective Jewish continuity, it was nonetheless under a new form, different from that which we can now term the "historic Jewish People", by which I mean *the Jewish People as an authentic actor upon History, and not as a reconstructed collective by the modern state.* The nation is a collective entity which is specific to the modern state.

In fact, what happened with Zionism, was the same as what happened with the broader nationalism phenomenon in Western Europe: the mass return of a collective (national) identity to inform the concept of individual, abstract citizenship. This phenomenon triggered among Emancipated Jewry, the Zionist movement that Herzl claimed to have created. The discovery of the continuity of a Jewish collective among emancipated Jews by European societies was the façade in which Europe clothed its anti-Semitism and constituted the driving force behind the emerging aspiration for a Jewish *Nation*.

The acknowledged failure of the status granted to individuals by the Emancipation is similar to the way in which countries that adopted human rights' ideology discovered, through experience, that the "social contract" was an unworkable ideal. The developer of its theory, Jean Jacques Rousseau, was himself aware from the outset of the logical unfeasibility of his model. Rousseau pronounced the national process as standing in total contradiction with his own logic. Baffled by the recognition that the law might barely be obeyed by the individual citizens who authored it, he came to the conclusion that there was a need for a sufficiently powerful *authority* to obligate individuals. In his opinion, only religion was effective in this regard. And for this reason Rousseau reintroduced a religion—the "civil religion"—into his individualist model. Defined either as patriotism or as nationalism, from now on, this new religiosity would teach submission to a higher authority, and the sacrifice of individuals to the collective.

People and Nation

Zionism was therefore the only historical movement to fully assume the principle of the existence of a Jewish collective in modern times. The national form was superimposed over the reality of the Jewish People. Zionism was also the only Jewish movement to claim a political sovereignty for all Jews, in one country—the Land of Israel. In that sense, after the creation of world Jewish institutions (the first of this kind appeared in France in 1860, the *Alliance Israélite Universelle*), it represents the first and only way of asserting an all-encompassing Jewish People on the scene of modern states.

As in the European scheme, the national form in the State of Israel represented a new kind of collective identity, the only possible kind of a *collective existence* in a democratic system. I make a distinction between Nation and People. How should we understand this transformation? With the fall of the Old Régime, individuals were no longer required to pledge allegiance to the authority of a king or dynasty, i.e., to a particular person, but to an entire collective. In democracy, the ensemble of individuals thus became the sovereign. The King's substitute became a collective, and the pledge to authority became based necessarily on the group. The numerous groups that existed in the Old Régime's society had to withdraw, renounce their identity and their group structure, and *identify themselves with the new collective identity, in order to be part of the new society*. From then on, what related to a specific collective identity belonged to the private domain, to individual choice. At that point, a national identity came into existence. What did it consist of? Initially, it was a voluntary project: the new regime wanted to banish the old world, destroy it and give birth to a "**new Man**." The French Revolution sought the "regeneration" of humankind, and in particular of Jews...But the *new Man* was not so new. After a profound conflict, the constitutive elements of the previous identity were in fact reintegrated: including, the basic anthropological, religious, and cultural characteristics of the dominant group (those of the king and his court). The politics of the absolutist monarchy had installed a centralist system before it was actually formulated, so that the fusion of populations was already ongoing. This process was ultimately experienced unfavorably by the minorities, whose members became citizens and had to adjust to the central model: an identity model, *with far greater impact than a simply political, constitutional model*. Their entire existence became politicized. For these people, citizenship represented not only a renunciation of their collective status, but also alienation from their own identity. *National identity was a radically different identity from their former community-based identity.*

The nation produced by Zionism was an *Israeli* nation, more than a "Jewish" nation, in the sense that the term "Jewish" refers to the "People." This distinction (Israeli nation / Jewish People) is justified—not only because of the presence in the Israeli citizenry of Israelis who are not Jewish — but also because Jewish Israeli citizens themselves belong to their nation, according to political, cultural, and existential categories that are not exactly identical to the category of "members of the Jewish People." The state's criterion for membership makes the difference.

The relationship between the Israeli and Jewish dimensions, however, remains confused, since today the load of the Jewish People is *de facto* carried by the Israeli nation. Jewish collective existence can be approached and understood only through the prism of the Israeli Nation. This does not preclude the fact that the condition of the Jewish People as seen through the Israeli Nation is always ambiguous and problematic. The ethnic conflict that has deeply marked Israel's recent history, and the conflict over religion that ravages contemporary Israel is better understood when the discrepancy between people/nation/Jewish/Israeli is taken into consideration. The arrival of "*Mizrakhi* ethnic identities" (*edoth haMizrakh*) on the Zionist scene represented an interruption of the historical-political transformation of the Jewish People into the Israeli nation. In this respect, a kind of temporal interference has taken place, as two levels of historic temporality collided within the same time frame.

The same is true of the war of religion that is tearing Israeli society apart. This conflict focuses on the status of Judaism in the Israeli nation and, indeed, the very definition of its historic identity. Zionism sought to create a new culture under the model of a new Man, produced by a melting pot absorbing waves of immigration. The "Jewish People" was supposed to disappear ("regenerated," which means, in this case, "normalized"), in the same way as — using the logic of the Emancipation and the Jews' regeneration. The Jews as a people and a cultural identity was supposed to give way to the individual and anonymous citizen. This is what we have defined as the logic of human rights, a logic in which the citizen, and therefore the State, defines the *Man* — contrary to what the Declaration of Human and Citizen's Rights would have us believe.

Today, nationalist venture has proven a failure: the rise of particular identities indeed illustrates the return of the logic of people into the logic of the state. In democratic regimes the world over, the state is receding and the nation-state is declining as the basis of identity. Modernity is melting like snow beneath the sun. The convergent freeze created by the centralist state, which covered up a former reality, is thawing, and collective identities are reappearing. The most fascinating *persona* in this process is surely the resurrection of Orthodox Great Russia, re-emerging after a period of 70 years of Communism.

In the wake of all of the above, a post-Zionist current is developing, with its characteristic hatred of the nation and of the state. Post-Zionist ideology, which can be related to post-modernism, is not free of internal contradictions. In fact, post-Zionism represents a historical regression. While imagining itself to be post-modern, post Zionism ignores the contradictory experience of modernity; it perceives itself as returning to the standards of the Enlightenment era, without integrating the lessons of the two intervening centuries. Its supporters engage in apologia for the ideology of human rights and democratic individualism, as if nothing had transpired over two centuries—both for the Jews, and for a Europe shattered by the experiences of two totalitarian regimes and the Holocaust. The Shoah is a highly disturbing phenomenon—not only, but particularly for the Jewish People—because it refutes their theory: human rights and democratic citizenship failed to save the Jews. It is the lesson of the destruction of the Jews as a people, in the heart of a storm born in the democratic West. This, therefore, is why they engage in a violent attack against the Jewish People and against memory. Post-modernism is neither a scientific nor an equitable assessment of reality, but an ideology that distorts it. It is also without a future, unless as the purveyor of catastrophe.

The Present Configuration

Such is the configuration of the "Jewish People" at the beginning of the 21st century. The core of the questioning of its identity resides in the relationship that must be established between the Jewish People and the Israeli nation—two forms of collective identity that are in competition over the definition of the collective condition. This problem concerns not only the Israel-Diaspora divide and, in particular, the relationship between the American Diaspora (demographic, cultural and political center of the Jewish Diaspora) and the State of Israel. It also concerns the Israeli nation itself, through the definition of the relation between its national identity with its various components—as well as with Jewish identity.

It concerns, in a different way, Western European Jewry, particularly in France where there is a type of identity mid-way between that which prevails in the United States and Israel. The "community" form of this identity can indeed be compared to the national kind, since the essential characteristic of the Jewish community in France until the 1980s was its centralism. It embodied all sectors of Jewish opinion (although this is decreasingly the case today), as is the case in Israeli society, *in a perfect parallel* with the French centrality of the state. This is very different from American Jewry, which consists of diverse networks that converge at the top. Unlike Israel however, French Jewry is still characterized by its relationship with Judaism, and is therefore closer to the "Jewish People." Through its fiery Zionism, it also identifies itself with the "Israeli nation."

Our basic hypothesis is the idea (and more than an idea) that the "Jewish People" is not an archaic remnant from the (pre-modern) past, an obstacle preventing the Jewish world from progressing. This assertion can indeed be often heard: of Judaism being an archaic religion or the Diaspora being an obsolete phenomenon. What clearly contradicts such an opinion is the objective global crisis of the nation-state and its civil religions today—and of Zionism itself. This does not preclude that fact that the assessment of decline and obsolescence of the Diaspora can be justified at other levels (this is my opinion). One would expect that the status change resulting from sovereignty would necessarily lead to an adjustment of the Jewish religion and of the Jewish People. *It is evident that the Israeli arrangement of Jewish existence can no longer be the same as that of the Diaspora — but the "Jewish People" could also continue in a modern State.*

Yet Judaism (as a system of ideas and creeds) and world Jewry (including Israeli Jewry!) prove today that they have been unable to adapt to the new reality. The criterion for evaluating the current situation is not only produced by the new reality of Israel — it stems also from the "historic Jewish People" itself. According to the doctrine of the Exile and the Return, which somewhat constitutes Israel's charter, the Exile was never perceived as continuing after the Ingathering of the Exiles — which is a phenomenon that occurred objectively, with the establishment of Israel. From this perspective, the contemporary Diaspora, which co-exists simultaneously with the Return, can *ipso facto* no longer be in exile, in *golah*. The additional issue is that, in light of this doctrine, it would never have been imagined that during the return of the Exiles to Zion, the returnees' link to Judaism (as a culture and an identity) would be questioned — as is the case in the modern State of Israel. All of these tensions between ideals and realities, however, cannot alter the permanence of the Jewish People and of Judaism.

A different type of politics and existential strategy should be invented to account for the permanence of the Jewish People and Judaism. For the time being, this remains a utopic vision. On the one hand, the normality of the sovereign Jewish collective — the exclusive privilege of Zionism — constitutes an irreplaceable value for Jews, allowing them to be the actors in their own history, and not the passive victims of their enemies or defenders. On the other hand, the "normalization" of the Jewish People, which is also a central axiom of Zionism, constitutes a problematic ideological project. Adjustment to sovereignty and State should not bankrupt the identity of the historic Jewish People, provided, of course, that the latter can adapt — which presupposes a reform of the "Historic Jewish People". *The drifting apart today of the two poles of the Jewish collective (Diaspora and Zion, religious and anti-religious) may unfortunately demonstrate that the situation is not moving in the desired direction.*

The Definite Identity Criterion of a Jewish People

The Jewish People possesses an identity inherited from history, and its reality is exemplified in the problems described above. In fact, the Jews' normalization, as understood by an entire current of opinion, *in Israel and even in Diaspora*, helps us understand the fundamental characteristics of Jewish identity. There is an alignment of the Jewish People with the existential terms of autochthony. In ancient Athens, citizens believed that they were born from earth and that their identity was one with their land and their state. Such an idea is completely foreign to Jewish history and to the Judaic intellect. Herein lies the axial criterion of Jewishness. Autochthony is the implicit "affirmative" side of the idea of the "negation of *galut*," which has so long been important in Zionist ideology. This idea is still defended by post-Zionists: when they contest the legitimacy of the "Law of Return," the strongest constitutional symbol of the State of Israel's link with the Jewish People, and when they seek to abolish the Jewish national character of the state, the neutralization of the history of a Jewish People and of Jewish culture in the national education system. They seek simply to return to Year 0 of the Emancipation of the Jews—as if nothing has happened since that point in time. Moreover, in this respect, the post-Zionist critique of the nation-state principle constitutes a political regression, viewed against the perspective of the achievement of the political sovereignty of the Jewish People. This, in light of the creation of the State of Israel, which represents the correction of the failure of the Jews' modernization and opened up a political framework for the salvation of the Jewish collective. As stated above, *in modern times, only the State of Israel (and not the American Diaspora) has illustrated the concrete existence and possibility of a Jewish People, encompassing all its components.*

The question of identity, as posed here, is totally different from the question of the place and the power of the religious establishment in Israeli society. Post-modernists and post-Zionists deliberately merge this issue with the fundamental problem raised above, in order to confuse the debate. *The identity of the Jewish People, while intrinsically related to Judaism and its culture, is not identified with rabbinic power* (if there is such a thing, since it has been centralized only by the modern Nation-State). In Jewish political tradition, religious and political authorities have generally been distinct and separate. At a purely practical level, on the other hand, the existence of a strong religious core in Israeli society constitutes a political and electoral reality, and should command respect, if one is a democrat. Because of it, it is politically impossible to disassociate Rabbinic power by democratic means from the Judaic dimension.

The most enormous paradox in Jewish history today is that, in the State of Israel, as part of the experience of Jewish sovereignty, the "Jewish problem" could reemerge. Yet this time, the issue is no longer about Jewish individuals, but about the very essence of this People, after it became free and independent. We can define the issue more precisely as the question of survival and continuity of the *Historic Jewish People*, within the *Israeli nation*. Contrary to what is generally believed, this problem will become increasingly relevant as the relative weight of the Israeli center increases—henceforth comprising the demographic majority in the Jewish world.

This problem undoubtedly is tied to the existence of a Diaspora which lives outside the framework of a Jewish state, but nevertheless in the political framework of the democratic nation- state (because Jews are citizens of democratic states). It is also and primarily connected to the original relationship of Jewish identity with the land, through the autochthony principle — the general criterion of collective identities of peoples and even more of nation-states. Here we touch on a permanent, structural element of the Jewish People, be it in exile or settled in the Land of Israel — a fact that is related to the essence of its collective identity and that has ensured its continuity and survival in contradictory circumstances, such as the dispersion and destruction of its state and religious institutions.

Contrary to what might be asserted by some currents of Zionist thought, Judaism did not "preserve" the People during their exile, to the point that it became obsolete when the exile was over. Certainly, it gave them the means to adapt to hostile circumstances (the Diaspora), but this could be achieved only by drawing upon an already existing dimension inherent to its essence — one that will not cease, as long as it exists. This dimension is the conscience of the exile, the system of values inherited from the doctrine of Exile and Return. *A distinction must be made between galut, a value of Jewish existence, which leads to a specific relationship to the world and golah which is the dispersion in the world.* The *golah* may end, but the *galut*, consubstantial with Judaism, may not.

This doctrine is not necessarily diasporist, i.e., favorable to the Diaspora. The Return is also important to it, but it is not the opposite of the Exile — rather, it is the direct product of it. Such a doctrine prevented the Jewish People from identifying completely with their places of dispersion, as well as with their place of settlement in the Promised Land. Today's Jews are, in fact, the descendants of Jews who remained faithful to this doctrine. Those who renounced it became one with their particular Diaspora location, with the local people, to the point of disappearance (here too, the American case is somewhat special — although not entirely so — because mobility within immense spaces without landmarks characterizes the relationship between the land and American identity.)

This exilic conscience ensured that the Jewish People would not disappear in exile: they possessed the resources to resist dispersion. In fact, because this conscience existed prior to the Jews' dispersion, the latter did not sound the death knell of the Jewish People. Furthermore, its effects are more powerful than dispersion — not only because it also contains the theme of Return, but because it also personifies a certain type of relationship with existence and with the world, which concerns the people as a whole, and not just the individual psyche. The first narrative of the Jewish People's origins is not their settlement, but the exodus from Ur in Chaldea, and from Egypt. Here lies an entire anthropology of Judaism.

This characteristic of exile is evident in all manifestations of Judaic civilization. It is exemplified, for instance, in the institution of the Levites according to the Torah, which draws a complete socio-political morphology of the Jewish People. The Twelve Tribes (a fluid population, depending on various censuses), at the time of the settlement in the Land of Israel, divide the Land between all the tribes—except one: the Levites. They do not receive any territory, only cities allocated equally by the tribes, and are therefore located in the middle of their territories. They are charged with the keeping of the Ark of the Covenant, of the Book of the Covenant (*Sefer Habrit*) and with the management of ritual. The Levites' status as a non-sedentary tribe, scattered among all the others, is thus demonstrably in line with the principle of "exile" within the sedentary state. As such, it constitutes a living obstacle to autochthony and to merging with the Land, with oneself. The prophets—whose main message consists of recalling the Covenant delivered in the desert to a sedentary people, who have forgotten it—were an outgrowth of the Levites. Talmudic Judaism went on to elaborate a new version of this schema.

In light of this wide-ranging politico-morphologic example, it is possible to assess the extent of the concept of exile. Exile may express a relationship beyondgeographic dispersion, since of course it operates existentially only when the People dwell in its own Land and is sovereign within it. Sovereignty is the *sine qua non* of the Levites' institution (while the opposite can be said, from a moral and existential point of view). Exile is not the antithesis of politics, but the basis of a different politics. In this respect, if one poses the question of the place of the Jewish religion in the Jews' collective existence, there is far more than exile at stake. Exile is only a symptom. The ideology of normalization we are discussing aims to eliminate this structural element in the Jewish People's condition.

The Concepts of *Peoplehood* and *Nationhood*

We can synthesize this representation by defining the Jewish being as existing a constitutive tension between immanence and transcendence. It can be better understood by looking at the two key concepts, namely: peoplehood and nationhood, and exploring the relationship between them. In specific terms, peoplehood designates the Jewish People as it *may* exist in the Diaspora, outside the framework of one territory and sovereignty of a State, but unified by the Covenant and its charter. Although Jews are spread across several countries and are citizens of various states, there *is* a Jewish People. Judaism's role in this process has been significant, for two reasons. Firstly, in terms of form, there is the fact that Judaism was formally delimited to the synagogue in the modern era and needed to redefine itself structurally as a denomination. Secondly, in terms of substance, insofar as Judaism has moved from a state of transcendence into one of immanence: Judaism is the only revelation communicated not only to one individual (Jesus or Muhammad), but to an entire people, without necessarily having a revealed and visible Divinity.

Since there is a People (a political dimension with the potential for sovereignty), *the principle of a nationhood* (with the institution of power and the state) *is therefore implied within it.* This finds a new shape in Zionism, which <u>reduces</u> the people to the state and the territory. The outcome is the departure from the constitutive tension between the transcendent and immanent dimensions of Judaism and Peoplehood, and a reduction of the Jewish condition to immanence alone.

This dichotomy, particularly in its present guise, is no longer absolutely ironclad: Judaism exists in a problematic equilibrium with nationhood, and is affected by the latter's normality and immanence. For their part, the two characteristics of peoplehood (religion and the relationship with the Jewish People)—two different ways of raising the question of transcendence, of what transcends autochthony—create a problem within the Israeli nation. Conversely, Israeli nationhood is a disturbing factor in the citizenship of Diaspora Jews who belong to a Jewish People *in* the Diaspora. Their affiliation to a peoplehood (which is not, in terms of Jewish identity, the opposite of nationhood) is identified as an affiliation with the Israeli nation and they are suspected of dual allegiance.

The tension between Peoplehood and Nationhood is actually one of both transcendence and immanence. It demonstrates that the Jewish People is the product of the synergy of these two elements, destined to articulate each other and never merge, yet also susceptible to dissociate without disappearing, as shown in the growing separation between Israel and the Diaspora. The image offered by the Jewish collective condition is one of duality—it is both external (spread around the world) and internal (in one country); both worldly (in the universe of immanence, of power) and extra-worldly (toward transcendence). Heavenly Jerusalem and earthly Jerusalem.

JEWISH SECTARIANISM
AND JEWISH PEOPLEHOOD

AMI BOUGANIM

Editor's summary

Ami Bouganim posits an unresolved tension between the demands of historical Judaism, as it developed over two thousand years of exile, and the demands raised by the proper functioning of the modern State of Israel. He characterizes the dominant paradigm throughout much of Jewish history as a rabbinical-Pharisee model that developed under conditions of the Babylonian exile, in order to enable the Jewish People to live a meaningful religious life outside their homeland. Bouganim examines the Pharisees against their historical counterparts, the Sadducees, and suggests that a similar underlying conflict may exist in the arguments between political Zionism and rabbinical Pharisaism in the modern State of Israel. He shows how the creation of the State has challenged the rabbinical Pharisee paradigm, while at the same time creating a laboratory for Jewish cultural creativity and renewal. Finally, he turns to Mordechai Kaplan's concept of peoplehood as a new means of conceptualizing Jewish identity in the modern world.

The establishment and consolidation of the State of Israel has been a crucial factor shaping modern Jewish existence. The State of Israel has gathered the scattered remnants of Israel from the four corners of the earth and armed them spiritually and militarily to confront their enemies. Whatever meaning we chose to attribute to the term, the State of Israel constitutes the "first buds of our redemption," whether or not we ourselves dwell in Zion. The existence of the sovereign Jewish state is an essential condition for the spiritual revival of the Jewish People, and the future of the people depends on the success of the state.

At the same time, the renewal of national and political sovereignty over parts of *Eretz Yisrael* significantly disrupts messianic narratives held by Jews, both in Israel and abroad. There exists an unresolved friction between the demands of historical Judaism, as developed over two thousand years of exile, and those raised by the proper functioning of a state that aims to be simultaneously democratic, open, liberal and Jewish—a state of all its citizens and the state of all Jews; a state that does not deny its Jewish heritage, although it often clashes with it.

A state cannot be torn between two authorities—in our case, sovereign and rabbinical; two legal systems—civil and halachic; and two structures of expectations—civil and secular, on the one hand, and messianic and religious, on the other. The eminent philosopher Yeshayahu Leibowitz sensed the theological and political quandary confronted by the State of Israel with every fiber of his being, and warned of the seeds of calamity that this entailed. Since he was a man of faith and a man of *Halachah*, he declined to state that this quandary stemmed from an overriding inconsistency between the founding principles of Judaism and the founding principles of a modern, democratic and pluralistic society. It is this inconsistency that we need to confront and grapple with, if we are to create the conditions for Jewish renewal, both in Israel and in the Diaspora.

I am not addressing here a Jewish version of the struggle between church and state, one that can eventually be resolved through concession by the religious parties, or the adaptation of the halachic system to meet the new conditions of Jewish sovereignty. I am describing, rather, a fundamental tension between Judaism, as we have known it for thousands of years, and the modern democratic state of Israel, as we have come to think of it today. This does not mean that Judaism is not democratic or pluralistic, or that it lacks the exegetical and halachic tools required to cope with scientific discoveries and technological developments. The source of the tension is that, whenever Judaism is mentioned, the reference is to a very specific paradigm of Judaism that assumes a model with a rabbinical, Pharisee, exile-like or Diaspora character—in its fabric if not in its content—one that is not necessarily compatible with the Zionist political model. It is this rabbinical-Pharisee model which shapes our Jewish sensitivity—both in the Diaspora as in Israel, as well as in the Liberal streams, just as much as in their Orthodox counterparts.

The rabbinical-Pharisee model will not admit any form of Jewish stateism, other than the Diaspora form that enabled the Jews to pursue their sovereign, theocratic life under the yoke of subjugation to other nations. Rejecting the Diaspora, with all its ills, its longing for Jerusalem, and its messianic expectation of the ingathering of the exiles changes little. In exile—from the Babylonian Exile onward—the Jews developed their system of beliefs, opinions and laws. The rabbinical-Pharisee model assured them the most appropriate conditions possible for life under a direct theocracy—albeit with certain limitations of sovereignty, under the yoke of subjugation to other nations. It allowed the Jews to exempt themselves from the political prevarications inherent in the reinstatement of sovereignty, and to survive tough competition from other paradigms of Judaism. These included: the Sadducee paradigm, which disappeared with the destruction of the ritual institutions of political sovereignty, or semi-sovereignty, over *Eretz Yisrael*; the Sadducee-Karaite paradigm, which enjoyed dominance over the rabbinical-Pharisee model for a considerable period of Jewish history; and, above all, the Christian-Pharisee model, which threatened to devour it. When we speak of Judaism today, we essentially mean the **rabbinical-Pharisee model**, which seems ostensibly irreconcilable with the **Zionist political** model.[1]

This paper will begin with a survey of the inception of the rabbinical-Pharisee model, in order to understand why it is at such odds with the Zionist political model. We will view the Pharisees in light of their historical counterparts, the Sadducees, and consider that the conflict between these two groups may lie behind the arguments between political Zionism and rabbinical Pharisaism in the modern State of Israel. We will next show how the creation of the State has challenged the rabbinical Pharisee paradigm, while at the same time creating a laboratory for Jewish cultural creativity and renewal. Finally, we will turn to Mordechai Kaplan's concept of peoplehood as a new way of conceptualizing Jewish identity in the modern world.

The Rabbinical-Pharisee Model

It may reasonably be assumed that Rabbinical Pharisaism was born during the Babylonian Exile, from where it migrated to *Eretz Yisrael*, clashing with Sadduceean circles. The movement originally emerged as an attempt to adapt the Law of Moses to conditions of life in exile, and to enable Jewish continuity in these circumstances. It entailed a creative effort to adjust the Biblical worldview: adapting the significance of a Torah no longer suited to the political situation in which the Jews found themselves; adapting their chosen ness, which had been fractured by their expulsion; adapting laws and regulations to suit them to the new reality, and so on. Pharisaism thus commences with the exiles' response to the destruction of the First Temple, with all this implies in theological terms; this trend would be further reinforced with the survival of the exile communities following the Return to Zion, the political changes in Judah, the destruction of the Second Temple, the defeat of the Bar Kochba rebellion, and the abandonment of *Eretz Yisrael*, the Land of Israel.

From the outset, Pharisaism appears to be an attempt to separate the Jews from other nations and an endeavor to preserve the Scriptures, accompanied by commentary. It is apologetic in its essence, leaving room only for the yearnings for a past era; it is also apostolic, even as it directs its principle

---

[1]   Unraveling the theological and political maze in which the Jewish People finds itself demands that we redefine such concepts as exile, *Golah*, Diaspora, Pharisaism, Saducism, and so on. In this article, "Exile" refers to an involuntary existential situation accompanied by a sense of alienation from one's surroundings and yearning for different surroundings; *Golah* refers to the theological and social conditions of Jews in exile who experience their condition as exile; Diaspora refers to communities and groups of Jews outside the borders of *Eretz Yisrael*, the Land of Israel.

efforts toward the communities of exiles. It develops an Oral Law intended to clarify the meaning of the Written Law and brings it down from Mount Sinai, in order to strengthen its status in the face of its detractors. Above all, Pharisaism was intended to offer new forms of life and a new ritual language. To its founders and adherents, after the destruction of the Second Temple even more than before, it constitutes a development of the pure faith in one God Who chose Israel to disseminate this message among the nations of the world, uprooting idol worship and preparing people's hearts to accept the Divine yoke. In so doing, it develops a survival strategy for the Jews, based around messianic scenarios of an all-embracing redemption, and, unwittingly, sparks historical thought as we know it today. *Eretz Yisrael* becomes the object of nostalgic yearnings, and the more these longings become part and parcel of Jewish liturgy, the more Utopian seems the idea of return to Zion. The exile itself does not remain a curse and a shame, but is raised rather to the level of a theological and political framework serving the mission of the dispersed Jews. Moreover, the alienation of exile permits the direct acceptance of the Divine yoke without the mediation of kings or priests, to the point where the *Golah* may be understood as the melting pot of Pharisee theocracy. Indeed, over 1,500 years later, much of Kabbalistic literature is devoted entirely to variations on the paradoxical status of a people chosen to be exiled from its own land, in order to fulfill its mission and realize the promises of its chosenness.

It is reasonable to assume that both the Sadducees and the Pharisees represented a range of views along the spectrum that existed among the Jewish public. The Sadducees hailed mainly from the more prosperous classes and were attracted by the Temple worship. They included both priests and Israelites, zealots and Hellenizers, the faithful and the assimilated. In all probability, they were not as insensitive, degraded, or obsessed with power and honor as depicted by their opponents.[2] Nor were they incorrigible conservatives, unprincipled collaborators, or uncompromising zealots. Moreover, much of what we know about them is sourced in their polemics with the Pharisees.

As far as one may gauge from the writings of the Pharisees themselves, their struggle with the Sadducees was too crucial to be understood as a campaign for public support, or for key positions in Temple worship or the work of the Sanhedrin. Theological, political, cultural and social issues divided the two movements, although they tended to unite in the face of a common

---

[2]   The academic community is unable to agree on the status, beliefs and role of the Sadducees. Some perceive them, in classic Pharisee tradition, as a cult of priests and their associates committed to Temple worship; others, as intellectuals interested in Greek culture and appalled by the positions of the Pharisees. There are even those who have characterized them as nationalist extremists who fought the Romans to their last. See Ben-Zion Katz, *Pharisees, Sadducees, Zealots, Christians*, Tel Aviv: N. Twirsky, 1948 (in Hebrew).

external adversary. The Pharisees returned from exile, charged with their pure faith in God, equipped with Midrashim that talked to the people—parables of comfort that spoke of the resurrection of the dead, and uplifting parables of the coming of the Messiah. Their backgrounds were generally more modest and they favored the work of the Sanhedrin. They combined an acceptance of Divine providence with an enthusiastic and sometimes fiery *Hassidut* and merged as gifted interpreters of Moses' Torah. They favored a holistic religious approach, importing into *Eretz Yisrael* the "fences" they had developed in exile for the purpose of life in exile, and promoting these among the masses in Judah and the Galilee. Through their sermons, they highlighted their disagreements with the Sadducees in various spheres:

A Hermeneutic Dispute

As mentioned, the Pharisees interpreted the Written Law in light of the Oral Law and, despite pressure from their opponents, they managed to imbue the Oral Law with a status and role of clarification that was no less esteemed and authoritative than the foundation of the Written Law itself. They plowed through it with an interpretative license that allowed them to attribute meaning to the text *ad infinitum*. They developed an arsenal of exegetical tools and produced a mass of halachic rulings, viewing their rabbis as the heirs and continuers of Moses, and elevating their exegesis to the level of revelation.

The Sadducees, for their part, railed against their gimmicks, inventions and parables. They were horrified by Pharisean exegetical enthusiasm, rebuked them for their appalling deviations from the written text, and perceived in them signs of distortions of the original meanings. They did not accept the tradition that the Oral Law was given to Moses on Mount Sinai, and abhorred the desecration of the Written Law. Yet they did not balk at all acts of interpretation; they themselves did not interpret the Torah literally. Even according to their opponents, they were open to their social environment and some of them were exposed to Hellenic wisdom; they were neither *Hassidim* nor ignoramuses. They were no more bound to the literal sense of the text than their adversaries and they were not afraid to exercise their own discretion.

A Principled Dispute

The Pharisees and Sadducees disagreed on all credos that were not sourced explicitly in the Torah and which the Pharisees had adopted over their years in exile, including the resurrection of the dead and the coming of the Messiah. These beliefs removed from Judaism its stoic rigidity and restraint, to offer comfort and compensatory answers for the masses: in an entire series of parables, they addressed extensively the reward that comes after death and the "world to come."

The Sadducees did not always have a response for their Pharisee counterparts, and found it hard to contend with their success. Instead of the reward of the world to come, they offered resignation to fate—in the discussion of Antigonos of Sokho[3]—, or even submission to the unfathomable will of God—in the case of Job. In place of the Pharisees' heaven and hell, they remained silent, since they could not examine the underworld. Instead of the resurrection of the dead, they preferred to speak of the eternity of the soul that finds its most concrete and convincing manifestation in the eternity of the dynasty, or procreation. Ahad Ha'am, philosopher of Cultural Zionism, interpreted their position on this matter as a commitment to the Eternity of Israel: They did not toy with the ideas of reward and punishment after death, but clung rather to life in this world, interpreting the survival and flourishing of the people as a victory over the death of the individual, called upon to sacrifice his life for the sake of the whole.[4]

A Ritual Dispute

The Pharisees introduced institutional changes that partly challenged the place of the Temple, the status of the priests, and possibly even the importance of the monarchy. They advanced the authority of the rabbi at the expense of the priest or king, encouraged prayer in the synagogue over the sacrificial offerings of the Temple, disseminated Torah learning among the masses, and made it a component of religious ritual. They were more attentive than their Sadducee rivals to the feelings of the masses and had no hesitation, in the name of the Torah, in introducing *de facto* reforms in the procedures for religious ritual. By contrast, the Sadducees adhered firmly to the concept of the sacrifices, for which they were disinclined to find alternatives.

A Political Dispute

Classic historiography emphasizes the political dispute between the Sadducees and the Pharisees by depicting, on the one hand, an aristocratic and conservative party that controlled public offices and maintained the integrity of the Temple worship, and, on the other, a populist and *Hassidic* party, revolutionary in many ways, that envisaged democracy within a popular theocratic framework. It may reasonably be assumed that the Pharisees, for their part, led the opposition to idol worship and foreign culture. They imbued their struggle with a prophetic and messianic dimension and frequent references to the coming of the Messiah and the era of peace, enthusing the

---

3   See *Avot*, 1:3.
4   Ahad Ha'am, "Flesh and Spirit," *At the Crossroads*, Judischer Verlag, Berlin, 1921, Vol. III, p. 228. (Hebrew)

masses with a wide variety of scenarios—political, apocalyptic and super-natural. Some even advocated a Torah of the heart through wonderful parables, recruited students from the margins of society, and provoked riots on the Temple Mount.

The Sadducees and the Pharisees were also divided in their attitude to authority and the monarchy. The Sadducees were the party of government; the Pharisees were the party of Torah, as galvanized through the Sanhedrin—if not the party of God. Both camps had their own extremists, sages and eccentrics. The Pharisees occupied themselves with a body of legislation to create the conditions for life under the yoke of other nations, rather than under Jewish political sovereignty. For them, the key political and theological principle was "*dina demalkhuta dina*" (the law of the state is the law)[5], in *Eretz Yisrael*, no less than in exile. This was a pragmatic and opportunistic principle enabling Jews to enjoy or accept the protection of another state without conceding the conditions of autonomy that allowed them to acknowledge the supremacy of the Divine dominion. The Pharisee's inclination to theocracy was fairly extreme: they were disinclined to make concessions, other than tactical ones, designed to satisfy the sovereign power; at times, it verged on religious anarchy. God is the Creator and God is the Sovereign.

In the final analysis, while the Jews experienced their exile as a curse and patiently awaited the Messiah, they nonetheless adapted their lifestyle and their expectations to the conditions of the *Golah*. Throughout this period, they cooperated with the alien powers, if only in order to ensure their sovereignty in exile, i.e. those conditions necessary to allow them to live their life according to the Torah and *Halachah*. Although imposed on them, the *Golah* thus constituted the fundamental and existential fabric through which rabbinical-Pharisee Judaism was woven—a fabric that remained dominant until the appearance of Zionism. God exiled the People of Israel in order to fertilize the nations of the world[6] and, wherever they were exiled, the Divine Presence went with them. In their exile, the Jews became a kingdom of priests scattered among the nations, to whom they brought the word of God.

To invoke more modern terms, rabbinical Pharisaism is post-stateist, not pre-stateist: it abandoned the political and historical arena and has no desire to return to it. In its political assumptions, therefore, it would accept Zionism only as a yearning or a sleight of hand on the part of Divine Providence. Indeed, Pharisaism may be regarded as a product of the Babylonian exile that developed in the *Golah* and requiring the conditions of the *Golah* to flourish spiritually, or even for the sake of its survival. If the Sadducees of the day, or today's secularists, were to impose a political system that disrupted its living conditions on Pharisaism, Pharisaism would then create the mental and often

5   *Baba Batra* 55b.
6   *Hagigah* 3a.

artificial conditions of exile in order to cope with its theological disruption, through that same political stateism.

When Raban Yochanan Ben Zakkai, the disciple of Hillel the Elder who returned to *Eretz Yisrael* from Babylon to revive the Torah[7], leaves a besieged Jerusalem for Yavneh and its Sages, he is motivated by the Pharisee doctrine. He was not abandoning his struggle against the Romans but, rather, choosing to employ different methods. However, he totally rejected the Sadduceean perception of Jewish sovereignty, opting instead to embrace the Pharisee position strongly. It may be assumed that the campaign against the Romans was led by zealots from all the camps but, in the case of the Pharisee camp, predominant were the unequivocal political and theological beliefs that Torah observance constituted *the* purpose of Judaism, and that religious autonomy would suffice for that purpose. The *Keter Torah* (Crown of the Torah) was deemed more important than the *Keter Malchut* (Crown of Power), in that the *Keter Torah* assured the Kingdom of Heaven, while the *Keter Malchut* led to its desecration. The Babylonian exilees developed mechanisms for social insularity and survival appropriate for Jewish life in exile, to the point that the *Golah* eventually became the most convenient theological and political framework for the realization of its prophetic and messianic mission. In the final analysis, while the Jews experienced their *Golah* as a curse and patiently awaited the Messiah, they adapted their lifestyle and expectations in response to the prevailing conditions of life in the *Golah*.

Pharisaism actually grew stronger throughout the Jewish dispersal, despite the difficulties of exile and the yearning for Jerusalem. Or, more accurately, the Sadduceean dimensions of Judaism—the challenge to the authority of the Oral Law; protest against the excesses of Kabbalistic exegesis; rejection of the concept of resurrection of the dead; politicization of the Messiah, and so on—became obscured with the continuing state of exile, with Pharasaism becoming the stable mold in which Judaism was cast. Exile was perceived as a disgrace and the longing for Jerusalem did not wane; however, a parallel process was set in motion that virtually justified exile, in no small measure under Kabbalistic influence. This gradually permeated intellectual circles, down to the great twentieth-century thinkers, such as Herman Cohen, Franz Rosenzweig and, closer to us, Emmanuel Levinas. Even those who immigrated to *Eretz Yisrael* and attempted to address the theological and political challenges represented by Zionism either recreated there the virtual sub-conditions of exile, or—in the case of the students of Rabbi Kook—developed messianic

---

[7]   The position presented in this article was not unknown to the Sages. As is well known, Resh Lakish stated that it was the Babylonians who, on repeated occasions, restored [the study of] the Torah in *Eretz Yisrael*: "At first, when the Torah was forgotten by Israel, Ezra came up from Babylon and established its foundation; when it was again forgotten, Hillel the Babylonian came up and established it; when it was again forgotten, Rabbi Hiyya and his sons came up and established it" (*Sukkah* 20a).

frameworks that allowed them to surmount, at least in part, the inherent contradictions between Pharisaism and Zionism.

The debate between the Sadducees and the Pharisees—the true debate, not its Phariseean version—thus vanished from the face of the Earth, leaving a significant displacement. However, it is true that one may still follow traces of Sadducism in the thinking of such eminent figures as Maimonides, the leaders of Reform Judaism, and even Yeshayahu Leibowitz. Neo-Sadducism, if not Sadducism, was characterized by:

- A particular interest in writings that may be classed as Sadduceean—the Psalms, Job, Ecclesiastes, etc.;
- An unfailing and scrupulous examination of the written word, in order to elucidate the meaning of the text;
- An emphasis on the legislative purpose of the Torah, at the expense of its ritual function; and
- A focus on natural Providence, rather than supernatural Providence, together with a disregard for phenomena of a miraculous nature.

The conflict between Sadducism and Pharisaism lies, perhaps, behind arguments between political Zionism and rabbinical Pharisaism in the modern-day State of Israel. Rabbinical Pharisaism is completely or partially unwilling to accept Jewish national sovereignty, since this impinges on its exile-based *Weltanschaung*.

The Political Zionist Paradigm

It is generally accepted that the establishment of the State of Israel dictates a change in the paradigm of Jewish existence, and hence the change in the Jewish historiography that has prevailed since the destruction of the Second Temple. After two thousand years of exile, during which the Jews pursued their spiritual and religious life under "the yoke of the nations," a sovereign framework recognized by the nations of the world has again been established, wherein the Jews can build their own sovereign public space in the framework of an independent state. For the most part, this public space claims ownership of the Jewish heritage, its treasures and symbols. It is developing a Hebrew-Jewish culture that draws inspiration from Jewish sources and seeks a special status within the global Jewish presence, because it has established governmental institutions answering to the authority of an elected government that is committed to the vision of the renaissance of the Jewish People. A solid Jewish majority has been created, due to mass immigration of Jews from the world over, along with their immediate naturalization and maximal integration into its social, economic and cultural life. Wars have been waged for the survival of the state, operations and struggles launched to save Jews in distress, and to free those persecuted because of their Judaism. Finally, the capital of Israel sits in Jerusalem, which has symbolized the focus of longing and/or renaissance for the Jewish People throughout the generations.

Yet we need to acknowledge that, after over a century of Zionism and sixty years of Israeli sovereignty, Jewish theology continues to be essentially rabbinical-Pharisee, with an orientation that reflects the Diaspora, if not exile. Given rabbinical Pharisaism's hegemony over Jewish philosophy, Jewish thought remains almost entirely apologetical in its confrontation of the challenges posed by: a hostile environment, alien culture, a negating or competing Christianity, an offensive Islam, adverse philosophy, or even a sovereign Jewish ideology such as Zionism. Halachic rulings, to focus on the most significant component of the rabbinical-Pharisee paradigm, have not yet undergone the changes demanded by the reinstatement of Jewish sovereignty, nor have they "vanquished" Israeli Law, in one manner or another. Indeed, rabbis, philosophers and politicians all offer their opinions on issues of the Israeli reality, and even pronounce rulings on the most burning of them: yet the Zionist revolution itself has failed to challenge the foundations of the rabbinical-Pharisee *Halachah*. Precedents created over two thousand years of Halachic rulings in exile, intended for life in the *Golah*, may well require more than sixty years of independence for that *Halachah* to begin to adjusting to the new theological and political reality; and the parallel legal systems employed in Israel will continue to guide our lives for a considerable time to come. However, the reality of Israel, together with the processes of cultural, social and political transformations, is nonetheless molding contemporary allegorical exegesis, and may reasonably be expected to steer halachic rulings increasingly toward sovereign directions, rather than exile-oriented ones.

For the Jews of the Diaspora, the establishment of an independent Jewish state also poses a challenge—whether they are among the supporters or the detractors of Israel as a state. Beyond any religious and ritual commandment or categorical demand on the part Zionism, it owes its primary impact to Israel's geographical presence in a land redolent with memories that have been preserved in Jewish tradition and the Jewish way of life, as well as to its spiritual and cultural achievements: the revival of Hebrew as a language of speech and creativity; spiritual and cultural dynamism in the many fields of pan-Jewish creativity, including the production of Israeli-Jewish emblems and ceremonies that have been adopted by Jewish communities around the world; constitutional decisions, relating both to civil life in Israel and to Jewish lifestyle worldwide.

Despite significant signs of alienation, Jews find it difficult to remain indifferent toward Israel. For some, Israel, as the state of the Jews, is struggling for its existence and its security against enemies seeking to destroy it; for others, it is implementing a policy of settlement that deprives another people of a homeland. For some, it is gradually but resolutely realizing the vision of the ingathering of the exiles, developing a democratic Jewish society and fostering spiritual, religious and cultural renewal; for others, it is attacking the spiritual and moral assets of Jewish heritage. For some, it constitutes the first chapter in a new stage of the history of the Jewish People necessitated by their circumstances before and after the *Shoah*, and constitutes even the first blossoms of their redemption; for others, it is a closing chapter in the annals of the Jewish People—even the beginning of its spiritual decline. For some, Israel appears to be a creation that unifies, or with the potential to unify, the different parts of the Jewish People; for others, it represents a source of dissension among the same Jewish People.

Whatever the case, the establishment of a Jewish state in *Eretz Yisrael* and around Jerusalem—a state of the Jews and/or of the Jewish People—has transformed the circumstances of Jewish existence. Through its very existence, the State challenges the political and theological legitimacy of the Diaspora, even though Zionist discourse and action no longer place emphasis on the negation of the Diaspora as once was the case. It challenges the geographical, political and spiritual Jewish map that has prevailed for two millennia and demands that Jewish communities adopt a different perspective on themselves and other communities. Even were Israeli national institutions to proclaim that the prosperity of the Jewish communities constitutes a value in its own right and an important component in the spiritual strength and security of the State of Israel, Israel would nonetheless continue to embody the ultimate location for the realization of the spiritual, religious, cultural and social ideals inherent in all the streams of Jewish heritage that has never denied Jerusalem, despite its rabbinical-Phariseean fabric. Israel is not just another Jewish community, but a political entity where decisions are made by a Jewish majority and off their free will. On the one hand, it belongs to its citizens; on the other, it belongs to all Jews.

I cannot assess precisely what place Israel holds in the symbolic space of the American Jewish community—the largest and most influential of all—and in the topology and psychology of each of its members. I can only reiterate that Israel features prominently in the Jewish heritage of all streams of Judaism and especially within the rich symbolism of Jerusalem, as the focus of Jewish yearnings since the Destruction of the Temple: a longing for a different, more fulfilled life, and for a different, reformed world. *Eretz Yisrael* figures as the Promised Land, *qua* the Land of Zion and Jerusalem, the site on which the innermost hopes of the Jewish soul would find their realization. Jews did not make frequent pilgrimages to Jerusalem; instead, they visited it within their souls. To this day, Jerusalem represents an address for prayers, hopes and supplications; throughout the Jewish Diaspora—in the United States and Canada, in France and Russia—it forms the backdrop to Jewish life.

However, while desolate Jerusalem impaired the joy of the Jews, rebuilt Jerusalem has yet to clarify its role in their contemporary existence. It is evident to all that even American Jews cannot abandon their longing for Jerusalem, nor their support for it, without risking the loss of the firmest foundation for their existence as Jews. Disconnecting the symbolic and/or political bond leaves them only the options of either living as ultra-Orthodox Jews in protected environments or constituting a new stream of Judeo-Christianity.

Strengthening the connection between Israel and the Diaspora is, in any case, of reciprocal interest. On the one hand, without bonds to the Diaspora, Israel will be at best a nation like any other; on the other hand, without its connection to Israel, the Diaspora will disappear through the assimilation process by Jews, as individuals. Israel stands only to benefit from flourishing Jewish communities in the Diaspora: through their political and economic support, and the breath of fresh air that they provide. It needs therefore to accept that it is a small nation, dependent on market and political forces beyond its control, and that it must therefore open itself still further to Jews, enchanting them and creating bonds to unite them with it.

The Diaspora, for its part, owes a paradoxical and symbolic debt to the Israeli phenomenon. More than Zionism liberated the Jews in Zion from the Diaspora, it liberated the Jewish *Golah* from the shame of exile. The Jewish state gave the Diaspora a national pride, presented it with political, social and cultural challenges, and introduced an element of creative competition. Israel is located at the heart of modern Jewish existence and discourse, at the center of Hebrew-Jewish creativity, and at the core of contemporary Jewish symbolism. Overall, it enjoys a prominent position within Jewish communal and emotional space. Indeed, Israel as a state has become no less a generator of identity in the Diaspora than within Israel itself, particularly among Jews who have abandoned religion and are not active in communal frameworks. This is apparent even in anti-Zionist ultra-Orthodox circles and post-modern intellectual groupings.

Nonetheless, the bond to Israel, just like the other components of Jewish existence, may weaken and even disappear. For better or for worse, Israel is in the news headlines the world over. Of all the nations of the world, it is the only one to attract such extensive criticism. The support of Christian Evangelist groups notwithstanding, Israel's very existence challenges Christian dogmas on the curse of the Jewish People and the prospects for its conversion. It also challenges the Islamic credo that the Qoran constitutes the final stage of Divine revelation. In the eyes of the nations of the world, Israel represents the transformation of Judaism from a faded religion negated by Christianity and Islam, to a renascent civilization that has returned to the international arena, where it currently figures as an exception to the rule. Its claims re-sound with particular dissonance in an era when monolithic nation states are opening themselves to other nationalities, cultures and religions—especially the United States, a country that was founded on the principles of multi-nationalism, religious pluralism and multiculturalism. Jewish ears are not deaf to this dissonance.

A New Political and Theological *Midrash*

Israel constitutes a laboratory for Jewish cultural creativity in numerous spheres. It has to address numerous challenges and respond with original solutions. This is particularly evident in areas relating to everyday life. Criticism from intellectuals in the various Jewish communities aside, research and intellectual creativity in Israel are actually broader-based than those in the most vibrant Diaspora communities, and their existential ramifications are particularly significant for Jews *qua* Jews.

On the face of it, the Jewish People's existential questions, or those of the Jewish individual, demand a new *Midrash* to revitalize society and community, law and *Halachah*. This would undoubtedly contribute to a clarification of the theological and political horizons within which individual Jews would be able to ask the questions that interest them, or those that guide or impinge on their lives as individuals and as Jews. Naturally, everyone has his or her own questions and each individual has his or her own answers. Nonetheless, a new political and theological paradigm is required to channel these answers, however different, into one single fabric and thus foster a sense of belonging to a single people.

I believe that, in the specific case of the Jews, contrary to other peoples, the theological and political package cannot be disassembled, either in Israel or in the Diaspora, and that this is precisely what makes the Jew so original. Thus, from whichever theological and political perspective we propose, the individual Jew would be able to grapple with a more or less closed set of questions, to which secondary questions would be added, depending on the individual's socio-cultural background, economic status, intellectual factors and age. The core cluster comprises four principal questions:

1. The Attitude to God

God stands at the foundation of the Jewish question and behind Jewish meaning—whether or not He is the Creator of the world; whether or not we believe in His existence and Providence; whether He is a cosmic entity or a moral ideal; whether He dwells in the Heavens or is inherent in nature; whether He is revealed in the human heart, in their intellect or in Scripture; whether He hears prayers or conceals His face. Judaism pursues the poetics and symbolism of the concept of God as manifested in the verse that states

"I am that which I am" (Deuteronomy 13:16). Behind this enigmatic declaration lies an entire palimpset of interpretations written in the ink of wonder, despair and hope, and their complexity only increases.

2. The Attitude to the Ethos of Torah Study

The commandment of *Talmud Torah* (to study the Torah) has acquired a place of respect among all sections of the Jewish People—whether for the sake of Heaven or for reward; whether the study is liturgical or investigative in nature. Today, we recognize the importance of the search for meaning in general: it fuels research, philosophy and creativity, whether in the realm of Religion or Science; it explores textual archives from which it derives its insights, including those that form the basis of scientific hypotheses.[8] In their search for wisdom, some base themselves on the wisdom of the Greeks, others on poets; others on the Prophets (Hermann Cohen), the great leaders of Hassidism (Martin Buber), or the Sages (Emmanuel Levinas). It is texts which document the marvels and enlightenment that attribute meaning, and Jewish meaning grows with interpretation, in a spiritual, loving, and sympathetic affinity for the Biblical, Talmudic, rabbinical, philosophical, and literary canon. In other words, the search for Jewish meaning demands fidelity to the Bible as a sacred and/or classic text that has established and shaped identity in light of Talmudic, rabbinical and philosophical exegesis, whether we define ourselves as the People of the Book or a literary people, whether the written word binds us, or sets us free.[9] Being Jewish thus emerges as a quest of infinite dimensions, sometimes well grounded, sometimes cumbersome, into Jewish issues within our search for human meaning.

3. The Attitude to the Commandments

Jewish tradition teaches that there are 613 *Mitzvot* (precepts) incumbent upon Jews—whether we perform most of them or a few of them; whether for the sake of Heaven, or for personal reward; whether they are deemed to be acquired human behavior or magical acts; whether they are perceived as traditions or Commandments; whether or not they have a rationale be-hind them. Hermann Cohen, who sought a *Halachah* that would be more acceptable than the rabbinical one, noted, "Those who have not sampled the yoke of Halachah cannot comprehend that it is carried like a ladder to the Heavens."[10] Yeshayahu Leibowitz went even further, in an attempt to reduce Judaism to the observance of the *Mitzvot*. On a different, more existential

---

8   Cf. Popper, K., "Une Epistémologie sans sujet connaissant", in *La Connaissance objective*, Aubier, Paris, 1991, p. 232.

9   See Ahad Ha'am, "The Torah of the Heart," *At the Crossroads* Vol. I, p. 93 (in Hebrew).

10   Cohen, H., *Religion de la Raison*, XVI, p. 509.

and poetical note, Rabbi Soloveitchik presented the *Mitzvot* as the quasi-mathematical definitions of Jewish existence.[11] For Mordechai Kaplan, the observance of the commandments infuses poetical significance into a routine existence that might otherwise become alienated. Freed from the shackles of rabbinical tradition, he proposes that we regard them as, "Jewish poetics in action."[12] Whatever the case, the *Halachah* places limitations and boundaries in all matters relating to the satisfaction of natural needs, from food to sex.[13] It integrates the individual Jew within the historical Jewish collective, at the price of restricting his or her inherent possibilities as a human being. It shapes his or her space and time; it defines his or her attitude to others and to God; it colors his or her life.

The Attitude to *Tikkun Olam* (Repairing the World)

The desire to 'repair' or improve the world appears to survive even among those who emphatically reject Jewish tradition, filling the void resulting from the absence and silence of God as if the longing for His proximity were transformed, nonetheless, into a longing for a better world without Him. Stefan Zweig, who offers postmodernist views on the Jews, puts the following words into one of his characters, Benjamin the lamp-keeper: "It is terrible to be the person on whom God calls all the time and who never realizes his wishes; the one to whom He makes the promises that He fails to keep." *Tikkun Olam* is driven more by longing for the return of the God who has concealed His face, than by abstract ideals for a better society, or the love of mankind.

A Cultural and Political Paradigm

Even before the establishment of the State of Israel, Mordechai Kaplan sought a political framework that would ensure the continuity of the Jewish People. He was seeking not beliefs and opinions, arguments and justifications but, rather, that cultural and political ethos, beyond the theological and political, which he termed 'civilization'. He accept neither the Orthodox approach which emphasizes the principle of Judaism, in one way or another, in order to impose it on the

---

[11] See Y.D. Soloveitchik, *The Man of Halachah*, Jerusalem: Department for Jewish Zionist Education, Jewish Agency for Israel, 1979, pp. 28–30 (Hebrew).

[12] "...religious poetry in action. The normal human being is exhilarated by any kind of ritual which gives him a sense of unity with the larger life of some group. In sharing that life, his own is redeemed from its dull and drab routine." M. Kaplan, *Judaism as a Civilization*, New York: Schocken Books, 1967 (1934), p. 434.

[13] See E. Simon, "Totality and Anti-Totalitarianism," in *The Right to Educate and the Duty to Educate*, Jerusalem: Sifriat Hapoalim, 1983 (Hebrew).

Jews, nor the Reform approach which emphasizes the best of Judaism, in one way or another, in order to make it attractive to Jews who might otherwise not be interested. Kaplan faults Orthodoxy for ignoring the needs of the moment and the Reform movement for sanctifying them. Both somehow act to reduce Judaism to a religion, while Kaplan sought to expand its canvas to encompass all social, communal, cultural and religious phenomena.

Addressing the renewal of Jewish civilization, Kaplan attempts to reconstruct a Judaism shattered by the Emancipation. Before the Emancipation, affiliation to the Jewish People was a precondition and guarantee for securing the World to Come and it was the sense of being chosen, inherent in the promise of Redemption for all Israel, which forged a sense of common destiny. Affiliation with the Jewish People would be rewarded with Redemption, and the Torah was, "the *lettre de patentes* which bestowed nobility upon his people, and, therefore, upon him" for every man and woman in Israel.[14] Following the Emancipation, affiliation with the Jewish People ceased to be an inevitable assumption and was sometimes even unacceptable. Faith in the Redemption was not as steadfast or deep-rooted as in the past and Judaism, as the Mosaic religion, had difficulty keeping its place behind, alongside, or in front of, Christianity. Intermarriage and assimilation ravaged the Diaspora Jewish communities; affiliation with the Jewish People could no longer offer the expectation of reward or recompense in the World to Come.

Kaplan asked the question that has since been raised continuously by American Jewry: "What shall henceforth be the status of Jewry as a collective entity vis-à-vis the rest of the world?"[15] Unlike Ahad Ha'am, Kaplan prioritizes the Jewish People above Judaism, in that he perceives Judaism to be necessary to ensure the strength and success of the Jewish People, rather than Jewish continuity, in order to ensure the perpetuation of Judaism. He even ranks the People higher in importance above Judaism, or, to adopt a more traditional phraseology, above the Torah. Kaplan is convinced, furthermore, that the Jewish People constitutes a unique spiritual and national entity. Following Ahad Ha'am, he bases his process of *Tikkun* on the concept of nationhood or, more precisely, pseudo-nationhood, castigating the rejection by Reform Judaism, at that time, of any element of nationhood as national suicide.[16] Like Hermann Cohen's students prior to the establishment of the State of Israel, Kaplan initially distinguishes between nationhood and nationalism. *Nationhood*

---

[14] "The Jewish people was to him not an abstract or invisible entity which demanded loyalty and gave little or nothing in return, but a living nation which conferred upon him a privileged status in the order of creation, believed in him, and assured him bliss eternal. The Torah was to him the lettre de patentes which bestowed nobility upon his people, and, therefore, upon him." Kaplan, M., *Judaism as a Civilization*, p. 12.

[15] M. Kaplan, *Judaism as a Civilization*, p. 227.

[16] "This surrender of Jewish nationhood is a new kind of suicide, suicide on a national scale." M. Kaplan, *Judaism as a Civilization*, p. 120.

suggests affiliation to a defined group that preceives itself as a nation; *nationalism* refers to a struggle designed to advance nationhood, i.e., to strive to create a framework that will benefit and facilitate its proper development. Kaplan's nationhood is similar to that of Hermann Cohen, although without the hostility toward Jewish nationalism, particularly in its Zionist manifestation, that epitomized Cohen's positions. Kaplan is even inclined to speak of an international Jewish nationhood, based *inter alia* on a national home or nation state, but without confining himself to stateist nationhood. He adopts Ahad Ha'am's approach in speaking of, "a new type of nation—an international nation, with a national home to give them cultural and spiritual unity."[17]

The reality of the Holocaust and the creation of the State of Israel, however, change everything for Kaplan. In 1954, he feels the need to qualify the comments he made in 1935. The situation is now entirely different. The State of Israel has been founded on the ashes of the mass annihilation of millions of Jews. American Jewry, for its part, was situated at the apogee of a shockwave and the dawn of an awakening which, some decades further on, would be considered pseudo-nationalistic. Kaplan rejects the concept of nationhood, proposing instead the concept of peoplehood. In the preface to a new edition of his book *Judaism as a Civilization*, he writes: "The concept 'nationhood,' as applied to the Jews, has come to be closely identified with statehood, and was, therefore, in need of being replaced by the concept 'peoplehood.'"[18]

Jewish peoplehood, according to Kaplan, and as it emerges after the establishment of the State of Israel, seeks to be a post-nationalist stage in the history of the Jewish People. It posits the achievements of Jewish nationhood while striving to avoid its pitfalls; it will be legitimate only insofar as it contributes, in the spirit of Ahad Ha'am, to the continuous renewal of the Jewish People. Jewish Peoplehood thus supplies the infrastructure for a new religion that views this world as the arena of Redemption, speaking to the Jews of the Diaspora no less than to Jews in Israel, and assuring self- realization for each Jewish man and woman in this world, both as a Jew and a human being. Moreover, Kaplan does not confine himself to a doctrine; he also seeks institutions, including the reinstatement of the Sanhedrin as an institution representing the entire Jewish People,[19] capable of making a declaration of the caliber of the Basel Declaration, as well as the establishment of a parliament representing all sectors of the Jewish People.[20]

In a series of articles written after the establishment of the State, Kaplan frequently employs the term 'Jewish peoplehood.' Equally interestingly, he refers to his amended doctrine as 'New Zionism': the contribution of the Diaspora in

[17] M. Kaplan, *Judaism as a Civilization*, p. 232.
[18] M. Kaplan, *Judaism as a Civilization*, p. IX.
[19] M. Kaplan, *A New Zionism*, New York: The Herzl Press & The Jewish Reconstructionist Press, 1959, p. 184.
[20] M. Kaplan, *A New Zionism*, p. 128.

general, and American Jewry in particular, to Israel.[21] For Kaplan, Zionism is charged with its own theological mission: it came into existence to address the challenges of the transition from a religion dependent on the World to Come, and which assumes a supernatural God, to a religion of this world that perceives humans as its sole standard. It rejects the follies of supernatural faiths and other worlds, sometimes to the point of totally removing God from religious human considerations. Kaplan may thus be considered to have introduced, in his own way, the same anthropocentric revolution that characterizes modern attempts to remove religion from the supernatural labyrinth.[22] His brand of Zionism aims not merely to ensure refuge for persecuted Jews, but also to provide an answer to the theological revolution that has transformed the perception of Redemption from the supernatural state—awaiting the Messiah—, to a political and spiritual one.

Kaplan formulated the Jewish Question in cultural and political terms, advocating the renewal of Jewish civilization. He did not offer a new Jewish theology, nor did he anticipate the transformation of the entire world into a single civilization, fueled by scientific and technological advances and the media revolution. Those changes taking place in the Jewish world mean that his questions are back on the contemporary Jewish agenda, compelling us to seek a response better suited to the theological and political status of the Jewish People within the globalized world currently emerging before our eyes. On the one hand, Israel should reject the Pharisee theological and political perspective that is eroding its stateism, yet without denying its Jewish heritage; on the other, Diaspora Jewish communities need to develop a positive perception of the Jewish People that represents a function of positive considerations—a new *Midrash*, dialogue with other faiths, and a model society—rather than negative ones, as it has in the past, such as: Anti-Semitism, distressed communities, or support for Israel. In communities where the lifestyle continues to reflect exile (even if those Jews are not conscious that their presence in the Diaspora constitutes an existential or symbolic form of exile), rabbis and thinkers have to address the Pharisee theological and political paradigm in their rulings, simultaneously with the existence of an independent Jewish state that claims to be fulfilling part of Judaism's messianic and political visions. In other words, just as the political Zionist paradigm demands sovereign decisions, the rabbinical Pharisee paradigm necessitates pronouncements for exile. The cross-fertilization between these two halachic legal systems can thus ensure a continued dialogue between Israel and the Diaspora.

---

[21] "The idea of the peoplehood of world Jewry and the indispensability of Jewish religion may have to be imported from American Zionism." M. Kaplan, *A New Zionism*, p. 104.

[22] "To the Jew, therefore, God is the God of the Jewish People, insofar as it is for him a medium of salvation. If he is a traditionalist, he believes that its was of life was revealed by God. If he is a modernist, he regards its way of life as revealing God." M. Kaplan, *A New Zionism*, p. 114.

The lesson to be gleaned from Kaplan, then, is twofold: American Jewry cannot achieve a spiritual and religious renaissance without formulating a theological and political model of the Diaspora that incorporates the political existence of Israel, and without avoiding the painful lessons from Europe. The State of Israel, for its part, needs to accept the revolution that its creation has enacted in the theological and political status of the Jewish People and become a symbolic and existential anchor for the Jews of the Diaspora. And this, if only to found its existence in the theological and political narrative that addresses God and the Jews, in an era that has included experiences of both Holocaust and Redemption. The Israeli experiment, with both its successes and failures, is noteworthy in its own right, fascinating large sectors of Jewish society who view the transformation of a muddle of immigrants into a model society as the most significant challenge facing the Jewish People. Above all, it allows us to raise controversial issues that rabbinical-Pharisee Judaism was reluctant to address and to provide creative answers that may appeal, not just to the Jewish People, but to mankind as a whole.

A SOCIOLOGIST'S GUIDE FOR BUILDING JEWISH PEOPLEHOOD

EZRA KOPELOWITZ

Editor's summary

Ezra Kopelowitz begins with the notion that Jewish Peoplehood is generated only in the context of living a rich Jewish life. To show how a connection is built between an individual and the Jewish People, he considers four levels of analysis: the social rituals that characterize day-to-day interactions; the educational, religious, and social events of Jewish life; the institutions within which these events occur; and the realities of Jewish communal life in Israel and the Diaspora. He draws upon examples from Jewish life in America and Israel to show that most Jewish experiences are conceptualized as "closed events" that have little obvious connection to the rest of the individual's life. He argues that for Jewish Peoplehood to thrive, there can be no distinction between "Jewish belonging" and "real life." Rather, Jewish experiences need to be translated into patterns of interaction that will occur even with Jews who are not immediately present, thus forging a connection with the Jewish People at large.

I propose what at first glance is an obvious thesis: Jewish Peoplehood is generated in the course of living a rich Jewish life. A Jewish lifestyle might be secular, humanist, religious, socialist, Conservative, Orthodox or Reform. What matters is that a person lives a Jewish life that goes beyond participation in an occasional event or membership in a particular institution. When a person lives a rich Jewish life, he or she will feel part of the Jewish People. We would be hard-pressed to find a mainstream leader in the Jewish world who will disagree with this assertion, and yet many of the events and institutions of Jewish life are not designed to encourage individuals to adopt a rich Jewish life style.

The call we are hearing from Jewish leaders and institutions today is pointing us to new and more exciting forms of life cycle ceremonies; experiments in Jewish media, music and culture; changes to the synagogue service; Jewish travel programs to Eastern Europe or Israel, and more. The problem is that the connection between making a particular event or program more meaningful to an individual and the creation of a rich lifestyle is not automatic. While administrators, educators, policy makers and rabbis should bend over backwards to make their programs and institutions relevant, interesting and meaningful, we must always ask how these same programs and institutions help create a sense of belonging to the Jewish People. In the rush to adapt Jewish life to the meaning needs of individuals, we often forget that a rich Jewish life necessarily includes the group dimension, which is a by-product of living a rich Jewish life.

My goal is to "bring the group back in" to the discussion on Jewish continuity.

- A prayer service might be spiritually uplifting, but does it promote a sense of belonging to a larger group—a sense which extends beyond the people immediately present?
- Does the prayer service impart knowledge and skills which motivate and enable the individual to pray with other Jews who live elsewhere and belong to different religious movements? If so, what are the qualities of the prayer service that enables Peoplehood? Likewise, do the organizers of a trip to Israel move beyond the concern that individuals in the group enjoy themselves, and also stress the connection between the tourist and the larger Jewish People? If so, how does the tourist experience contribute towards building Jewish Peoplehood?
- Do new forms of Jewish media, art and culture do more than just stimulate individuals to "engage with their Judaism"? Do they enable the consumer of popular Jewish culture to identify with other Jews worldwide? Do they help foster a sense of Peoplehood?
- What must be present in the events and rituals of Jewish life for the individual to take the experience to other arenas of everyday life, and hence to continually reinforce the connection to the global Jewish collective?

In this chapter, I seek to explore the elements of a rich Jewish life that enable Jewish Peoplehood, drawing on sociological theory and many concrete examples from Jewish life as it is currently lived in Israel and the Diaspora. I will demonstrate how, once we isolate these elements, we can then translate our insights into forms of educational, religious and other types of programming that will build Jewish Peoplehood.

This chapter is divided into four sections. We begin with an examination of the rituals we use in our daily face-to-face interactions with others, some of which enable a connection between an individual and the Jewish People. We will then look at how Peoplehood rituals integrate into the educational, religious and social events of Jewish life. Next, we analyze the institutions within which these events occur. In the fourth and final section, we look at the different realities of Jewish communal life in Israel and the Diaspora, and the implications for building Jewish Peoplehood.

Step One: Face-to-Face Relationships and Jewish Peoplehood

The first step in analyzing how Peoplehood is forged is to consider why an individual in the course of everyday life would come to identify other Jews as members of a common people, even though they may never actually meet one another. In *Imagined Communities,* Benedict Anderson[1] laid the groundwork for this type of analysis when he asked: "How is it that people are able to identify with millions of others in a nation-state such as France or England without ever meeting face to face? Why would someone regard a total stranger in the context of everyday life as a fellow compatriot—a Frenchman or Englishman?" Anderson argued that modern nationalism is tied to the development of national languages that came about with the invention of the printing press. For example, when people all over a country pick up the same morning newspaper, written in the same language, focusing on the same news stories and presented in the same format, they internalize a sense of involvement in a common group enterprise that did not previously exist.

As other sociologists Erving Goffman[2] have noted, reading a newspaper, like many other everyday activities, is an example of a social ritual—a repetitive form of behavior that occurs in a predictable fashion and enables us to communicate with others. This definition of ritual includes most activities we undertake in everyday life, from prayer, to shaking someone's hand, or waiting on a line to board the bus.

In considering how Jews come to identify with one another, then, we need to understand the qualities of social rituals that enable participants to imagine they are part of the Jewish people. With this goal in mind, we start off with the following definition of a social ritual that builds Jewish Peoplehood:

A Definition of a Social Ritual that Builds Jewish Peoplehood

Jewish Peoplehood is forged when face-to-face social interactions between Jews are structured in such a way, that:
(1) the individuals involved identify with Jews who are not immediately present
and
(2) skills and knowledge are imparted that motivate and enable the individuals to participate in future interactions with other Jews.

The emphasis in the above definition is that the ritual enables identification with, and the possibility of interaction with, Jews who are not immediately present in the context of the face-to-face relationships an individual experiences

---

1   Anderson, Benedict. 1991. *Imagined Communities: Reflections on the Origin and Spread of Nationalism.* New York: Verso.
2   Goffman, Erving. 1982. *Interaction Ritual: Essays on Face-to-Face Behavior.* New York: Pantheon Books.

in everyday life. Social rituals capable of building Jewish Peoplehood must enable individuals to identify with Jews who are not present in their everyday lives. To accomplish this, the ritual structures face-to-face interaction in a manner that is replicable—namely, the form of interaction can be done with other Jews in different times and places. Hence, the ability of the individual to imagine membership in the Jewish People, despite the fact that almost all the other members are people he or she will never actually meet. This imaginative ability is what makes Peoplehood possible.

In order to build Jewish Peoplehood, a social event must include rituals that enable participants to transcend their immediate context and imagine that they are joining with Jews elsewhere who are participating, have participated or one day will participate in a similar event.

To understand how Peoplehood rituals enable this type of transcendence, we need to consider the manner in which rituals bring people into contact with one another. A group of Jews may come together to pray, play soccer, or experiment with Jewish art, to give just a few examples. But we are interested in these social events only insofar as they generate a sense of belonging that extends beyond those who are immediately present. If the participants leave the event simply having had a good time with each other, but no greater sense of group participation is generated, then the goal of forging Jewish Peoplehood has not been achieved.

Example One: The Passover Seder

The Passover Seder serves as an example of an effective Peoplehood ritual. The Seder, narrowly defined, is no more than a meeting of friends and family members who sit around the table and share a common meal. Yet something happens at the Seder that transforms the smaller group sitting around the table into one part of a larger group of Jews who also participate in the Seder. When people sit around the Seder table they are aware that there are others located elsewhere who are also eating the Passover meal. The awareness of participating in a larger act that includes others who are not physically present transforms the physical space of the room and the table around which the diners sit into a forum for sharing a sense of membership in the Jewish People.

The Seder builds Peoplehood in that it *structures face-to-face social interaction in such a way that enables the possibility of interaction with other Jews who are not immediately present*. It enables transcendence[3] in that participants literally transcend the physical confines of the table around which they sit and become members of a larger group.

---

[3] My use of the concept of "transcendence" draws inspiration from Swanson, Guy E. 1967. *Religion and Regime: A Sociological Account of the Reformation*. Ann Arbor: The University of Michigan Press.

When do social rituals enable transcendence? French anthropologist, Maurice Bloch[4] provides an answer by looking at the qualities of a song. Bloch argues that when people sing together they must accept the existence of a larger group framework. Successful singing requires common knowledge of the words and agreement to sing them together, keeping the same tune and rhythm. The members of the singing group conform to a social framework that extends beyond the immediate group. The result is the reproduction of culture and the creation of a broader social group, in that all the singers know that they can continue to sing the same song with other members of the extended cultural group in different contexts. Hence, the power of song—the ability to participate in the life of a social group, both in the context of face-to-face interaction and, at the same time, to be part of a larger group of people who are not actually present at the given moment.

Beyond the need for shared knowledge, an additional dimension of singing in a group is that individuals necessarily suppress their personal preferences. Such preferences are of secondary concern. The success of the event is itself the source of meaning, after which it might be appropriate to ask if the individual identifies with all aspects of the ritual—although one is not dependent on the other.

An individual might not fully identify with the words of the song, but will nevertheless sing, for he or she finds value in being part of the larger group.

Example Two: Singing Together on a Teen Travel Program

Of course, not every singing experience is an effective ritual. Harvey Goldberg provides an illustrative example of an educational event in which the use of song failed to generate the Peoplehood experience. Goldberg is drawing on ethnographic research he carried out among a group of young American Jews on a summer trip in Israel.

> The knowledge or ignorance of a specific song may seem like a peripheral detail, but the following notes, taken from the end of the four days of archeological work, accompanied by challenging and fun climbs through the Beit Guvrin caves, suggest otherwise.
> The guide had just finished taking us around the vast and almost cathedral-like "bell-cave." The guide suggested in the bell-cave that they take a group photo, and that they sing. The group started to sing something—in English—and the guide mentioned that she thought something in Hebrew would be appropriate. Some people suggested *Hava Nashira* [a particularly sonorous melody], but others said they did not know it. The guide came up and tried to organize things, suggesting the *Kol HaNeshama* hymn [associated with the Reform synagogue in Jerusalem]—but they also said that some people don't know it.

4   Bloch, Maurice. 1974. "Symbols, Song, Dance and Features of Articulation: Is Religion an Extreme Form of Traditional Authority." *Archives Europeenes De Sociologie* XV:55–81.

Another suggestion thrown out was the Safari cheer. Debate went on for 3–5 minutes. The guide sings *Hava Nashira* a bit and tries to teach it. Her attempt doesn't last long, with only partial participation. Then kids began laughing at her conducting motions—and she says: "Forget it." Someone else throws out: "Row, row...zyour boat," and this catches on—in a round—for a while, but things break up after a couple of times. Picture-taking does take place, but in smaller groups and quickly—not involving the whole Safari.

The lack of a shared musical repertoire—in Hebrew—appropriate to the occasion, deprived the group of a "summing-up" memory culminating several days of a successful "learning through participation and fun" program.[5]

Goldberg's example illustrates the failure of a Jewish educational opportunity to produce a Peoplehood experience. These young Jews did not share enough common knowledge in order to claim membership in the Jewish group, nor did they have the desire to coordinate their individual actions through song. The default choice of "Row, row...your boat," signals membership in Western culture, but not in the Jewish People. The result is that the young participants on the summer trip happen to be Jews, but in the context of the social ritual that Goldberg describes, they had no sense of belonging to the Jewish People.

Beyond the need for shared knowledge, an additional dimension of singing in a group is that individuals necessarily suppress their personal preferences. An individual might not fully identify with the words of the song, but will nevertheless sing, for he or she finds value in being part of the larger group.

The goal of participation is to make the ritual succeed and confirm the value of membership in the larger social group. *An individual's personal preferences are of secondary concern. The success of the event is itself the source of meaning, after which it might be appropriate to ask if the individual identifies with all aspects of the ritual—although one is not dependent on the other.*

We only need to think of the oft-stated argument by liberal or secular Jews that they cannot participate in a traditional prayer ritual because they don't believe in it or identify with its message, in order to comprehend the significance of the claim made in this chapter. If every prayer must meet the meaning requirements of each individual saying the prayer, then it is unlikely that the prayer will promote Peoplehood. To the extent that the prayer ritual, like a song, succeeds in connecting individuals to a larger group, then the individual must first prioritize the fact that the ritual enables membership in the larger social group, and only afterwards ask: "Do I personally identify with the content of the prayer?"

Another important aspect of Peoplehood rituals is that they include within them an acceptance that the authority to determine "authenticity" or "meaning" is located outside of the immediate control of any one individual. To

5   Goldberg, Harvey. 2002. "Hebrew in a NFTY Safari." *Presented at Department Seminar, Department for Jewish Zionist Education, Jewish Agency for Israel.* http://www.jafi.org.il/education/moriya/newpdf/HarveyGoldberg.pdf, p. 8.

live in a group requires the acceptance of "restricted rituals"[6] which members understand as obvious to the very essence of belonging. If you don't do the ritual *and do it correctly*, you become an outsider.

People who have more experience or expertise in the rituals of Jewish life will also have greater authority to introduce change.[7] However, even those with greater knowledge and experience must reference other members of the group who are not present in the immediate situation when they introduce change. The value of the ritual is that it is replicable. Thus, if the participants are to engage in the same ritual with Jews elsewhere, then change to a given ritual can only be slow and gradual, or it won't be recognized as Jewish by others. Change the song too radically, and other Jews won't be able to sing along in the future.

What is clear is that for an educational, religious or any other type of Jewish event to promote Peoplehood, its content can't entirely suit the tastes of individual participants. The Peoplehood rituals that make up a social event demand a degree of conformity, so that the Jewish content of the event will be recognizable by Jews who are not immediately present. If the goal of the event is to engage participants in Jewish spirituality, but the individuals don't come out of the event able to join with other Jews in prayer, then the cause of building Jewish identity might be served, but not the goal of generating Jewish Peoplehood. The same can be said for the above-mentioned participants in the Israel travel program. To the extent that they ended the trip with an enjoyable experience, but without the ability to sing Hebrew songs with other Jews, we can argue that the trip did not enable the forging of Jewish Peoplehood.

Step Two: Pluralism and the Social Events that Build Jewish Peoplehood

Social rituals (such as the singing of a song) take place in the context of broader social events (such as an Israel teen trip). The event, like the ritual, has the potential to forge Jewish Peoplehood. In order for this to happen, the people at a social event need to draw on a base of common knowledge. They need to feel that they are interacting with one another in a culturally coherent fashion that is reproducible in other social contexts.

If we are to understand how social events enable Jewish Peoplehood, we need to move beyond the metaphor of song to the larger act of making music.

---

6   Douglas, Mary. 1982. *Natural Symbols: Explorations in Cosmology.* New York: Pantheon Books.

7   Liebman, Charles S. 1999. "Post-War American Jewry: From Ethnic to Privatized Judaism." Pp. 7–17 in *Secularism, Spirituality, and the Future of American Jewry*, edited by Elliott Abrams and David G. Dalin. Washington, D.C.: Ethics and Public Policy Center.

David Sudnow[8] explores the cultural fabric of different types of social events by comparing the act of making music in an orchestra and jazz ensemble. An orchestral performance requires near total conformity of each musician to the larger group and the demands of the conductor. In contrast, the music of a jazz ensemble more closely resembles a conversation, in that each musician has room to express his or her individuality, while at the same time listening carefully to the overall rhythm of the group. It is both by expressing individuality and by remaining attuned to the group that the member of the jazz ensemble is able to produce a coherent form of music that is replicable and recognizable to others.

The orchestra and jazz ensemble serve as apt metaphors for two different types of Jewish social events: the ceremony and the conversation, respectively. A ceremony is a form of face-to-face interaction that is highly scripted, has a clear beginning and end, and occurs at a fixed point in time. Like an orchestra, it requires that all members conform to the goals of the group and its leader. The ceremony promotes a symbolic connection between the participants in a face to face interaction and other Jews. A conversation, in contrast, is an actual face-to-face meeting that allows for social interactions that are loosely scripted. Participants in a conversation need to account for the differences between them. One will respond to the other, as one jazz musician listens and responds to the other, developing a conversation around a common cultural rhythm. The success of a conversation depends on the actual interaction between different types of Jews and the concomitant feeling of connection of one to the other that emerges.

Jewish social events may be categorized as resembling either the orchestra or jazz ensemble, or as something in between—but, in all cases, the interaction between participants must produce a sense of connection to Jews who are not immediately present. For this to happen, the knowledge and skills which are reproduced and refined in the course of the social event must be recognizable and applicable to other situations.

Example Three: Israel Day at American Jewish Summer Camps

The difference between the use of ceremony and conversation to promote Jewish Peoplehood is apparent in the different ways that Jewish summer camps organize an event generally referred to as Israel Day. The goal of the event, which is a standard part of the educational program of many Jewish summer camps, is to promote a connection between the campers and Israel, as well as to use the connection to Israel to define the camp as a Jewish institution.

---

[8]   Sudnow, David. 1979. *Talk's Body: A Meditation Between Two Keyboards*. Middlesex, England: Penguin Books.

Wolf and Kopelowitz[9] asked summer camp directors about the role Israeli staff—often known as the *mishlachat*—play in planning and implementing Israel Day. The directors tended to view the Israelis as representing "Israel" and "Israelis" to the campers in both a real and symbolic sense. When asked about the significance of the Israeli presence in the camp, they all agreed that the Israeli staff make palpable for the camper what is otherwise a distant reality, sharing a specific educational style, ways of behavior and the spoken Hebrew language.. However, the directors followed one of two very different approaches when it came to the question of what roles they assigned to the Israel staff in organizing the day.

In some camps, the Israeli staff take the role of representing Israel in a highly ceremonial way, while in others the camp director encourages more informal forms of interaction that are intended to promote an Israeli-American conversation within the camp. The ceremonial orientation encourages the Israeli staff to invest time in planning camp-wide events that are rich in symbolic value, such as a commemoration ceremony for victims of terrorist attacks. The goals of these events are to emphasize the symbolic importance of Israel in the life of the camp, an act that is enhanced by the involvement of Israeli staff in running the events. Of importance is that in the Israel ceremony, the Israeli staff usually performs a role analogous to the conductor in the orchestra.

In contrast, the second approach de-emphasizes the symbolic and ceremonial role of Israelis in the camp and instead emphasizes the interpersonal dimension. Israel Day is important, but it is one of many ways in which the Israeli staff connect at the emotional level with campers and other staff. These interactions are most important, however, when they take place in the course of everyday life. Through the "little moments," as opposed to ceremonial events, the directors expect members of the camp community to learn about Israel. The privileging of the conversational approach is demonstrated in the following words of one Camp Ramah director:

> I think that the real nature of the question [is] [h]ow do you build *shlichut* [Israeli mission overseas]? It doesn't come from Yom Israel [Israel Day] or from these big *tekassim* [ceremonies]. It comes from the day-to-day regular interactions the kids have. You get to know each other and then [the campers] say, "We want to know about you. I am going to ask you. You were in the army? What did you do? You were in the *tzanchanim* [paratroopers], did you go to the West Bank? Were you ever shot at that you had to kill somebody? Do you know somebody who was killed in a *pigu'a*? What does your family know?" From those individual interactions that have nothing to do with being a *shaliach*...So then you build that strong *kesher ishi* [personal connection] and then they invite each other during the year. My campers e-mail my *shlichim*, they send

9   Wolf, Minna F., and Kopelowitz, Ezra. 2004. "Israeli Staff in American Jewish Summer Camps: The View of the Director." Jerusalem: Research and Development Unit, The Department for Jewish Zionist Education, The Jewish Agency for Israel.

messages with them. It is not just when things happen in Israel, when there is a *pigu'a* [terror attack]. But when there is a *pigu'a* the kids know somebody in Israel and they write to them and say, "gosh, I hope you are okay." Then they get back this message, "It's a very sad thing, but that happened in Haifa and I live in south Jerusalem"...It is from those *kesharim* [connections] that you get...*shlichut*.[10]

Example Four: Peoplehood and Informal Jewish Education in American and Israeli Schools

My research on Jewish education in Israeli schools and Israeli education in American Jewish schools also shows a spectrum of ceremonial and conversational strategies. When it came to the Israeli system, I focused on three schools, HaSharon, Bar Lev and Brenner, that—relative to other Israeli *mamlachti* [non-religious] schools are outstanding in the resources they devote to Jewish education. I found that—HaSharon tends to adopt a ceremonial approach and BarLev tends to adopt a more conversational approach, whereas Brenner falls somewhere in the middle.

> HaSharon seeks to promote an emotional connection between its students and other Jews, both past and present, but with no expectation that the educational experience will produce actual social relationships. The school's goal is to foster a sense of symbolic and emotional identification, rather than interpersonal connection. The desired result is Benedict Anderson's "imagined community," a group whose members might include millions of individuals (or more) spanning large periods of history and disparate geographical areas. Such a group exists because of the ability of its members to imagine their connection to one another, in spite of the fact they may never meet in face-to-face relationships.
> BarLev falls at the other end of the Jewish education spectrum, deemphasizing the symbolic/emotional connection between the individual student and the Jewish People, and instead uses educational activities as a means to foster actual social relationships in which the participant comes to feel a concrete sense of obligation to maintain a relationship with either another individual or social group. Here the emphasis is not on the imagined community of millions of people, but rather concrete social relationships in the present.
> The differences between HaSharon and Bar Lev's educational goals appear in the informal educational events sponsored by each school. HaSharon often sponsors school-wide activities involving many different grade levels. The activities tend to be in-school ceremonies that stress the symbolic dimensions of the events in question—i.e., Holocaust, Jewish life cycle and Zionist holidays, or prayer. In comparison, only 25% of Bar Lev's (as opposed to 57% and 47% for HaSharon and Brenner respectively) informal activities are ceremonial. The majority of the informal educational program at Bar Lev occurs in the course of conversational learning in the Bet Midrash, during research projects, and on school trips. All of these venues stress the experiential and hands-on

---

[10]   *Ibid.*, p. 14.

dimensions of learning, with relatively little emphasis on ceremonial events having to do with bar-mitzvah or Jewish/Zionist holidays.[11]

Research I have conducted on Israel Education in community day schools in North America[12] shows a similar spectrum of ceremonial and conversational strategies. *Table One* below presents a list of informal educational activities included in the survey and the percentage of schools that encouraged their students to participate in that activity "to a great extent." The research shows that all the community day schools sponsor ceremonial events that stress a connection to Israel. Thus, for example, 100% of the community day schools covered by the survey conduct Israeli Independence Day ceremonies and encourage their students to participate.

Table 1: *Informal Education Events/Activities*
(Kopelowitz 2005a, p. 9)

Orientation of event is to:	Symbolic vs. Social Orientation	Event	Percent of schools that encourage students to participate in the activity "to a great extent"
Israel	Symbolic	Yom Haatzmaut Ceremony	100
Jewish culture	Symbolic	Holocaust Ceremony	78
Religion	Symbolic	Daily Prayer	74
Local Community	Either	Participate in Local Community Events	74
Israel	Symbolic	Yom HaZichoron Ceremony	70
Israel	Symbolic	Donations to Israel	70
Religion	Symbolic	Tu Beshvat Seder	65
Israel	Symbolic	TuBeshvat Tree Plant/Israel	64
Israel	Social	Connection to Israeli School	47
Israel	Social	Connection to Israeli Youth	47
Israel	Symbolic	YomYerushalayim Ceremony	36
Israel	Symbolic	Terror Victims Ceremony	35
Israel	Symbolic	Donate To Terror Victims	32
Israel	Symbolic	Israel Day Parade	30
Religion	Symbolic	Shavuot Learning	20
Israel	Social	Aliyah	15
Israel	Either	Demonstrate for Israel	15

11   Kopelowitz, Ezra, Yaffe, Meir, and Weiss, Barak. 2005. "How to Determine a "Successful Jewish Education" for Secular Jews in Israeli Mamlachti Schools—Part Two: From Practice to Theory." Ramat Gan: Panim for Jewish Renaissance in Israel, p. 10.

12   Kopelowitz, Ezra. 2005. "Towards What Ideal Do We Strive? A Portrait of Social and Symbolic Engagement with Israel in Jewish Community Day Schools." Jerusalem: The Department for Jewish Zionist Education, The Jewish Agency for Israel and RAVSAK.

In contrast, a minority of schools encouraged their students to participate in events classified as being unambiguously oriented towards creating the interpersonal/conversational dimension between American and Israeli Jews. These include events in which schools encourage their students to participate in partnership programs, events that create connections to Israeli youth, or programs that encourage Aliyah. All three types of programming aspire to go beyond the goal of fostering an emotional/symbolic connection to Israel, and attempt to build actual ongoing social relationships between the student and Israelis and/or Israeli society. Yet these types of programs are far more rare than their more ceremonial counterparts.

Step Three: What is the Goal? Educational Intervention or Everyday life

We have seen how social rituals take place in the context of social events. In this section, we will look at how social events in turn take place within the context of various types of Jewish institutions.

An educational or religious institution might succeed in creating a powerful Peoplehood experience in the form of a ceremony or conversation, but all too often that experience ends when the participants return to their everyday lives. The educational or religious event is treated as a form of intervention, rather than as a type of behavior that is reproducible in the future, or in other aspects of the everyday life of the individual participant. For example, the Israel Day celebration in a Jewish school is very rarely tied into a continuous engagement with Israel, whether through discussions of current events, pen-pal programs or a trip to Israel.

For a synagogue, school, community center, or any other Jewish institution to promote Peoplehood, it must empower its members to leave an educational event and continue to interact with other Jews in the institution and the local, national and international Jewish community using the knowledge and skills gained from participation in the event. The extent to which Jewish institutions succeed in this goal varies widely. Often, a similar event can either fail or succeed, depending on the institution in which it takes place, as the following example demonstrates.

Example Five: The Liberal Prayer Service—Is it an Educational Event or an Event which is Part of a Rich Jewish Way of Life?

Prayer takes place in several different types of Jewish educational contexts. For the purpose of this analysis, we will consider two such contexts—the synagogue and the Ramah camp.

In many ways, one of the most important institutions in American Jewish life—the liberal synagogue—is, at least in terms of the prayer service, often a negative force in socializing the average congregant into a lifestyle capable of generating a significant sense of Jewish Peoplehood.[13]

A primary motivation for those who design and run many liberal prayer services is the desire to facilitate attendance of non-observant Jews. While this is an important goal, the unintended consequence is often that the prayer service becomes an educational event, rather than a natural part of living a rich Jewish life.

The primary change that the liberal prayer service introduces involves reducing the obligation on individual congregants to own the materials and acquire the knowledge necessary for participation in a wider communal and religious life. The synagogue provides *kippot* and *tallitot*, page numbers are announced, and a stage-audience relationship is created by elevating the rabbi and cantor to dominant role within the prayer service. If the service includes a choir and organ, the "audience" assumes an even more silent and passive posture, in relation to those who stand on stage and perform. The result is an experience of the prayer service as theater or edutainment, rather than an experience that integrates into a rich Jewish lifestyle.

On one hand, the lower the obligation, the easier it will be for less knowledgeable Jews to participate, and hence the greater the chances of pulling them into the orbit of religious life. On the other hand, over the long term, the theatrical nature of the contemporary liberal prayer service limits the ability of the synagogue to impart the skills necessary for the individual congregant to confidently pray with other Jews, without the props and support provided by the clergy.

Another notable innovation of the liberal prayer service is the segregation by age group. There are children, teen and adult prayer services, and most educational activities focus on the younger generation. In the effort to cater to non-observant families, the synagogue makes it acceptable for parents to send their children to a prayer service without participating themselves, displacing the family as an integral religious unit. Less observant or irreligious families are relieved of their obligation to move between their home and synagogue in a manner that includes all members of the family.

The single-generation prayer service speaks to a larger phenomenon in contemporary Jewish life, in which religion and Jewish education are primarily aimed at children.[14] Both clergy and educators come to think of their

13   Parts of this argument were developed in Kopelowitz, Ezra. 2001. "The Logic of Numbers vs. The Logic of Souls: The Quandaries of the Contemporary Conservative Synagogue and their Implications for Jewish Communal Continuity." *Conservative Judaism* Fall edition.
14   Gans, Herbert. 1958. "The Origin and Growth of a Jewish Community in the Suburbs: A Study of the Jews of Park Forest." Pp. 205–248 in *The Jews: Social Patterns of an American Group*, edited by Marshall Sklare. New York: The Free Press. Gans, Herbert J. 1979.

institutions as a means to intervene and save the younger generation from the surrounding secular society and the non-observant home environment. Ironically, by separating the child from his or her family, the distinction between the synagogue or educational institution and "the rest of life" is further exacerbated.[15]

The prayer service also takes place in Ramah summer camps, but here it tends to be far more effective.

Like other Jewish summer camps, Ramah summer camps remove children from their families for two months a year, in order to give them an intensive Jewish experience that many will not receive outside of the camp.

As Steven M. Cohen[16] shows in research on Ramah alumni, from the perspective of the Conservative movement, the camps simultaneously produce success and failure. On one hand, the camps produce individuals who are confident in the liturgy and seek to join the synagogue and other Jewish institutions for themselves and not only for their children. Yet, on the other hand, the alumni express alienation from the typical Conservative synagogue. Cohen brings the following citation from Seymour Fox to illustrate the larger problem.

> We didn't achieve an effective transition between the rarefied atmosphere of Ramah and the camper's home community...After a summer at Ramah, campers found it hard to return to a [synagogue] service that suddenly seemed stilted and complacent, and to a rabbi who seemed formal when contrasted with the informality and warmth of the camp. We even had youngsters who refused to attend synagogue services after camp because the service no longer felt authentically Jewish to them.[17]

The success of the Ramah camps illustrates the failure of the liberal prayer service which enables easy entry for those without knowledge and skills.

"Symbolic Ethnicity: The Future of Ethnic Groups and Cultures in America." *Ethnic and Racial Studies* 2:1–20. Sklare, Marshall. 1979. *Jewish Identity on the Suburban Frontier: A Study of Group Survival in the Open Society*. Chicago: University of Chicago Press.

[15] Bekerman, Zvi. 2005. "Paradigmatic Change: Towards the social and the cultural in Jewish education." Pp. 324–342 in *Educational Deliberations, Studies in Education dedicated to Shlomo (Seymour) Fox*, edited by M. Nisan and O. Schremer. Jerusalem: Keter. Bekerman, Zvi, and Kopelowitz, Ezra. 2007. "The Unintended Consequence of Liberal Jewish Schooling: A Comparative Study of the Teaching of Jewish Texts for the Purpose of Cultural Sustainability." in *Cultural Education <> Cultural Sustainability: Minority, Diaspora, Indigenous and Ethno-Religious Groups in Multi-Cultural Societies*, edited by Zvi Bekerman and Ezra Kopelowitz. Mahwah, New Jersey: Lawrence Erbaum Publishers.

[16] Cohen, Steven M. 1999. "Camp Ramah and adult Jewish identity: long-term influences on Conservative Congregants in North America." Pp. 95–129 in *Ramah reflections at 50: visions for a new century*, edited by Sheldon A. Dorph. New York: National Ramah Commission.

[17] Fox, Seymour with Novak, William. 1997. *Vision at the Heart: Lessons From Camp Ramah On The Power Of Ideas In Shaping Educational Institutions*. New York: Council for Initiatives in Jewish Education and Jerusalem: Mandel Institute, p. 42.

Although there is no research data to back up this point, it is commonly assumed among the Conservative leadership that many Ramah graduates join Orthodox synagogues or set up alternative *havurot*, rather than join mainstream synagogues. At Ramah, the camper experiences prayer and Judaism as part of a rich Jewish life style; and many of the campers search out that way of life outside of camp. However, at their home synagogues the camper finds a prayer service that focuses on a Jewish experience confined to the four walls of the institution. For example, when a stranger enters an Orthodox synagogue on Shabbat, it is likely that he or she will receive an invitation for a meal. Such an invitation is rarely extended at the average Conservative or Reform synagogue, because very few members sit down as a family unit for a Shabbat meal at home. If people are not eating Shabbat meals in their homes, then a stranger in a synagogue will not receive an invitation for a meal. More importantly, if there is not a natural continuity between the synagogue service and the home on such a basic element as eating a Shabbat meal, then a key element of living a rich Jewish life is missing.

At Ramah, the camper learns that membership in the Jewish People requires knowledge and skills that enable a holistic Jewish life. For a Jew who desires a full Jewish life, the liberal prayer service as it is experienced in most American synagogues does not offer a compelling alternative, as its primary role is to enable access to the less observant, rather than to promote an expanded sense of participation in the life of a Jewish community, and from there the Jewish people.

The contrast between the synagogue and the Ramah setting demonstrates is that a synagogue, school, community center or any other Jewish institution will promote Peoplehood only insofar as it empowers its members to live a rich Jewish life. They need to be given the social networks, knowledge and skills gained from membership in the institution in order to be motivated and able to interact with other Jews in the local, national and international Jewish community, which is the subject of the next section.

Step Four: Peoplehood is about Living a Rich Jewish Life in the Context of Community: Divergent Challenges in the Diaspora and Israel

The final level of analysis in this paper is the level of community—a geographical area in which Jews move from one institution to another (from home to the bus, to a walk on the street, to school, to work, to synagogue, to a restaurant or sporting event etc...). There are many different types of Jewish communities. For the purpose of this analysis, we shall contrast Diaspora and Israeli communities, broadly defined.

The Diaspora Challenge for Building Peoplehood—
Drawing the Individual into a Rich Jewish Lifestyle

In the Diaspora, a large part of Jewish life is lived in a local geographical community. Jews do not tend to live in segregated neighborhoods; rather, an individual interacts with other Jews while working out in the gym at the Jewish Community Center, hanging out at the local kosher pizza parlor, shopping at the kosher aisle of the supermarket, attending prayer services at the synagogue, and participating in Jewish voluntary organizations such as the Federation, the Jewish old age home etc. Jews who live this lifestyle also tend to send their children to Jewish schools, summer camps, youth movements and trips to Israel. Most importantly, these same people who live a full Jewish life will confidently and eagerly seek out interaction with other Jews, which is a pre-condition for Jewish Peoplehood.

The Diaspora challenge is to pull people out of a Jewish experience that is confined to the home, or a synagogue experience that does not go beyond the occasional prayer service. Jewish Peoplehood is built as Jews participate in the everyday rituals and social events that make up a rich Jewish life. Any initiative that seeks to build Jewish Peoplehood must be predicated on drawing the individual into this lifestyle.

It is not enough to provide Jews with a place to work out at the JCC, or to provide a spiritually uplifting prayer service, or to offer a trip to Israel. All of these activities might strengthen Jewish identity, but if they do not provide the individual with the tools to interact with other Jews in other contexts and indeed encourage such participation, they do not build Jewish Peoplehood. The prayer service must enable the participant to seek out and pray comfortably with other Jews elsewhere. Likewise, the Jewish community center or Israel trip must provide opportunities to acquire knowledge of Jewish current events and culture, as well as chances to network with other Jews that will spill out of the community center or beyond the trip itself. A successful Peoplehood-building experience needs to affect other areas of everyday life as it is lived in both the context of geographical community and beyond.

The Israeli Challenge—Moving Individuals from a Passive
to Active Jewish Lifestyle

In Israel, the challenge is both similar and different from the Diaspora. Israelis also need to live a rich Jewish life in order to connect to the Jewish People, but the starting point for understanding how to build such a lifestyle is very different.

The difference between the Israeli and Diaspora experiences is in the nature of Jewish community. Whereas in the Diaspora the geographic community is primarily experienced as a local phenomenon, in Israel the concept of Jewish community is first and foremost a national experience. Israeli Jews, young and old, continually interact with other Jews in the multiple contexts of their everyday lives. Being Jewish is in many instances something that exists in the background—as an obvious experience that happens as one lives in the public sphere of the Jewish state, which includes public holidays such as Holocaust Remembrance Day, the Day of Remembrance for Fallen Soldiers, the public aspects of the various religious holidays that mark the calendar year, army service, and the nationalist aspects of soccer and basketball, among other possible examples.[18] Even mundane events, such as boarding the bus and choosing a seat, reinforce the sense of Jewish belonging when one needs to decide whether or not to sit next to a Palestinian passenger, who reflexively, is assessed for the possibility that he or she might be carrying a bomb.[19]

These examples of Jewish life in Israel show that Israeli-Jewish belonging can be lived without any formal work on the part of an individual. Whereas in the Diaspora one must decide to belong to a Jewish organization and pay membership dues in order to express a connection to Judaism and the Jewish community, in Israel one connects by simply living life. Thus, while Jewish belonging is an active decision in the Diaspora, in Israel it is for many Jews a passive by-product. Indeed, as anthropologist Shlomo Deshen points out, Israeli Jews need to actively reject the Jewish aspects of public life in Israel if they wish to disown their Jewishness.[20] Rejection, not affiliation, is what requires Israeli-Jews to make an explicit decision to act.

The challenge for building Jewish Peoplehood in Israel is to bring Israeli Jews from living a passive to an active Jewish lifestyle. The need for the transition to an active Jewish lifestyle is evidenced by an interesting discrepancy in the answers of secular Israeli Jews to survey questions about Jewish belonging.

Survey data shows that Israeli Jews feel that they are part of Jewish People. The 2000 Guttman/Avi-Chai survey, the only comprehensive national survey on this subject, shows that Israeli Jews express a high level of Jewish identification. 82 percent of the Israeli Jewish public answered that given the chance they would choose to be born again Jewish; 95 percent feel that they are part of the Jewish People; and 70 percent state that Jews in Israel and abroad share a common destiny.[21]

18   Kopelowitz, Ezra. 2005. "Who is the Young Israeli Jew: Changing Leisure Habits and "Jewish Education." Jerusalem: Research and Development Unit, The Department for Jewish Zionist Education, The Jewish Agency for Israel.

19   Kopelowitz, Ezra. 1996. "Equality, Multiculturalism and the Dilemmas of Civility in Israel." *International Journal of Politics, Culture and Society* 9: pp. 373–400.

20   Deshen, Shlomo. 1998. "Yom Kippur: Between Flight and a Search for Secular Content [Hebrew]." *Panim* 7:48–54.

21   Levy, Shlomit, Levinsohn, Hanna, and Katz, Elihu. 2002. *Belief, Observances and Social Interaction Among Israeli Jews, 2000 (Hebrew)*. Jerusalem: The Louis Guttman Israel Institute of Applied Social Research, Israeli Democracy Institute.

In a 2002 study, we asked 20 to 30 year-old secular, traditional, and religious Israeli Jews similar questions about their Jewish identity, with similar results. Yet, when we asked, "If you were born abroad, would you choose to be Jewish?" the numbers dropped drastically, with only 35 percent of the secular respondents answering in the affirmative.[22]

Why did the secular participants in the study give positive answers to questions that touch on Jewish pride and identity, but a largely negative response to the question about the ability to imagine being born a Jew abroad?

An answer: For most secular Israeli Jews, being Jewish is first and foremost associated with practices that occur as a result of living in Israel. These practices are not easily replicated in the Diaspora context. In other words, the secular Israeli Jewish concept of Peoplehood is largely limited in their imagination to living as a Jew in Israel. Whereas the traditionalist and religious Jew practice "Jewish" rituals and customs at home or in a communal framework in a manner that is similar to Diaspora Jewry, the secular Israeli Jew does not have a similar frame of reference. Being Jewish is too much about living in the public sphere of the Jewish state, which we described above as a largely passive form of Jewish lifestyle. Enter the home, or areas of life in which one has direct control, and little to no explicitly Jewish content informs everyday life.

Thus, on one hand, we have among secular Israeli Jews the reverse of the well-known Diaspora formulation of taking off a *kippah* when leaving home. The American Jew is often characterized as being a Jew at home and a worldly person in public. In contrast, the Israeli Jew is a Jew in public, though not necessarily in private. As such, the public Jew is a uniquely Israeli phenomenon. But, in both the Diaspora and in Israel, any attempt to reach out Jews on issues of Jewish Peoplehood and Israel-Diaspora relations must reflect an awareness of these public-private distinctions. In both contexts, a rich Jewish life *that is explicitly* chosen as part of everyday private decisions remains the key to building Jewish Peoplehood in Israel.

Conclusion

This chapter began with the example of song as a type of social ritual that builds Peoplehood. For Jewish Peoplehood to remain a possibility Jews must be able to sing together as Jews, or to engage in equivalent types of social rituals. Peoplehood rituals require knowledge and skills that go beyond the particular face-to-face encounter and enable interaction with other Jews who are not immediately present.

---

[22]   Kopelowitz, Ezra, and Rosenberg, Lior, forthcoming. "Israeli-Jews vs. Jewish-Israelis: The Public and Private Ritual Basis of Israeli Jewish Identification with the Jewish Diaspora," in Harvey Goldberg, Steven M. Cohen and Ezra Kopelowitz (eds.). London: Berghan Press.

We then looked at social rituals in the context of broader social events and showed that—whether in the form of ceremony or conversation—social events, like rituals, will succeed in enabling Jewish Peoplehood to the extent that they enable individuals to acquire knowledge and refine skills that, in turn, encourage interaction with other Jews who are not present at the particular event. The Peoplehood ceremony or conversation is not limited to an "educational intervention," but rather empowers individuals to participate in the broader Jewish community. It is not enough to pique interest in Jewish identity, which is what most educational and religious programming are currently designed to do; rather, the curiosity generated by successful educational and religious programming must be explicitly translated into stable forms of Jewish living as a matter of policy.

In the American context, the case study of the liberal prayer service illustrates how an individual may feel comfortable and have a meaningful experience, yet still leave the synagogue without the knowledge, motivation and skills needed to interact with other Jews in other places. In order to build Peoplehood, institutions and the programs they run have to approach Jewish life as a continuum that is lived as people move from one institution to another. For example, if synagogues, schools and summer camps focus on the family, rather than the child, these institutions will more likely become a natural extension of the home, rather than a place where parents leave their children for a Jewish education. If the entire family is involved in Jewish life, then it is also more likely that the family members will move between the home and the various institutions that make up their Jewish life, in a manner that increases interaction with different types of Jews in a natural, continuous and empowering (from the perspective of Jewish Peoplehood) way.

Likewise, as educational programming should not focus on a classroom or particular event, so the experience of "Jewish tourism" to Israel or elsewhere should not be limited to the trip itself. The tremendous resources that are currently devoted to subsidizing Israel travel tend to be channeled into one-time programs, with little attempt to use those programs as means for encouraging individuals to live a rich Jewish life. My suggestion is to subsidize fewer participants on Israel programs, but to insist that when an educator returns from a professional development program, or a student returns from an Israel Experience program like Birthright Israel, or a lay leader returns from a Federation *shabbaton*—the sponsoring organizations would work with local communal institutions to make sure there a continuation of the experience back home. Do the social networks built with fellow participants on the trip and Israelis continue? Do the ideas and enthusiasm generated during the trip have a natural framework within which to play themselves out in local communal frameworks? The answer needs to be *yes*.

In the Israeli context, the question of how to devise effective Peoplehood building must be adapted to the Israeli experience. On one hand, in the past decade strategies for Israelis Jews have gained increased attention.[23] Institutions from the Jewish Agency to the Ministry of Education, the Community Center Associations, the Army, youth movements, and an increasing number of third-sector organizations, are investing heavily in educational outreach to secular and religious Israelis on the topic of Jewish Peoplehood. On the other hand, little systematic thought is given to the defining features of "Israeli Jewish Education." Many of the programs resemble their Diaspora equivalents, which focus on strengthening knowledge about Jewish ritual and sacred texts. Time and some research will tell if this is an effective strategy for a secular Jewish population who live in a world filled with rich Jewish associations that are rooted in the public Israeli experience. An alternative strategy, currently pursued by a very small minority of public figures and educators, is to focus on the lack of public discourse and debate among secular Jews concerning the Jewish character of Israeli society and to create new forums and opportunities for this type of intellectual engagement. One option that has received a fair amount of attention in both Israel and the Diaspora is the use of the "*mifgash*," encounters between Israeli and Diaspora Jews in the context of youth travel programs, such as Birthright, professional exchange programs between educators and others, and sending young Israelis to work in Diaspora communities.[24]

The success of these Israeli-Jewish educational initiatives ultimately rests on the same principle applied to Diaspora Jewish education. The common challenge is to make the Jewish knowledge and skills gained in a particular educational, cultural or religious setting relevant to life that the person lives after the program or event. While the above statement might seem obvious, in many—perhaps most—cases, educational and religious institutions work in the opposite direction. Education and religion are conceptualized as closed events. The participant takes part in an event and then returns to "reality."

---

23 Kopelowitz, Ezra. 2003. "Between Mifgash and Shlichut: Paradigms in Contemporary Zionist Education and the Question of the Ideological Relationship between Israel and Diaspora." Jerusalem: The Department for Jewish Zionist Education, The Jewish Agency for Israel.

24 Bar-Shalom, Yehuda. 1998. "Encounters With the Other: An Ethnographic Study of the *Mifgashim* Programs for Jewish Youth, Summer 1997." Jerusalem: The Charles R. Bronfman Centre for the Israel Experience. Bar-Shalom, Yehuda. 2003. "Research Evaluation—Project Gvanim, The Development of Educational Centers on the Topic of Jewish Peoplehood in Teacher Training Colleges (Hebrew)." Jerusalem: Research and Development Unit, Department for Jewish Zionist Education, The Jewish Agency for Israel. Bram, Chen, and Neria, Eran. 2003. "Veni, Vedi, Ii: Israeli 'Shlichim' Identity Encounters," in U.S Jewish Summer camps [Hebrew]. Jerusalem: Research and Development Unit, The Department for Jewish Zionist Education, The Jewish Agency for Israel. Feldman, Jackie, and Katz, Neta. 2002. "The Place of the Jewish Agency in Mifgashim Between Israeli and Diaspora Youth: Cultural Differences, Administrative Practices and Hidden Ideological Positions." Jerusalem: The Department for Jewish Zionist Education, The Jewish Agency for Israel. Kopelowitz, Ezra. 2003. "Between Mifgash and Shlichut: Paradigms in Contemporary Zionist Education and the Question of the Ideological Relationship between Israel and Diaspora." Jerusalem: The Department for Jewish Zionist Education, The Jewish Agency for Israel.

The educational and religious event is not structured so that the participant regards it as an extension of, rather than a temporary retreat from, everyday life. From the policy perspective, this is not a good use of resources.

All the examples in this chapter argue that for Jewish Peoplehood to thrive there can be no distinction between "real life" and "Jewish belonging." From the perspective of Jewish Peoplehood, there can be no clean distinction between the educational event, synagogue life, the family, Jewish tourism and the rest of everyday life. Jewish institutions and programs must consciously work to enable individuals to enter and exit their institutions as part of a fluid movement from one Jewish context to the next. The more movement the better, with each organized Jewish experience designed to motivate the individual to leave the institution and search for more. When that happens, the Jewish People becomes an economic resource, a massive social network, a gateway to emotional fulfillment and spirituality and the source of the songs we sing with our children.

A NEW UNDERSTANDING OF PEOPLEHOOD: THE JEWISH CONVERSATION

LAURA GELLER

Editor's summary

Laura Geller argues that Jewish Peoplehood may be understood as the sense of connection and responsibility created by people who share a story, or are part of an ongoing conversation. This sense of peoplehood is lacking among liberal American Jews today, who no longer share, as their parents and grandparents once did, an identity shaped in response to anti-Semitism and identification with Israel. In order to create this sense of connection today, we need to teach all Jews to view their personal experiences in light of the Jewish story, the narrative that unfolds through our liturgy, ritual, theology, and history. To this end, we need to create programs that encourage them to participate in an ongoing conversation with Jews from all over the world. These conversations may take place over sacred texts, thereby enabling individuals to see the Torah of their lives as a dimension of the Torah of tradition. Alternatively, they may take place over art and literature, and over the internet or face-to-face. Most important, our challenge today is to help these conversations become powerful enough that they engender a sense of connection that leads to obligation for each other.

What does it mean to be part of the Jewish People? Does being Jewish imply a sense of responsibility for other Jews? Is there is any truth to the Jewish claim: *Kol Yisrael areivim zeh lezeh* (all Jews are responsible for each other)? The answers to these questions used to be clearer than they now seem to be, particularly among the liberal American Jewish community.

For much of the second half of the 20th century, Jewish identity was shaped both in response to anti-Semitism and vicariously through identification with Israel. The shared experience of anti-Semitism was common ground for Jews who were quite different from each other. An American Jew from Beverly Hills with a memory of being excluded from a country club could relate to the stories of Jews from the Soviet Union who were denied the freedom to live as Jews. Second-generation American Jews remembered their parents' stories vividly enough to be moved to help Jews in other countries who wanted to flee persecution. Images of the Holocaust were fresh enough to motivate American Jews to support efforts to rescue Jewish populations around the world in need of help. Those American Jews who remembered the creation of the State of Israel and the miraculous victory of the Six Day War believed that they had the responsibility to insure that Israel would always be a refuge for Jews, perhaps because they still harbored the fear that they themselves might someday need a refuge. There was a sense that being Jewish meant you had some connection to and responsibility for other Jews, wherever they lived. Rabbi Joseph Soloveitchik speaks of this as a "covenant of fate."

But, in North America, particularly for non-Orthodox Jews born after the Six Day War who are already third- and fourth-generation American, this "covenant of fate" and the sense of responsibility that it engenders no longer seem to exist. Younger Jews have had no real experience of anti-Semitism. They feel completely comfortable and fully enfranchised as Americans. Many have family members who are not Jewish. For some of them, Jewishness is a cultural attachment, manifest in the foods they eat and the books they read. For others, Jewishness is a personal spiritual path, giving meaning and purpose to them as individuals and perhaps to their families, but with little if any communal dimension. Jews who define identify in these ways have hardly any sense of obligation to other Jews.

To them, Israel, which was a source of pride to their parents and grandparents, is problematic at best or, at worst, not even a conscious factor in their lives. The image of Israel that might have been presented to them as children, "a land without a people for a people without a land," is no longer viable, and they don't know enough to find a meaningful alternative world view. They are more likely to visit Europe or Central America than to visit Israel, and their college-age children are more likely to take a year abroad in Central America than in Israel.

This kind of Jewish identity does not bring with it a sense of Jewish People-hood. "Peoplehood" suggests membership in a larger community where something is held in common. Realistically, what does a secular left-wing Jew in Los Angeles have in common with a haredi Jew in the West Bank? What links a Jew by choice, converted by a Reform rabbi, with a Habadnik in Russia? Very little. To add to the problem, being Jewish for many North American liberal Jews is only one of many dimensions of identity, and not necessarily the most important. An individual might describe himself or herself simultaneously as a Jew, an American, a feminist, a Prius Owner, a yoga practitioner, and a listener to public radio. Any of these descriptions might create a limited sense of community, but not enough to instill a sense of obligation to the others who share this identity. So, while liberal Jews might well assert that they are part of the Jewish People, it is an identity that doesn't suggest responsibility for other Jews.

If one doesn't feel that all Israel is responsible for one another, in what sense is one really part of the Jewish People? Judaism might be an individual spiritual path, a family memory, an identity that one moves in and out of around times of transition or loss, but not a sense of belonging to a people. This kind of Jewish identity is clearly meaningful for individuals and families, but the kind of community it creates is limited and temporal, linking the individual to his own syngagogue or her own *chavurah*, perhaps, but not the larger Jewish world, and certainly not to Israel. It is a far cry from Rabbi Joseph Soloveitchik's covenant of destiny, a vision of a Jewish future that requires an on-going commitment from all Jews. If "peoplehood" involves a connection to a community that is powerful enough to exert a claim or demand a responsibility from an individual, this kind of Judaism does not include "peoplehood."

To put the problem in another way, the classic understanding of Judaism—where God, Torah and Israel are all one—no longer seems to be true. Liberal Jews in North America are paying attention to God and Torah, but not to the third dimension of the triangle. Jews are actively exploring their connection to God through attention to spirituality, healing and the creation of compelling worship experiences. They are drawn into meaningful connection to Torah through wonderful initiatives, like the Experiment in Congregational Education, Wexner, Meah, and the serious adult education that is taking place in synagogues and university classes all over North America. The one piece that seem to have fallen out of the triangle is Israel—that is, the Jewish People.

A Judaism missing any one of these elements is impoverished. Therefore, it is important to refocus our efforts on strengthening Jewish Peoplehood, on finding ways to help Jews feel connected to other Jews, however different from each other they might be, and increasing the sense of responsibility and obligation that comes from that connection.

This challenge is both theoretical and programmatic. Let me begin with the theoretical. In a world where we see ourselves as autonomous selves, the very idea that others, particular those we don't know, can make a claim on us, is almost counter-cultural. Yet other people make claims on us all the time. Our partners, our children, our parents expect us to be there for them when they need us, and we respond, not because we are forced to but because we want to. The obligation comes out of the relationship. The beginning of responsibility is relationship. For the idea of peoplehood to make sense to this generation, it must be framed in terms of "being in relationship," having enough that connects us, that we feel a sense of wanting to respond.

Today, as throughout Jewish history, the primary chord that connects Jews to each is other is the Jewish story. This story is both cosmic and personal. On the cosmic level, it is a story of creation, revelation and redemption, and of a covenant between God and a people. This is the story that unfolds through liturgy, ritual, theology and history. The challenge is to help people link their own personal experiences to this larger narrative, transforming their personal stories into Jewish stories, so they can discover a connection between the Torah of their lives and the Torah of tradition. Through that connection can come a connection with others who share the story. This story, then, will become the beginning of a relationship.

Here, the classic article by Robert Cover called, "Nomos and Narrative" is helpful. For Cover, obligation, or law, emerges out of stories. He suggests that there is there a narrative common to all Jews that is compelling enough to create a sense of obligation. This insight enables us to reframe the concept of "peoplehood" to mean a sense of connection and responsibility created by people who share a story, a powerful story that not only brings meaning and purpose to our individual lives, but also creates an obligation to the others who share the story.

For example, almost everyone sometime in his or her life has an experience of feeling stuck. To label that "narrow place" with the Hebrew word for Egypt—*Mitzrayim* (literally: the narrow place), enables the individual to feel a connection to the master Jewish narrative of *Yetziat Mitzrayim*. The Jewish story brings a deeper meaning to the personal story. The rituals of Passover and the telling of the personal story within the larger story of the *Hagaddah* can become a bridge to understanding oneself as part of a larger collective, an interpretive community. That explains the power of the many different kinds of *haggadot* that have emerged over the past few decades in North America, ranging from feminist to twelve step/recovery, to give just two examples. As a person begins to hear echoes of his or her experience in this foundational Jewish ritual, it might lead to the beginnings of connection with other Jews who also celebrate Passover, albeit in very different ways.

Another example is the ritual of *tashlich*, the symbolic casting off of our sins on *Rosh Hashanah* that is achieved by means of throwing bread crumbs or stones in a flowing body of water. Once observed primarily by Orthodox Jews, now more and more non-Orthodox Jews are finding meaning in a ritual that offers a symbolic casting off of negativity or regret. We each have a story of beginning again, of second chances, of forgiveness. To tell that story, to act it out on the beach or by a reservoir, makes it more than our own story...and links us to others telling similar stories. In Los Angeles, on *Rosh Hashanah* afternoon, one can see black-hatted Hasidic Jews sharing the beach with clearly non-Orthodox Jews all "throwing away their sins." However these groups might view each other, there clearly is something they have in common. A shared narrative links them and might perhaps lead to a connection that carries with it some mutual responsibility. Who knows? They might actually talk to each other!

Our first challenge, then, is to find ways to help Jews tell their stories within the larger Jewish story. This larger Jewish story is an ongoing Jewish conversation. To quote Richard Siegel, Director of the National Foundation for Jewish Culture,

> "Judaism is fundamentally a conversation. Sometimes, it's a conversation with God. Jewish prayer, after all, is literally a conversation between us—as individuals—and God. Very often, it's a conversation with the past. Think of the Passover Seder as a conversation that has been going on for millennia. More often, however, these days at least, it is a conversation with the present...And, therefore, I would posit that where we have robust conversations about things Jewish, we will also have meaningful Jewish identity and living Jewish

communities. And conversely, if we want to nurture meaningful Jewish identity and living Jewish communities, then we should work on cultivating the Jewish conversation."[1]

This insight deepens our re-definition of "peoplehood." *"Peoplehood" can be understood as the sense of connection and responsibility created by people who share a story, or are part of the same ongoing conversation.*

- How is conversation created?
- What would we need to do in a liberal American synagogue to create the kind of Jewish conversation that would make enough of a claim on those participating that they would feel connected to other Jews around the world?
- How would we have to change the education that begins in synagogue Early Childhood Centers and continues in our family education programs and in our day schools and religious schools?
- What should we teach about Israel?
- How ought we to acknowledge the complicated realities that constitute modern Israel and Israeli politics?
- How could we use the book clubs, arts programs and visiting scholars that are so much a part of adult education to introduce the richness of Israeli culture and world Jewry to our congregations?
- What kinds of new liturgies, prayers for Israel, new rituals or new norms for how life cycle rituals ought to be celebrated could deepen the conversation that would lead to a sense of peoplehood and therefore responsibility?
- What kinds of *b'nei mitzvah* twinning programs could cultivate Jewish conversations with young people around the world?
- What could we do at every baby naming that would create the expectation that this child grow up to be an active participant in the Jewish conversation?
- How do we translate the *sheva berachot* at a wedding into a meaningful way to link this couple with other Jewish couples around the world?

There are many ways to answer these questions, and many creative and exciting answers that are being given today. In many cases, these answers involve conversations over sacred texts, which is the "Torah" part of the triangle. Through Torah study, we are actually talking with commentators who lived in different times and places, and with Jews in our own time who are studying the same pages. We are thus learning to see the Torah of our lives as a dimension of the Torah of tradition, and *vice versa*.

---

[1]   Richard Siegel, *Jewish Culture News*, November 2006.

Speaking from personal experience, one example of the power of the conversation with sacred texts is the program created by the Board of Rabbis in Los Angeles called "Meeting in Torah." For several years, the Board of Rabbis has organized an evening program near Shavuot where Jews from many different synagogues gather with rabbis of different denominations for text study in English around the themes of Torah and revelation. While initially the program primarily attracted Jews who were affiliated with the synagogues with rabbis connected to the program, this year the Board has embarked on a more ambitious program called "One People, One Book." Through advertisements in the local Jewish press and through mailings connected to synagogues and community groups, the Board of Rabbis and the Jewish Community Library have challenged Jews in Los Angeles to read the same book (in this case, Milton Steinberg's *As a Driven Leaf*) and to discuss it in groups with other Jews. The Board prepared four text studies related to the themes of the book that could be taught by a Jewish educator in a class, or used by lay people in a book club or *chavurah*. The program was inaugurated by a community-wide event in the fall with a keynote address, followed by inter-congregational *chevrutah* (partnered) learning, and it concluded with a similar program in the spring. In my congregation, where we have approximately 1,000 member units, almost one hundred people read the book in different classes or *chavurot*. One actually reported discussing the book with a stranger in Starbucks, whom she noticed reading it! A Jewish conversation...a new relationship, and the beginning of peoplehood!

There are many other examples across the United States of successful programs of adult Jewish education, some requiring a major commitment, such as the *Meah* program in Boston, or the Wexner Heritage Foundation, and others which are less intense. Encouraging more serious adult Jewish education in all of its forms is a first step toward enabling adult Jews to develop both the skills to be part of the conversation, as well as the passion to understand why doing so is so important. A hopeful trend is the flowering of Jewish studies at universities around the country, where many Jews (as well as non-Jews) are introduced to the intellectual Jewish conversation and learn the skills to continue it later in their lives.

After inviting Jews into the conversation and giving them the tools to have something to talk about, the second step in promoting conversation is to lift up the dimension of peoplehood that deepens the conversation around Torah. It must be made more transparent that Torah study is *not only* about personal intellectual or spiritual growth, but *also* about being connected to a community of other people who also study Torah. We need to teach explicitly that, because of the Torah we have in common, we have responsibility to each other.

Conversation with sacred text is just one dimension of the Jewish conversation. Other versions of the Jewish conversation emerge through Jewish art, film, music and theater. The response to Mel Gibson's "The Passion" was a Jewish conversation; so was the controversy over Steven Spielberg's "Munich." The episode of the popular television program O.C. that introduced Christmaka led to Jewish conversations. The range of Jewish magazines, from *Heeb* to *Commentary*, are all part of the Jewish conversation. The richer the conversation, the more possibility of a sense of peoplehood that might lead to a feeling of connection and responsibility. In order to strengthen peoplehood, then, we have to both deepen the conversation and expand the circle of those involved. This challenges us to support the artists and intellectuals who are creating Jewish art and culture and to give them the opportunity to deepen their own Jewish knowledge and identity so that it might be reflected in the work that might spark these conversations.

The process of peoplehood also challenges us to expand the conversation to include Israelis and Jews from other countries. How can we import and export the films, art, music and theater being created by Jews around the world, so that we all have some of the same things to talk about? There are Jewish film festivals now in many countries around the world; seeing a Jewish film set in Berlin, or Tel Aviv, or going to a Jewish Culture Festival in Krakow provokes conversation and a sense of peoplehood with Jews, not only in Israel and in the US, but with Jews who live all over the world. The more people understand that we are like each other, and that though we live in different places, we still talk about the same things, the more we will develop a sense of being part of a People.

These questions suggest both theoretical and programmatic challenges to Jewish educators. They also lead to imagining other dimensions of the Jewish conversation that could be deepened enough to lead to real connections among Jews. For instance, social justice work in a Jewish setting provokes Jewish conversations. The work of an organization like the American Jewish World Service, which took such an active role in the tsunami relief efforts, or in responding to the genocide in Darfur, gets people talking about the responsibilities Jews have in repairing the world. Participating in a process of faith-based community organizing, nourished by the Jewish Fund for Justice, where members of synagogues, along with members of churches, unions and schools, talk "one on one" with every member of the congregations about the impulse to engage in social justice work, is literally to be part of the Jewish conversation. The Jewish college students who spend their spring break in Central America with Jewish organizations building houses and studying Jewish texts about *Tzedakah* are deepening their Jewish conversations. If more American Jews knew the work of Israeli NGOs in the developing world, there would be more conversation and more sense of peoplehood. If there were more projects that brought Israeli, American, European and other Jewish young people together to do social justice work around the world, there would be a deeper sense of peoplehood. And, out of that sense of peoplehood, could come responsibility to each other.

Because ultimately, people talk when they are together. The more shared experiences we have, the deeper the sense of community and peoplehood. As powerful as Birthright trips are for those American Jews who experience them, they would be more powerful if there were more opportunities for interaction between the American young people and their Israeli peer group. Jonathan Ariel has suggested a different kind of Birthright trip, with half the participants Israelis recruited from the army. What a wonderful opportunity for Jews from around the world, including Israelis, to join in the same conversation. Israel trips that don't bring Israeli, American and Jews from around the world together are a missed opportunity. When you have a friend in Israel, you care about what happens there. When you know a Jewish person in Poland, you read the newspapers with a different eye.

Israel trips provide one important opportunity to deepen the conversation with Jews from around the world; Jewish summer camps offer another. Going to a Jewish camp is not only one of the best ways to connect a Jewish young person to Judaism; it can also be, some of the other campers or counselors are Israeli, one of the best ways to connect that young person to Israel if. Meeting Jewish kids from other countries reinforces the idea that Jews can live here or there, and that wherever they live, they all connected, part of the same community of kids who can talk about camp. Hence: Peoplehood, and then perhaps responsibility to each other.

An example of a successful program that brings together Jews of different locations is the LA-Tel Aviv Partnership. Through it, people who have the same interests in Tel Aviv and in Los Angeles come together to do projects or to share expertise. Americans have a lot to teach Israelis about hunger and food insecurity; the Partnership has organized several seminars in Israel on this. Tel Avivniks have a lot to teach Angelinos about managing trauma and crisis; the Partnership has organized conferences in LA around this topic. Through these gatherings, people enter into an ongoing conversation, and they keep talking after the meetings are over. Perhaps the conversations could be deepened by shared engagement in other versions of the conversation—text study for example—rooting the shared work in a Jewish conversation about *tikkun olam*, the repair of the world.

There are different ways to have Jewish conversations. Most effective are face-to-face conversations, but it is also important to nurture the many different kinds of conversations that go on over the Internet, through list serves and chat rooms and on-line study opportunities. Just as more and more of our young people are meeting their partners online, through conversations facilitated by organizations like J-Date, so also more and more of them could discover a sense of peoplehood through online conversations.

Now, of course I recognize some of the problems with the idea of people-hood being linked to an ongoing conversation. One problem is language itself: what language? In fact, the language seems to be English, even, increasingly, in the study of sacred texts, now that so much is translated so well into English. But much is lost in translation...and not everyone in the conversation speaks English. Could Hebrew ever become the language of our conversation? Personally, I doubt it, but the question remains significant. Second, does the content of the conversation matter, or is it enough that Jews are talking to each other about Jewish things? Art, even bad art, provokes conversation. So, what are the standards or parameters that might help us to decide what kinds of conversations to support? And what are the strategies that could deepen conversations, link different versions of the conversation to each other, reminding people that these conversations are ultimately part of the cosmic Jewish narrative, a narrative that ultimately connects us Jews to other Jews—however differently we define our Jewishness? Finally, what are the challenges for those of us working in North America to provide opportunities for those conversations to take place? How can we encourage the Jews we work with to be part of an ongoing conversation?

These are some of our challenges: to help Jews tell their stories within the larger Jewish narrative, so that they understand they are part of an ongoing Jewish conversation; to give Jews the skills to participate in those conversations; to support the artists and the intellectuals who are creating the Jewish culture that people want to talk about; and to expand the circle of those in the conversation; and to find ways deepen the conversations enough to create as sense of connection that leads to responsibility for one another. Then being part of the Jewish People will have real meaning.

It is a slightly new take on an old Jewish joke. Max is a deeply religious man. He prays fervently, and he has a powerful sense of God in his life. Of course he comes to synagogue every Shabbat. Sid, on the other hand, is an atheist, but he too comes to synagogue every Shabbat. The rabbi knows both men well, and one day says to Sid: "I understand why Max comes to shul every Shabbat. But why do you come? You don't even believe in God!" Without missing a beat, Sid replies: "Max comes to shul to talk to God; I come to shul to talk to Max."

We don't all come to shul anymore. But we still need to find a way to enable Max and Sidney, Irina and Lior and Baruch and Stacey to keep talking. We need to find ways to remind them all that their conversations are part of a larger narrative that links them to each other, to Jewish history and to a Jewish future. Most important, we need to help those conversations become powerful enough, that out of that conversation might come a sense of connection that leads to obligation for each other, and, together, for the world at large.

AGAINST THE CULTURAL GRAIN: JEWISH PEOPLEHOOD FOR THE 21st CENTURY

RIV-ELLEN PRELL

Editor's summary

Riv-Ellen Prell explores the tension between universalism and particularism that has characterized the Jewish People since the modern era of Jewish history began in the eighteenth century. She argues that these poles of identity have now been eclipsed by questions of boundaries: Who has or should have the authority to decide what it means to be Jewish? Does anything unite the Jewish People? Prell contends that these questions may be best answered by turning to a notion of Peoplehood, a project which requires the essential conditions of pluralism and a sense of a shared past. Finally, she shows how feminism provides a model of pluralism that can serve as a basis for the construction of Jewish Peoplehood in our own age.

Since the modern era of Jewish history began in the 18th century, many Jews have been characterized as living between "universalism" and "particularism" in negotiating their lives. If we understand these classical tensions, over-simplified as they might be, we may grasp how unique our present moment really is, and, in so doing, consider and re-consider the terms in which we understand what it means to be a Jew and part of the Jewish People.

Until the modern period, Jewish history was marked by a strong sense of particularism: Jews were characterized by their unique history and destiny and, as such, considered themselves (and were considered by others) to be set apart from other nations and cultures. Jews' embrace of a universalist outlook, which began in the post-Enlightenment period, was initially centered in Europe as the home of Western ideas and movements born out of the Enlightenment. The significance of universalism was different for Western and Eastern European Jews, because of the dramatic differences between these regions and nations and how Jews were located within them.[1] Likewise,

---

[1]   For a discussion of these contrasts, see Michael A. Meyer. *Jewish Identity in the Modern World*. Seattle, 1990.

universalism meant one thing in the context of the development of Reform Judaism, another in literary and artistic endeavors, and quite another in political movements.[2] Nonetheless, universalism, at its most general level, meant that Jews embraced an understanding of themselves as (largely) transcending their religious or national particularism. Whether they were united in a class struggle or committed to humanity or humanism, a universalist vision claimed that Jewishness did not exclusively define or in any way limit the lives of European Jewry.

After centuries in which Anti-Semitism defined the political, economic, and social realities of Jews, it is no surprise that the ideas and social movements that redefined society and human experience would be enormously appealing to many Jewish intellectuals, as well as young men and women. Some scholars have argued that these utopian dreams of a world without national, cultural, or religious barriers might be understood as the embodiment of a Jewish messianic vision in the secular world.[3] Hence a people whose very existence depended for centuries on the fickle tolerance of others would readily include those who eagerly embraced visions of social and economic justice that transcended any form of human difference.

Jews were also associated with another form of universalism designated by the pejorative term "cosmopolitanism." Because they lacked a nation of their own, they were slandered as people who were loyal to no one and unable to live as normal citizens. Though the slander was itself a form of Anti-Semitism, it is worth understanding the ways in which cosmopolitanism, in a neutral sense, was linked to many Jews' ready embrace of modernity. One cannot help but be struck by the extraordinary presence of European Jewry in the foreground of every cultural, intellectual, and scientific movement of the late 19th and early 20th centuries. Jews were central to questioning traditional boundaries and borders of knowledge and experience. As pioneers of new theories of society and new forms of music, art, and literature, they certainly drew on their lives as outsiders to the dominant culture. Even for those Jews to be found in universities, medical schools, and artistic circles, most were aware of their difference from others, and of their vulnerability because of it. Their motivation to invest in cultural change seems self-evident. Whether promoting the rationalism of science or questioning traditions of realism, Jews were willing transgressors of traditional hierarchies and assumptions about social and intellectual life.

Jews who relished the potential freedoms of life in European cities, where they might pursue education, culture, and political activism, were often impatient with the demands of Judaism, with the limits on their freedom, and a way of life that was often judged as "primitive" or "Oriental" by the

---

[2]   An overview of these events may be found in Meyer, *op. cit.*
[3]   For a discussion of these contrasts, see Meyer, *op. cit.*

larger society. At best, for some, Judaism belonged in the private realm of family and, perhaps, synagogue.[4] As citizens of a nation, or of the world, Jewish cosmopolitans and Jewish radicals pinned their hopes on a world of rationalism, or freedom, or justice, or all at once. Universalism promised Jews a world that would have no reason to discriminate against them, a world in which difference might ultimately wither away to leave in its place a utopia of equality and justice.

Universalism was, of course, by no means appealing only to Jews, nor only to Europeans. It spoke powerfully to all sorts of groups and peoples who imagined a world of humanity and cooperation, who believed in the possibility of human beings transcending race, class, and, for some, nations and religions. Jews were one of many groups advocating universalism, on the grounds that it was the dangers of embracing cultural uniqueness which brought groups into conflict.

Although universalism was a powerful force in the modern period, in the opposite camp were those Jews who continued to hold on to their uniqueness as the defining feature of their identity. The Jewish particularists of modernity counted secularists, as well as observant Jews, among their numbers. They imagined that the future would maintain their Jewish uniqueness as central. Zionists, Jewish socialists, and others who combined Judaism with modernity or politics, looked to history, language, culture, traditions, or Jewish law, as the irrefutable foundation of Jews' lives. Whether Jewish life was best defined as lived out in a nation, or as a culture, a people, or what was considered in the West to be a religion, its Jewishness was pre-eminent. The absence of difference was not an ideal for particularists, and offered little to recommend it. For them, particularism was the state of human existence, and Jewish normality was best realized through it. All groups, they argued, had markers of identity; there was nothing about culture, language, or beliefs that were incompatible with the modern world.[5]

These struggles took form in many nationalist, religious, and political movements for the first third of the twentieth century; then the Holocaust and the Declaration of the State of Israel silenced many of these debates and conversations for Jews. What could universalism possibly mean in light of genocide? As political and social contexts changed after the Second World War, the nature of Jewish discussions of identity also changed, creating the unique set of conditions that characterize our own age.

---

4   See Jonathan Frankel. *Prophecy and Politics: Socialism, Nationalism, and the Russian Jews 1862–1917*. Cambridge, 1981.

5   See David Biale, "A Journey Between Worlds: East European Jewish Culture from the Partitions of Poland to the Holocaust," In David Biale, ed. *Culture of the Jews: a New History*. New York, 2002.

New Poles of Identity: Borders and Boundaries

The mid-twentieth century marked the start of a shift in the politics of Jewish identity.

With the end of the Cold War era, in which the world was divided by two super powers' spheres of influence, particularism and nationalist identities began to reign supreme. Long-suppressed groups re-emerged to provide demands for political autonomy and national territories. The resurgence or new visibility of what is called religious fundamentalism, which is assertively anti-liberal and anti-universalist, appears to underline the power of particularism and be the ultimate eulogy for modernity.

However, the present moment, which some have termed "post-modern," is full of challenges to nationalism or religion as the ultimate particularism. Indigenous peoples, for example, claim global identities as they preserve languages and customs that do not recognize boundaries. Nations no longer hold people of a common heritage or a shared history. The identities of late 19th century Europe do not serve many groups effectively. The world is too complex and too diverse to imagine classical particularisms—territory or religion—as the only foundation for a people.

With the shrinking of the world through globalization, mass migration, and people everywhere united by shared media and shared consumption, new identities have emerged, purveyed by movements that are neither nationalist, nor religious, nor even political. Ideas about freedom and identity are closely tied to music, clothing, dancing, sports and to a myriad of markers that may be simultaneously local, national or transnational. From the point of view of the global market, there really are no boundaries or unique identities at all.

That very mobility, in both a physical and cultural sense, has had a profound impact on ideas about authority and hierarchy, and has created a remarkable polarization that simultaneously makes, for example, religious authority more attractive to some and more irrelevant to others. It is not surprising, then, that rampant secularization and fundamentalism co-exist, particularly in the West.

In short, given the world in which we live, for Jews as for other peoples, the particular and the universal trip over one another, as what is local, what is universal, what is national, and what is transnational, are no longer easy to locate. For example, rather than escaping Jewishness and championing universalism, as another generation did in the United States and Europe, one may instead practice and claim Jewishness precisely as one wishes. There are few external constraints on Jewish life. In the United States Jews may define themselves in many ways: by their generation or their music, for example. Moreover, they may define themselves as Jewish and/or as belonging to any other number of religions. And so, rather than asking if people should be Jewish, or if Jewishness is meaningful, the most common questions today regard where the boundaries of Judaism lie.

Who has or should have the authority to decide what it means to be Jewish?

These questions of boundaries lead us to ask:

- Does anything unite the Jewish People?
- Looking into the future, will American Jews remain Jewish in recognizable ways?
- Will Israel continue to embody a Jewish state?
- Is there a sense of a global Jewry without shared definitions and boundaries, and what are the implications?
- How do we think and act as Jews in a "global" world?

Ironically, borders and boundaries also form critical questions facing the State of Israel. The meaning of nation and nationalism has certainly shifted since the late 20th century. Some Israeli activists and scholars today are extremely critical of the nation state as a just or meaningful form of social life. What is a Jewish state and what does its Jewishness entail, are among the most compelling questions of the moment. The classical view of Zionism as a vision for world Jewry has not been realized and, perhaps more disturbing at this juncture in history, is the realization that North American Jews' sense of connection to Israel is declining. Zionism, Judaism, Jewishness are ideas and realities all very much at stake for Jews.

Jews are by no means the only people of the world beset with these questions of borders and boundaries. Immigration, intermarriage, religious conversions, and resurgent fundamentalism are experiences that Jews share with many other cultures in which religion, ethnicity, and nationalism are expressed away from "home," and home and culture and religion are all remade in the process. The new century demands new identities that, as noted above, scramble older ideas. There are novelists, activists, artists, and scholars who celebrate the end of identities bounded by single forms of group membership, such as nation or religion. They celebrate the borderland as the most creative and promising site for culture. They deny the legitimacy or inevitability of boundaries for identity.[6]

Jews today have many ways to identify Jewishly. Nation, religion, ethnicity and culture are all legitimate ways of describing Jewish experience in the 21st century. However, these ways of marking identity leave many Jews uneasy. Those who are least vexed are the "extremists" at both ends of the spectrum: those who claim that Judaism is "anything," and those who see Judaism as a set of practices shared with only the like-minded. But, for the solid middle of world Jewry, there are many concerns about the significance of Israel to American Jews, about the viability of liberal denominations, about the extent

---

6   Gloria Anzaldua was the first scholar to conceptualize the border as the critical place of study in *Borderlands/la Frontera: the New Metstiza*. San Francisco, 1987.

to which Jewish in-marriage is necessary for the future of Judaism, about the salience of Zionism for younger generations of Israelis, about the impact of Jewish extremism on Israel, and about whether there can be a cultural Judaism in the absence of communal ties among Jews. These questions are raised in light of Jewish history, the effects of the Holocaust, the importance of Israel, and the total freedom enjoyed by Jews in the United States. Jews are asking new questions in new formulation to answer a very old question— "Who are we?"

The Project of Peoplehood

I suggest that there has never been a more pressing moment to return to a Jewish idea that seemed to fade in the face of nationalism and fundamentalism, the notion of peoplehood. As other essays in this volume note, the idea is associated with Ahad Ha'am, who offered a language for group affiliation that suggested connection across time and space.[7] Peoplehood, as Ahad Ha'am realized, draws on multiple forms of authority and provides competing versions of association, affiliation, and destiny. As a concept, it has functioned for Jews within the world of divine authority, as well as working class radicalism—for people who rejected the idea of the nation, and for people who built a Jewish nation. Peoplehood is also certainly evoked in Jewish liturgy as a link that unites all Jews "from the four corners of the world."

Although there are many rich images and ideas on which we can draw to fully engage with the notion and necessity of a Jewish Peoplehood, we must first acknowledge that peoplehood is a project rather than a thing in and of itself.[8] What Peoplehood means or how it is acted upon will always constitute an historical process, one that changes over time. It is imagined, rather than simply lived. It is self-evident that Jewish Peoplehood has been continually redefined and contested, not only in modernity, but in all periods of Jewish history. While the idea of the Jews being *a people* certainly suggests sharing a "fixed essence," there is no question that defining the contours and meaning of peoplehood was constantly under construction, and will always be lived through challenges and contestations about what it means to be part of the Jewish People, and about how those conversations, visions, and formulations of it might unfold in the 21st century.

---

[7]   See Steven Zipperstein. *The Elusive Prophet: Ahad-Ha'am and the Origins of Zionism*. Berkely, 1993.

[8]   Paula Hyman notes that assimilation is a "project" in her book *Gender and Assimilation in Modern Jewish History: The Roles and Representation of Women*. Seattle, 1994. Her term influenced this understanding of peoplehood.

In today's world, the project of Jewish Peoplehood can offer new ideas about membership and belonging that neither erase the boundaries of Jewish distinctiveness, nor make that distinctiveness an end in itself. Peoplehood can serve Jews well because they are a transnational, Diaspora people, as well as people within a nation. It is a formulation of Jewish experience that may best reflect the situation of world Jewry today, and provide not only what historians have called a usable past, but also a usable understanding of Jewish experience for the future.

We must first ask where the project of Jewish Peoplehood stands today. It has: a *nationalist* dimension, embodied in the State of Israel and its claim to be the homeland of the Jewish People; an *ethnic* dimension, claiming that Jews are a people within pluralist nations that recognize other types of diversity; and a *religious* dimension, claiming that Jews practice Judaism. These claims co-exist, as they have for over a century, although often uneasily. It appears that the connections *between* the dimensions are weakening—that the nationalist and the ethnic, or the religious and the ethnic, or all three, imply or support one another—or even any two—may be less salient than in the last half of the twentieth century. In addition to the weakening of connection among Jews, the nature of connection is also changing. Younger men and women find membership and commitment troubling. Attachment to Israel is empirically on the decline in the United States, as is synagogue membership. If there was a consensus about Jewish life in the United States in the 1950s, or one about Israel after 1967, none seems to be emerging today.

Even the nature of identity and identification is shifting. The effects of connections that are more transitory and individualized are complex. What may be gained in these newer formulations, is the participants' greater investment in the ability to shape Jewishness to him or herself, or to their micro-communities. On the other hand, what may be lost is both the larger sense of Peoplehood and tolerance for those Jews who differ and function, either inside or outside of the micro-communities.

The project of Peoplehood, then, must go against the current cultural grain in the 21st century even while being a product of it. Just as the universalism/particularlism formulations were played out within modernity—responding to its issues, context, and formulations—so must our current ideas reflect our time even while being in tension with it. Peoplehood simultaneously and paradoxically asserts that Judaism and/or Jewishness is the irreducible core of one's life *and that* it takes forms that differ from one's own practice or world view. I therefore propose two key dimensions to the current project of Peoplehood that are essential to building both depth and breadth in identification. The project of Peoplehood requires first and foremost a commitment to pluralism and, secondly, a context in which Jews who define their Judaism/Jewishness differently from one another can find a common vocabulary and symbols to articulate a shared past, in service of the future.

Pluralism: The First Condition of Peoplehood

Peoplehood requires an understanding that Judaism is plural, Jewish life is varied, and Jewish experience is multifaceted. Narrow and isolationist views have will not serve the Jewish people well; Peoplehood requires mutual recognition among all Jews.

I suggest, therefore, that *Jewish Peoplehood is not for all Jews*. It will only work among Jews who assert the importance of shared and overlapping concerns which may not be identical. Jewish Peoplehood will be unlikely to flourish in the context of any extremist view, right or left, ultra-orthodox, or adamantly syncretistic. It will not work for Hasidic Jews in Borough Park who refuse to acknowledge the Reform synagogue in their community. Likewise, it will not work for those forms of liberal Judaism which are syncretistic with both Eastern religions and Christianity. These forms of Judaism do not allow for a peoplehood that is built upon the acknowledgement of change and diversity, as well as shared and common practices.

Constructing History: The Second Condition of Peoplehood

The project of Peoplehood situates pluralism within shared memory and history, which are articulated through collective enterprises, in which visions of the past are shaped into programs for the present as well as for the future. Jewish Peoplehood neither does nor did require a notion of Jews sharing a contiguous territory, but it did imagine a shared past of common events, ancestry, unique language, and a common store of texts. In truth, the texts were not always common, the languages varied, the events were redefined and held different meaning or no meaning in various parts of the Jewish world. However, a mythological sense of a shared past was and is critical to forging a sense of mutual investment in one another.

Memory of that past has been constructed in varied ways, much to the advantage of the claims of Peoplehood. Liturgy is a powerful medium for a memory of a common past, in such unique forms as the Passover Seder and in prayer. Liturgies frame historical experiences and provide a common sacred language for shared loss and displacement. Because memory is central to culture, it is, to assert the obvious, dynamic—and thus, the modern claims to Peoplehood have been shaped to reflect varied political and social ideas. However, history and memory do not necessarily require a single trajectory. The contestation over the substance of the history of the Jewish People is a project of Peoplehood. Virtually every project of cultural reclamation depends on memory, thus on formulating history. What is essential to Peoplehood in this century, is to begin to shape historical memory together as a people in order to entertain a vision of the multiplicity of Jews and ways of being Jewish, for the present and the future. It is to ask the meaning of that history, and how Jews understand questions of justice and personal responsibility.

There are many ways of constructing a sense of shared history and many different contexts in which to do so. The Zionist youth movements of the 1930s to the 1940s, the denominational summer camps begun in the 1950s, and currently Birthright Israel, have all demonstrated in parallel and different ways that peoplehood happens in artificial communities that emphasize the power of experience. In these settings, the memories of Jewish People are made into a vision for the future.

Peoplehood will be formulated in different modes in the 21st century, since all forms of association are changing. Knowledge of Jewish Peoplehood will be transmitted through the internet. Experiences of all types will be shaped by a virtual reality. Hence, the project of peoplehood should involve efforts to work collaboratively on creating historical projects that help to define a present and a future.

One such project might be the planning of a curriculum about Jewish Peoplehood.

- What would it mean to build multicultural, multilingual, transnational peoplehood in partnership with other Jews? What language would be used? What texts would be drawn upon? What stories would be told? And what possibilities would be envisioned?
- How would participants imagine being mutually intelligible to diverse communities of Jews?
- How would they envision shared pasts that led to diverse futures for one people?

Several topics would be central to any such conversation:

- How does one draw the boundaries of Jewish experience? No vision of Jewish Peoplehood can reasonably imagine a history of sealed borders, impervious to the cultures of others.
- What would it mean to envision the full diversity of the Jewish People as fundamental to peoplehood, without claiming that anything any Jew does is Jewish?
- How do North Americans, Latin Americans, Europeans and Israelis confront this problem?
- Can peoplehood best be understood in light of difference, in the permeability of boundaries, and in the process of setting limits on defining Judaism and Jewishness?
- What texts define the core of the Jewish historical experience?

Grappling with these questions would offer opportunities to imagine and teach history in a variety of settings. Initially, such a project would offer a way to learn and experience peoplehood. Ultimately, it would bring together groups who would find questions to pursue and experiences to share. Taking the transmission of history as a core project would allow remarkable conversations about how to build a future.

Jewish Feminism: An Example of Peoplehood

One of the most compelling recent examples of a plural, vibrant Jewish Peoplehood is embodied in Jewish feminism of the last three decades.[9] It is a surprising, but interesting model, despite the fact that it hardly resembles classical versions of collective identity. Jewish feminism did not begin as a self-conscious pluralist movement, although it was inspired by a larger American movement which, in turn, was transformed to speak to the lives of Jewish women (and subsequently men) in different denominations and, in time, in different countries. Jewish feminist ideas were spread to tens of thousands of women and men, by means of articles published in alternative magazines, conferences organized by activists, and trends in Jewish denominational and trans denominational movements. It engendered debates about law, leadership, family and social policy. It provoked backlash, which only further underlined its power. Its advocates persuaded others and changed institutions while, at the same time, some participants in those institutions felt pushed out and created their own.

Jewish feminism began in North America, spread to Europe and Latin America, and took on different and parallel formulations in Israel, because of the link between religion and state. The movement became a transnational phenomenon, engaging women and men in a variety of scholarly projects, dialogues, and conferences, as well as new forms of observance and new ways of praying and studying. No aspect of Jewish life and scholarship is untouched by Jewish feminism; no denomination has avoided engagement with it.

What might be most interesting about Jewish feminism, as a model of peoplehood, is that it offers a vision of Judaism for people who do not agree, but nevertheless find common cause. It was and remains built upon a serious engagement with Jewish law and Jewish texts, for people who have different relationships to those texts and their authority. Hence, it shares the library of the Jewish People, their forms of observance, and their institutions. Jewish feminism, in all of its manifestations, acknowledges that Western ideas have a relationship to Judaism and continue to shape its practices and traditions. However, Jewish feminists disagree about the extent of that influence or how it is to be understood. Because of different relationships to Jewish law and authority, not all Jewish feminists can pray together, nor can they all eat together. They certainly feel slighted and patronized by one another from time

---

[9]   See, Riv-Ellen Prell, ed. *Women Remaking American Judaism.* Detroit, forthcoming.

to time. However, they can and do study together, talk to one another, and act together as Jews for themselves and for the Jewish People.

Jewish feminism has a relationship to the Jewish People that also makes it an important model for peoplehood. The movement drew people to Judaism who felt marginalized, and deepened the engagement of those who had been put at its margins, both women and men. By finding new meanings, new issues, and new ways of reading texts, Jewish feminism made peoplehood more inclusive and more vibrant. Like many other social movements based on "identity," Jewish feminism re-imagines the Jewish People, while asserting its centrality to the lives of Jews. It offers a remarkable case study in why people do not leave the traditions that they criticize, and how they come to feel more committed to the tradition in the process of changing it. Jewish feminists are united by past and future: they live in a history that they are constantly forced to re-imagine. In that search, they have uncovered texts and traditions that were lost, but they have also argued that tradition and history must be re-framed or changed or understood differently, depending on one's commitment to *Halachah* [Jewish law].

Jewish feminism provides a model of plural peoplehood in another sense: it draws on principles of justice. From the Baby Boom thinker Rachel Adler, through the writer Cynthia Ozick in the 1970s, to the Orthodox Israeli theologian Tamar Ross in the 21st century, Jewish feminists have demanded that Judaism examine the marginalization of women and address it. They have insisted that Judaism must be inclusive within the norms of various versions of Jewish practice.[10] Jewish feminism then, like other forms of Jewish Peoplehood, asserts the centrality of certain principles to Jewish Peoplehood. Its pluralism is in service of certain values—the greater inclusion of all Jews, the practice of justice within Jewish law.

What is interesting about the model of Jewish feminism, is that it offers a way to build a pluralist peoplehood. One can imagine this transnational identification among progressive Jews, religiously or politically, who cross denominations and also include secularists. Together, they already draw on textual and political traditions that unite them. What is important, is that without including all Jews, many types of Jews are drawn together by affiliation, and by the need for forge a vision of Judaism and Jewishness that is more inclusive. What makes this version (or potentially versions) of peoplehood contemporary, is the very ways in which it transforms notions of particularism and universalism. Feminists' assertion that Jewishness is not an undifferentiated category was truly revolutionary. That Jews are also women and men, and that

---

[10]   Cynthia Ozick, "Notes Toward Finding the Right Question: A Vindication of the Rights of Jewish Women." *Lilith*, Vol. 6, 1979; Tamar Ross, *Expanding the Place of Torah: Orthodoxy and Feminism*. (Waltham: Brandeis University Press), 2004. Rachel Adler, "The Jew Who Wasn't There," Davka Magazine, 1971.

is a component of Jewish life and experience, spoke powerfully to issues in the larger society. The Peoplehood project embodied in Jewish feminism is one that broadens participation, focuses on identity in complex ways, and links Jewishness to justice. Jewish feminism, in some ways, followed a conventional path of cultural change and the development of a collective, plural outlook: it brought people together in conferences, in universities, in scholarship, and in ritual innovation. Talking, writing, and acting, itself produced a sense of peoplehood.

Conclusion

In an age where we are plagued with questions about boundaries and borders, the ambiguities and possibilities of peoplehood appear to be more relevant than ever. We must recognize both that the pluralism of the Jewish People is its great asset, and that the historical traditions of the Jewish People remain foundational to establishing Jewish Peoplehood, Jewish Peoplehood must be a project that works to bring people together, to create venues for teaching and experiencing connection. Jewish feminism, a model that has recently succeeded, may serve as a basis for thinking through these issues.

The project of peoplehood will not be easy. If Jewish Peoplehood is not for all Jews, then that should not be defeating on the face of it. Part of the diversity of Jewish experience of the 21st century will most likely include those who cling to the micro-worlds and those who seek to create big tents. If there is a Jewish identity to be found in peoplehood, it will occur in local environments, brought into conversation with other attempts to do the same thing.

At the core of my vision of peoplehood, is the frank paradox that Jewish life has changed and changes, and that its most powerful symbols are those that imagine both a continuous past and a future. This paradox is the human condition, which Jews have embodied for centuries. Seeking the right questions, the right conversations, and the right venues to bring Jews together, are the best way to live this paradox.

anything in Israel is completely secular) cultural center—and went off to ask questions, from a distance. Like many before me, beyond the student alibi, I was exposed to Parisian "spleen" in my eighth-floor "chambre de bonne"— a garret room—on Rue de Rivoli, at the Place du Châtelet. During my days of feverish writing, far from the tumult of the city below me, I dreamed of Jewish theater while composing prose and poetry. The pages filled with Hebrew letters, first in longhand, later in print, using the Hebrew typewriter that I found, my heart pounding with excitement, at "Chez Durant" on the Boulevard St. Germain.

In Paris, I disconnected from the collective Israeli biography, and from the protective envelope provided by the Israeli cultural leadership—those who set the national tone. I became an alien, a minority, an exile, akin to the Parisian street-corner vagabonds. Although I had traveled to the city of culture and freedom, the city of Piaf, Brassens, and expatriate writers, I was nonetheless exposed to yet another kind of foreignness, a Jewish one. I found myself in the heart of the Jewish-European historical entanglement, and during the periods when I traveled from Paris to New York and Princeton for research, I was exposed to the completely different experience of American Jewry: a Jewish community exceeding that of Israel in size, and in the process of creating a Jewish cultural alternative. In the works of American Jewish artists, I found an echo of my own search, and the friendly and creative relationships that I developed with them have continued to inform my work over the years.

However, I first needed to "settle my accounts" with Europe. The Université de Paris VIII Vincennes campus where I studied was a center for PLO gatherings, and within its corridors, Israel's right to exist was not necessarily recognized. And when I had to answer the question, "Where are you from?" I would receive the response, "But you don't look Jewish!" When I was a child, to my embarrassment, my mother's Holocaust survivor friends would praise my "Aryan" looks in a frightening manner. Suddenly, without my being prepared for it, the Holocaust was present in the City of Lights, in whispers, in the film, *The Sorrow and the Pity* that was being screened in the cinemas, or at the Paris Opera, where I worked as an assistant director, and where—to my astonishment—the hero's entrance in Wagner's *Parsifal* echoed Hitler's welcome at the 1936 Olympics—all against the backdrop of the murder of the Israeli athletes in Munich that same autumn, at the 1972 Olympics. All that drove a wedge of suspicion between myself and European culture. In my "chambre de bonne," I found myself reading more and more, in "block Hebrew," Buber, *Midrash*, the writings of Rabbi Nachman of Breslav. And the next autumn, in the middle of the Yom Kippur War, I founded the "Seven Beggars Troupe," mounting, for its world premiere, *The Harvest of Madness*, a theatrical adaptation of Reb Nachman's tales, named for the fable in which the king and his steward are informed that anyone who eats from the next year's harvest will go mad. They decide to eat from it anyway, but first they place identifying marks on their foreheads, so that when they see each other they will remember that they are mad.

As a child, beyond the secular-socialist atmosphere in which I was raised, I absorbed echoes of Jewish tradition through my father's family's deep roots in Ukrainian Hassidut.[1] However, in order to transform these roots into a relevant and useful asset, I needed to undergo a revolution of consciousness. My Parisian exile, together with subsequent encounter with American Jewry, enabled me to deviate from the Zionist aspiration to become, "a people like all other peoples", from the limited vision , "in favor of normality"—in the words of A.B. Yehoshua—and from the historical circle of "young culture" that sprang up on Tel Aviv's dunes—straight out of the Bible and the archeological foundation—while negating the "Diaspora" and its glorious creative enterprise.

The community of great Jewish teachers in Paris of the 1970s provided both the conceptual tools and the opportunity for a deep encounter between Judaism and Western culture. The voices of Manitou (Rabbi Leon Ashkenazi), quoting from the *Zohar* in a guttural North African accent, or the philosopher Emmanuel Levinas quoting from Rabbi Chaim of Volozhin in a Lithuanian accent—all against a background of Sephardi-Ashkenazi commingling, which was also unheard of—even in Israel—in those days. While, from the United States, came the first echoes of the *chavurot* and their innovative methods of study. A trip to Poland, into "my mother's story," in 1975, led to a commitment to the memory of the Holocaust, while the decision to observe Shabbat and *Kashrut*, though it ultimately dwindled into isolated gestures, nonetheless represented a radical violation of the secular Israeli taboo. Before leaving Israel to study in Paris, I had submitted a research proposal to the University of Tel Aviv on Jewish Theater. My request was immediately rejected, with the explanation that, "there is no such thing," a response reflecting the cultural zeitgeist. In Paris, with the encouragement of Professor Andrei Weinstein, I researched "Contemporary Sacred Theater" and its central theatrical elements of hassidic ritual;[2] my research trips led me to Jerusalem, Boston, New York and Paris, to the National Library, the JTS Library, and to encounters with Gershom Scholem, Rabbi Kook, and Rabbi Soloveitchik.

---

[1]   The family's hassidic roots, from the 19th century on, are described in: *Hayinu Kecholmim* ("We Were as Dreamers") (family saga), Carmel, Jerusalem, 2005; Mordechai Globman: *Sixty Years of Life*, printed by Shlomo and Nurit Govrin, 2000; and have been analyzed by David Assaf: "From Friend to Enemy: Rabbi Akiva Shalom Chayot of Tolechin's Road from Misnaged to Hassid", in *From Vilna to Jerusalem, Studies in the History of Eastern European Jewry in honor of Professor Shmuel Verses*, Jerusalem: Magnes Press, Hebrew University.

[2]   Michal Govrin, Théâtre sacré contemporain, thèse de Doctorat, Université de Paris 8, 1976; Jewish Ritual as a Genre of Sacred Theater, in: Conservative Judaism, Vol. 36 (3) Spring 1983, and in: www.michalgovrin.com (theater).

All this set the revolution in motion and turned learning, *lernen* for me, into an intimate part of my life and artistic endeavor. Only years later did this revolution spread to Israeli culture generally. During the mid-1970s, while studying in Paris, I experienced this revolution in a state of menacing solitude, as expressed in my poem, "Fathers"[3]

Fathers

Like a stone stopping a burial-pit
Their shadows close over the sky.
They greet each other with a handshake
As though it were an everyday thing.
Winds of other times emanate
From the points of their beards
And the urgent pigeon-wings of their pilpul
Make a cloudy canopy
Under the open sky.

Hanging by a thread, my fathers jostle together,
A sleeve of Hispania cloth permeated with the scent of jasmine
On an austere robe from the lands of years gone by
On a breeze bearing blows, payes and pelts
Smells of walled houses in Gentile cities
A screaming child
              Women
                  And pots

And their covenant of blood will close the heavenly ceiling
With joined hands.
They will not know that they were visited
By the fruit of their loins.

I went to Paris to study as an Israeli and returned as a Jew, with a different awareness of the "story" to which I belong.[4] I did not return to my city of birth, Tel Aviv, but rather chose to live in Jerusalem, where I enjoyed open access to the generation's great scholars: Gershom Scholem, Shlomo Pines, Rivka Shatz, Yosef Tal, Stefan Moses, Moshe Idel, and Yehuda Liebs, and where I found numerous other artists and students with whom to share my quest. At the same time, the dialogue continued with Paris—with Jacques Derrida, and with Haim Brezis, my future husband.

Nonetheless, an artist's real *Beit Midrash* is located in the depth of his or her creative work. This is learning through creating, and creating through learning. And it is located in *emunah*—faith—in the power of creative learning to innovate, to generate, and for *tikkun olam*—to repair the world. It comes

---

[3]   In *Ota Sha'a, [That Very Hour] Poems*, [Tel Aviv]: Sifriat Poalim, 1981.
[4]   A perception that I have discussed at length in my article: "The Case of the Jewish Biography," *Partisan Review*, 2001/1.

as no surprise that the Hebrew word *emunah*, is related both to *ma'amin* (a religious believer) and *oman* (an artist). And thus, I brought the fruits of my learning with these valued teachers and peers to theater rehearsals and to the writing desk. The essential biography of an artist, with its peaks and plummets, also takes place in the secret chambers of the creative endeavor. Usually, one does not see what goes on backstage. I will try in the following pages to reveal some of the dramas that have engaged me during my artistic career — in first person feminine.

2. A Jewish Avant-Garde?

A. The Search for Jewish Theater

Starting in the late 1970s, alongside my directing work in Israeli repertory theater, I staged experimental Jewish plays in the heart of the Israeli and international theater community, which, each in its own way, created new forms of Jewish theater.[5] In my artistic creations, the unique ritual nature of *Halachah* served as the basis for the development of a theatrical avant-garde. This was an implementation of the theory which I had formulated in my doctoral dissertation, based on a dialogue with the works of Antonin Artaud, Peter Brook and Jerzy Grotowski, on the one hand, and on a fresh reading of the hassidic traditions and writings. In this approach, the *mitzvot* constitute the material language of a cosmic theatrical event, which forms — existentially — its "actor", enabling him or her to participate in the creation and *Tikkun Olam*. And thus, a large number of my dramatic productions have been avant-garde directorial interpretations of aspects of *Halachah*, or Jewish ritual. In *Variations on Morning* (1980), which was performed on the walls of Jerusalem's Old City, and in which the audience was drawn into involvement with the actors-worshippers, the *halachot* of rising in the morning and the first pages of the *Siddur* — prayerbook — are the dramatic focal points. In *The Journey of the Year* (1982), the drama was based on the cycle of the Jewish year, its movement from creation through latency and redemption, to revelation and destruction, and again, to a new beginning. In the performance, which was conducted as a kind of theatrical journey, the audience went into *selichot* — penitential prayers — in a space cleared by

---

5   The community included Yossi Yizre'eli, the director and teacher; playwright Aliza Elyon-Yisraeli, who founded the "Jerusalem Theater Troupe" for women with Ruth Wieder and Gabriella Lev; the director and Far East scholar Yaacov Raz; and playwright Dani Horowitz, who also coordinated the First International Festival of Jewish Theater in Tel Aviv in 1982, at which echoes could be heard of similar creative activities taking place in the United States and in Europe, just as the work of Sonia Sara Lifshitz appeared in Strasbourg several years later, or that of Yehuda Morly, who immigrated to Israel from France.

bulldozers, then continued on to the sounds of a klezmer band from Rosh Hashanah to Yom Kippur, and on to the other stations, through the seasons and "acts" of the Jewish calendar. In *That Night's Seder* (1989), performed around a huge Seder table, the participant-observers (rabbis, painters, dancers, politicians, and writers, such as Aharon Appelfeld and Yossel Birstein) presented their interpretations of the Haggadah through a variety of media, all against the background of the first intifada. And, in 1993, after years of preparatory teamwork with the set designer and plastic artists Frieda Klapholtz, Doron Livne and Orna Millo, I established, in cooperation with artists from diverse fields in Israel and abroad, the *Gog and Magog Laboratory*, which ran for two years. The starting-point for this work was Martin Buber's historical-hassidic novel, whose stage version was performed at the Israel Festival. The artistic issues raised during this project (acting and prayer, song, dance, language, and story) served as the basis for the future work by the laboratory's participants, who include leaders of Jewish theater worldwide (Bruce Meyers and Serge Vaknin) and in Israel today (Eitan Steinberg, Etti Ben-Zaken, Baruch Brenner, Avi Asraf and Mendi Kahana).[6]

B. Between Hebrew and Jewish Literature

However, if Hebrew theater, which was created against the background of a culture lacking in theatrical tradition, originally drew for its inspiration on the entire range of Jewish life[7], then the new Hebrew literature became, primarily, the arena of Zionism's struggle against the Old World, and against its bookshelf, jam-packed with weighty religious tomes. The destruction of Eastern European Jewry, and the uprooting of the Jews from Arab and Mediterranean countries, only deepened this divide. The dominant stream of Israeli literature continued, for the most part, along this path—from Brenner through the "Palmach Generation", and the "Generation of the State" writers, and on to Oz, Yehoshua Kenaz (in the generation preceding mine), and my generation—Grossman, Castel-Bloom and writers of the "Want of Matter" school. Any reference to Jewish sources was limited to the literary dialogue— a fascinating one in itself—with, primarily, the Bible. The linguistic, stylistic, and thematic break with the Jewish people's religious-national creative heritage in the Diaspora remained almost total. Even the most eminent critics viewed Hebrew literature as the vanguard of the struggle for secularism—a struggle that was not untainted by political ideology.

---

[6]   Documentation of the work of *Gog and Magog* is housed in the IMEC archive in France, in the Academie Expérimentale des Théâtres collection and in The School of Visual Theater, Jerusalem.

[7]   Also, for example: the Habimah Theater's repertoire during its first years of activity as a drama studio affiliated with Constantin Stanislavsky's Moscow Art Theater. [See also]: B. Harshav: *Language in Time of Revolution*, Stanford, CA: Stanford University Press, 1999.

At the end of the 1970s, in the wake of my "Jewish French Revolution," I decided to mount a resistance to this dominant cultural stream. The Hebrew literary voices expressive of the "Jewish" dimension of whom I was aware, were few and included, in the generations that preceded mine, the poets Avot Yeshurun and Harold Schimmel, and the prose writers Aharon Appelfeld and David Shachar. I conducted a dialogue mainly with Bialik and with Agnon, with whom I had a sense of thematic and formal intimacy, across the generational divide. A visit to Agnon's workroom, its four walls covered with thousands of *seforim* containing his reading notes (Kafka and Mann are in the adjacent corridor), was one of the most meaningful writing lessons that I have ever experienced. And Bialik's poems, stories and essays always astonish me anew.

For years, my main literary dialogue took place with writers across the Atlantic who, like myself, were engaged by the aspiration to create a Jewish literary avant-garde. Present in the background was the American Yiddish literary tradition, and the preceding generation of American Jewish authors, writing in English. In relation to my own generation, thoughts that I could not share with my Israeli colleagues I shared, instead, with many American writers and poets, some of whom became my personal friends: David Rosenberg, Nessa Rappaport, Grace Shulman, David Shapiro, Cynthia Ozick, Grace Shulman, Alicia Ostriker, Jonathan Rosen. For a decade, my annual lectures at poet David Shapiro's seminar at Cooper Union in New York constituted an intellectual and creative laboratory on the encounter between *Halachah* and the artistic process.

C. A Poetics of Jewish Consciousness

The ideological-political Zionist-Israeli clash, which cut Hebrew literature off from its sources[8] and precluded any possibility of direct dialogue with these sources (whether out of a sense of continuity, or out of rebellion) also retarded the development of an original Hebrew avant-garde literature. This, at least, was my assumption at the time that the "sea of Torah" was flooding my writing desk with waves of language, and with a wealth of unique textual forms.

In the *Beit Midrash* of artistic creation, the "Jewish book" opened before me, with all of its linguistic layers and its multiplicity of genres — the book that had been composed over the course of hundreds of years and across a huge geographic and cultural expanse. And, in contrast to the European languages, which broke off from ancient Greek and Latin, the Jewish tradition bore, in all of its wanderings and amid the echoes of a multiplicity of tongues, and with its full literary and linguistic meanings, in continuous succession through the era

---

8 Bialik and Ravnitsky's work in collecting selected midrashic tales in *Sefer Ha'aggadah* ("The Book of Legends") also constituted a reaction to the cultural rift.

of contemporary Hebrew—via the Bible, the *Mishnah*, the *Talmud*, the *Midrash*, liturgical poems, prayers, the *Zohar*, rabbinical Responsa, the commentaries, the *Shulchan Aruch*, reflections, *Mussar*, Hassidism, invocations, missives.... A unique rainbow of linguistic colors. At the same time, the myriad layers of the Jewish book revealed to me a wealth of original literary genres which, by their very nature, reflect the human consciousness in a unique manner. Genres which, surprisingly, reverberate more strongly through the prism of scholarly or scientific innovation. And thus, brain research, artificial intelligence and postmodernism enable us to appreciate the Internet-like "hypertext" of the Gemarah or *Mikra'ot Gedolot* page, the behavioral language of the *mitzvot*, the realism of the rabbinical Responsa, and the stylistic pastiche of the *Zohar*—to name but a few.

And so, with a background embracing Bialik and Agnon on the one hand, and the voices of the Western avant-garde (Joyce, Elliot, Beckett...) on the other, together with a deep awareness of the strong affinity between the work of the writer and that of the interpreter-commentator, I began to excavate the "archeological site" of the "Jewish book." Rather than dusty fragments, what I found there were buried treasures of endless inspiration.

Thus, with the exuberance of a person formulating a manifesto, I turned the entire Canon of Hebrew writing, with its myriad linguistic and formal layers, into an intimate writing tool. And, as in the field of theatrical poetics in which I was able to innovate by transferring ritual artifacts and behavior within the theatrical space, the traditional textual forms and their language have formed the basis for my books, enabling innovation in the novelistic genre and in poetic structure. My novel *The Name* was written as a mystical confessional prayer addressed to *Hashem*; my book of prose poetry, *The Making of the Sea: a Chronicle of Interpretation*, was composed in a style reminiscent of a Gemarah or *Mikra'ot Gedolot* page, with a central text surrounded by commentaries; and my novel *Snapshots* presents the "wrenching story" of the modern Jewish saga through fleeting glimpses, succah-like in their transience—the succah constituting the heroine's architectonic inspiration.[9]

The early 1990s saw the beginning of a broad cultural revolution in Israel. Alternative Batei Midrash, mixed secular-religious learning frameworks, and women's Torah study institutes began to appear, while intellectual and creative ferment (in theater, cinema, art, literature) began to spread to the ranks

---

[9] For example: *The Name*, on its appearance in 1995 in *Hasifriah Hachadashah* / Hakibbutz Hame'uchad, Tel Aviv, generated a wave of attacks (mentioned in Helit Yeshurun's article, "The Wolves Attack"), while also earning serious appraisals and literary awards; my book of prose poetry, *The Making of the Sea: a Chronicle of Interpretation*, was rejected over the course of a decade by one publisher after another, with the explanation that "Gemarah is not literature," until it was finally published in 1997 by Harel, Jaffa, (and in an offset edition in 1999 by Carmel, Jerusalem) with original etchings by Lillian Klapisch, and has since been the subject of scholarly articles, a symposium, and three exhibitions—which also indicate the change in the cultural atmosphere.

of Orthodox Jewry which, up until then, had participated only minimally in Israeli cultural life. At the same time, the Israeli literary landscape changed as well. More and more works began to be published engaging the entire Jewish bookshelf, with an increasing depth and diversity of voices. And so, along with the developments taking place in the United States and in Europe, a broader context for the search for a Jewish literature — poetic, technical, and critical — emerged in Israel, too.[10]

3. Kol Ishah ("Woman's Voice")

If the existential and artistic return to the sources necessitated, at the outset, the breaking of the Israeli-secular taboo, my return to the sources as a woman writer required breaking an additional taboo. In contrast to Christian tradition — which produced many respected women writers — in Judaism, the woman's voice, the voice of "immodesty," was excluded from the Canon. Among the thousands of Jewish writings handed down over the centuries, not one book authored by a woman is to be found. (The few compositions with some partial female attribution, from the Scroll of Esther to the *techinot* (Yiddish prayers for women), being merely the exceptions that prove the rule). Perhaps because of this, unknowingly, my early books are filled mainly with masculine figures. However, as soon as women began to make their appearance in my writing and their voices began to reverberate — out of the fullness of women's experience — in dialogue with the sources, a spark was ignited. Its bright light illuminated a hitherto unimagined landscape, a portion of which I will now try to describe, in the limited space available here.

A. Eros

I wrote *The Name* as a prayer-novel, a kind of stream-of-consciousness that weaves the emotional and spiritual wanderings of its newly-religious heroine, a daughter of Holocaust survivors, together with traditional Jewish voices. I composed the heroine's prayer using the "inter-textual" method employed by composers of the traditional prayers and *piyyutim*, in which quotations from earlier sources are incorporated into the new work, in order to convey the author's mood. It was actually the voice of a woman saying the prayers that set off the erotic charge of the prayers' language. A charge that remains concealed by metaphorical distance, when the prayers are spoken in the voice of a man. I will quote here excerpts from the opening section:[11]

---

10 This school's richness and diversity of voices call for comprehensive and detailed research.
11 *The Name*, New York, N.Y.: Riverhead, 1998, pp. 3–5.

MICHAL GOVRIN

With the help of God

> *May it be Your will, HaShem, Holy Name, my God and God of my fathers, that my prayer come before Thee. For You hear the prayer of each mouth...*
> *And may You want me.*

Another forty days. And the body is already burning in Your fire.
Another forty days. Toward you. Body to body and breath to breath.

Everything is ready with me. With complete devotion. Until the last of the Days of the counting, until the Kingdom of Kingdom. Until the last coupling of purity.

> *And may it be Your will to accept me with love and desire. And may it be Your will to answer my plea. And may it be Your will that my little bit of fat and blood be like fat placed on the altar before You.*
> *And may You want me.*

When uttered by a woman, the statement, "And may it be Your will to accept me with love and desire" and the expression, "coupling of purity" transform the words of prayer into words of explicit devotion, body and soul.

In a somewhat different gesture, *The Making of the Sea: A Chronicle of Interpretation*, which was written at the same time as *The Name*, places the Hebrew language's Eros at the center. The book, which moves between death and love, and between Rio de Janeiro and Jerusalem, is actually a love poem to the Hebrew language, and to its primal erotic tension. It resonates with the voices of those ancient and later writers who composed in the Hebrew language—the tongue in which the *world* was created by the *word*—the power of renewed creation, in both divine and human speech: in blessings, learning, interpretation, or dialogue. The tension of creation echoes throughout the book between center and periphery, in a dialogue that alternates continually between entrance and acceptance, between masculine and feminine.

B. The Conjugal Nature of the Covenant

The writing of *The Name*, a novel which directly addresses God—the One Who "hears each person's prayer"—in the voice of a woman, shed new light for me on the conjugal nature of the dialogue inherent in the prayer of the individual Jew, and on the mythical union between God and Israel. The novel's heroine has stormy relationships with the men in her life: her father, her lovers, her fiancé, and the rabbis whose paths she crosses in Jerusalem. Yet her relations are no less stormy with the object of her prayers and passion: God. The "realistic resemblance" between the two kinds of relationship guided me in the writing of the sections where the heroine discerns echoes of her own life in the life of the "young couple," God and Israel, and in their evolving relations—from the "betrothal" that is, the Exodus from Egypt—the heights of untrammeled devotion—to the abyss of jealousy and unfaithfulness that climaxes with the worship of the golden calf.[12]

"We are your wife and you are our husband," says a Yom Kippur liturgical poem of the relationship between the Israel and God that stands at the center of the Jewish myth. Images of betrothals, nuptials and love between the *dod*, the husband, the Holy-One-Blessed-Be-He, or the *Zeir Anpin*, and the wife, the Shulamit, the *Shekhinah*, *Knesset Yisrael* or *Nukvah* describe the relationship between God and the Jewish People from the Bible onward, particularly in the Song of Songs, and through the entire range of the later literature. All of these contexts convey, in various styles, the story of God who creates the world in order to enter into a nuptial covenant with His chosen people, and of their passionate, erotic, far-yet-near relationship.

The myth of conjugality expresses the Jewish belief in a world that is continuously re-created through the union of its contradictory elements. But what is the "reality" behind this image? What "really" takes place in this ancient couple's secret chamber? And what has kept them together between a few instances of exaltation, across a history filled with persecution and destruction?

The prayer of Amalia, the heroine of *The Name*, bursts forth through the gaping wound of the Holocaust. During my work, voices rose up through Amalia: ancient echoes, particularly of women, or, more precisely, echoes of the feminine voice. This is the voice that erupts in the myth during times of crisis, hurling its protest up to the heavens, remonstrating with the divine attribute of *Middat Hadin* (Justice), and struggling to revoke the heavenly decree. This is the voice of those who insist on drawing God out of His hiding-place and who take it upon themselves to heal Him (See Reference 10). This is the voice of women: Rachel, Hannah, the Jerusalem of *Lamentations*, *Knesset Yisrael*, the *Shekhinah*, or the *agunah* (abandoned wife). But it is also the voice of certain male voices, those audible in moments of crisis: Moshe, Choni Hame'agel, R. Levi Yitzhak of Berdichev, or Rabbi Kalonymus of Piaseczno, whose work *Holy Fire* was found under the ruins of the Warsaw Ghetto. The protest's vociferousness succeeds, in the mythical moments of salvation, in reversing the divine decree, and in making words of solace heard. And with this same dynamism that exists between the masculine and the feminine attributes—the merciful, comforting God becomes a God with a womb, since the Hebrew word for mercy, *rachamim*, which is a fundamental Divine attribute, is related to *rechem*, the word for womb (Jeremiah 31:19-20).

Generations of male writers have succeeded in rendering the woman's voice in the Jewish myth beautifully, through fine analysis and their depth of empathy. They thus gave voice to the feminine attribute that is present in

---

12   Detailed discussion in: D. Shapiro, M. Govrin, J. Derrida, *Body of Prayer*, New York: The Irwin S. Chanin School of Architecture of the Cooper Union, 2001.
See also: M.Govrin, "Parashat Beshalach," *Likrat Shabbat*, Hadas Achituv and Eyal Picard, Kibbutz Ein Tzurim: Yaacov Herzog Center for Jewish Studies (forthcoming) (in Hebrew).

the world, and within themselves. However, for me, writing in the first person feminine drove home the magnitude of the challenge posed by the introduction of women into the Canon. I became a partner with God in formulating — out of the fullness of the feminine experience and consciousness — the feminine and the masculine attributes of humankind and of the world.

C. The Anti-Semitic Relationship — the Woman and the Gaze of the Other: the Jew as Object of Desire

It was while writing *Snapshots* that I came to understand just how essential the "gaze of the other" is to the mythical Jewish union — both the internal and the external gaze. The mythical Jewish perspective describes the Covenant between God and Israel as an exclusively conjugal relationship, one that contrasts with the relationship between God and the Gentiles: the chosen wife versus alien women. Moreover, the public display of the Covenant before the Gentiles — at times of joy, or of crisis and divisiveness; or the consideration, "What will they say?" — may be fundamentally regarded as factors in the Covenant's establishment. Nor does the act of keeping the couple's "secrets" serve merely to conceal the "mystery of Israel" from the Gentiles; rather, it increases, at the same time, the desirability of what is "hidden from public view."[13] From the external perspective of Christianity and Islam, religions which share Judaism's God, the Jewish claim to exclusive occupation of the place of the wife makes any other kind of union with God illegitimate — an "intolerable scandal."

And thus, in the quarrel over God — a quarrel rooted in love, jealousy or proprietorship — something develops which may be termed an "anti-Semitic union" between the Jew, God's chosen spouse, and those who seek to replace him or her. The Jew standing at the gates (of Torah, or of the heavenly palace) blocks the way to God, and those who wish to replace the Jew cling to him or her. In this coerced relationship, the Jew plays the role of the "loved-despised woman," the object of an archetypal passion, and provides the focus for the transformation of this passion into jealousy and murderous hatred (for which de Sade's orgiastic rituals can be used as a basis for description). In addition, alongside the Christian and Muslim relationship with God, each in its own terms, the "anti-Semitic relationship" — with its alternating love and hatred of the Jew — functions as a major component of identity ("Verus Israel" or the "Muslim" victory). In this conflicted, perverse relationship, the Jew crosses

---

[13]   For a discussion of the problematic nature of public knowledge of the mystery, see, for example: *Yoma* 54a; *Yalkut Tehillim* 702; *Midrash Bamidbar Rabba* 20, 22; see also: Regnault, F. "Notre object *a*" in *Ornicar, revue du Champ freudien*, no. 50, 2002, pp. 31–41; Trigano, S., "Le prophétisme et la fin de la modernité," *La Cause freudienne*, no. 56, [2004].

The subject is currently being discussed within the framework of the Locanian "Cartel" devoted to the subject of Anti-Semitism, whose participants include: Susana Huler, Claudia Idan, Nehama Gieser, Gerda Elata-Alster, Michal Govrin.

gender boundaries. Just as the mysterious rite of circumcision removes a portion of the Jewish male's sexual organ, so in the anti-Semitic relationship does the Jewish male, and particularly one who bears obvious signs of his Jewishness (a beard, a traditional prayer shawl, an IDF helmet, or their "detested" combination of settler-style *tzitziot* [ritual fringes], and an Uzi machine gun) become the object of devoted passion, no less than the Jewish woman.

The story of *Snapshots* takes place in 1991, but the anti-Semitism that was then rumbling under the surface of the European continent lies at the center of the world of Alan, a historian and Nazi-hunter and husband of Ilana, the narrator. Ilana tries, at first, to hold onto the Israeli faith in the "normality" of the Jewish People as "a people like all others." However, upon returning from New York, after a desperate night of love with her Palestinian director-lover, she takes upon herself the role of the Jew — the stranger, the pariah. From her son's sickbed she calls upon her dead father and sarcastically hallucinates the Jew as the object of passion, the great temptation, the Don Juan, man or woman.[14]

[Between two and three a.m.]
And perhaps Don Giovanni is also a Jew — after all, Tirso de Molina wrote *Don Juan* immediately after the great auto-da-fe of 1605 at the Piazza Real. Forty burned at the stake, and dozens of straw figures sent up into flame in representation of those who escaped the dungeons of the Inquisition. A thrilling scene for the impassioned balcony spectators, one meant to ease the labor of the frail Queen Isabella...
Perhaps Don Juan was one of the *anussim*, the forced converts, Father. Rabbi Yochanan. Escaped from the Inquisition, from one woman's arms and into another's. A mystic who openly denies the story of the Immaculate Conception. Disseminates among the women of Europe the law of Eros of the living God, who recreates the world anew each day through unions of man and woman.
Don Giovanni, student of Rabbi Akiva, of all those who burn on the pyre of love. Sings from amid the flames: And you shall love the Lord your God with all your heart. Viva la liberta!
David sleeps with his arms, legs outstretched. Yonatan still tosses and turns, with his three pacifiers. One in his mouth and two clasped in his fists.
And so, Father, we are also a late incarnation of Don Juan. Wandering with our dreams, ablaze with yearning. Peddlers loaded with bundles, notions, fabrics, books, pots. Our restless tribe's bearer of Eros. Unceasingly devoted, the yeast that rises the dough. Like those boys, lovely as the sun, who were exiled by Nebuchadnezzar, their legs bound, "and the Chaldean women saw them and dripped with lust. They told their husbands and their husbands told the king; the king ordered them killed. And still they dripped with lust. The king ordered that their bodies be crushed."

[After four a.m.]
The humming of the highway from afar. The dawn greys the suburb.

---

14   *Hevzekim (Snapshots)*, (a novel) Tel Aviv: Am Oved, 2002, translated from the Hebrew by Barbara Harshav, Riverhead Books, New York, 2007 (hard cover). Forthcoming paperback edition, 2008. pp.97-100.

The outbreak of the new Anti-Semitism, which adds a "blue star" to the yellow one, and which also denies the State of Israel's right to exist, makes it even more imperative that we learn to understand the many aspects of "femininity" that characterize the mythical Jewish male-female union and the anti-Semitic relationship. A portion of my ongoing work is devoted to this issue.

4. The Feminine Attribute of Halachah

The "*Beit Midrash* of creativity" led me to the question of whether the feminine voice and attribute of the Jewish tradition—in contradistinction to its masculine voice and attribute—remain purely within the boundaries of story and myth. Or do they also find expression in *Halachah* and in the 613 commandments—the "material holy tongue" of "yet in my flesh shall I see God" (Job 19:26)?

This question sent me on an investigation of the extensive halachic literature that deals with the *mitzvot*, the details of their observance, and their meanings, from the Torah through the Acharonim (the later rabbinical authorities). This investigation testified to the existence of two opposing and complementary attributes of the *mitzvot*, which may be referred to as the male and female attributes. On the one hand, the "male" attribute is described in the Tanach as representing strength, justice, action, constructiveness, penetration and ownership. The "female" attributes, by contrast, are described as those which "leave an open space," and as a moderating force of relativity: partialness, transience, changeability, incompleteness, conditional ownership, and a powerful affinity for the factor of time. It is in the *mitzvot* of Shabbat, the succah, and the sabbatical year, as I discuss below, where these female attributes are most manifest.

The male and female attributes are dependent on each other as part of a dynamic whole that continually renews itself. And at times (as, for example, in the blowing of the *shofar*),[15] observing a particular *mitzvah* necessitates a transition between the male and the female attribute.[16]

A reading from this perspective opens up new, fascinating, and even revolutionary avenues in the vast body of the halachic literature, and demands a thoroughgoing investigation. I will remain here within the bounds of the "laboratory of creation", and the way in which I observed in my books the existence of male and female attributes in the "fictional slice of life." I noted how these attributes had the ability to influence characters' lives, to generate events and conflicts, and how they lay at the basis of myths, ideologies and stories.

---

[15] Reb Nachman of Breslav, *Likutey Moharan*, 22; 60.
[16] Here I would like to express my appreciation to Haim Brezis for his enlightening remarks.

In my writing, I have focused particularly on the female attributes of Shabbat, the succah, and the sabbatical year.

A. Shabbat

The desire to enter the space of Shabbat drove the endings of *The Name* and *Snapshots*. Throughout the novel, the heroine of *The Name* likens herself to *Knesset Yisrael*, the *Shekhinah*, and Jerusalem; she dedicates herself as an expiatory sacrifice to *Hashem*, and prepares for a mystical union with Him on the night of Shavuot. However, in the throes of a crisis of faith and heresy, she comes to recognize the powerlessness of God. And at the end of the novel, which takes place on the Sabbath eve, she comes to terms with the imperfection of the world and of God. In the final pages, this realization leads her to an acceptance of herself and her memories, and to make her peace with a redemption that is transient and cyclical.[17]

Echoes of Shabbat can also be heard at the end of *Snapshots*. The book's final "snapshots" are set just after the Persian Gulf War, as the heroine is on her way to an international conference on architecture. She is in early pregnancy when she begins driving to her destination; she is happy about the pregnancy, although she does not yet know who the father is: her husband — the French Jew –, or her Palestinian lover. And on the way, on the Paris-Munich highway, she addresses her thoughts about the "Jewish feminine space," to her father, in a kind of soliloquy of solace:[18]

> The life that flutters within me, Father. Yesterday's ultrasound. The technician's hand gliding with the probe along the layer of gel on my belly. On the screen, a millimeter of tissue with a pulsating vein. The life that I had only expressed in my thoughts, in whisperings to you. I carry it with me again, for a time, your snapshots.
> (...) The presentation unfolds in my mind as I drive. — The aspiration that this also will not be something "constructed," but rather will present, over its various stages, a transient pattern. One whose unifying premise will reverberate differently in the mind of each member of the audience. (Can't restrain myself. Delivering an entire lecture to you as I drive. I will end up reading it all from your snapshots...) I will start out by talking about the sacred place that is never whole, that by definition cannot be perfect, as Solomon said at the dedication of the Temple: "behold, the heaven and heaven of heavens cannot contain thee; how much less this house that I have built?" And then I will mention all of the other sacred-open forms: the Tabernacle, sabbatical year, Shabbat. If I can,

---

[17] *The Name*'s concluding word, "Shabbat," is an allusion to Paul Celan's last poem, "Winemakers," which ends with the phrase, "on Shabbat," Paul Celan: "Rebleute" ("Des vignerons"), in *Enclos du temps*, Ed. Clivages. I addressed this affinity in my article, "Chant d'outre tombe" in *Passage des frontiers, autour du travail de Jacques Derrida*, Galilee, 1994, and in its Hebrew version, "Not the dead," *Chadarim* [10].

[18] *Op. cit.*, pp. 373–375.

I will linger for a moment over the idea of the Shabbat, and stress how, in the Kiddush, the blessing is for the very ability to refrain from completing, to cease working in mid-task; the freedom to let go: "Then God blessed the seventh day and made it holy, <u>because on it He ceased</u> from all His creative work, which God had brought into being to fulfill its purpose."

(And perhaps I will dare to speak in the name of the fear on the first nights of the war. And in the name of the mothers. To turn the discussion toward the softness that floods the body.)

After two already. Have to get out.
In any case we will continue this highway conversation, Father, streaking through Germany in the night.

B. The Feminine Place: the Succah and the Sabbatical Year in Jerusalem

In contrast to their Diaspora Jewish colleagues, Israeli writers cannot escape, whether early or late, a responsibility for Israel's dramatic reality, each in their own way. Jerusalem, whose beauty and secretiveness exert an unceasing magic upon me, Jerusalem the woman-city, the object of desire, the eye of the three-way inter-faith storm[19] — Jerusalem has become for me another prism through which the voice of woman reverberates. Will the feminine voices — or the feminine attribute in *Halachah* — be able to have an influence? To change reality? Will they bring about a revolution in the place of the woman in the mythical and the actual male-female relationship, beyond the trap of jealousy and fanaticism?: will they enable Woman to be both wife and woman of the world, and Jerusalem to be at once the place desired by *Hashem* (Psalms 132:13, 14) and "a house of prayer for all people" (Isaiah 56:7)? Will the feminine attribute be able to bring about a revolution in political discourse? In the words of Ilana Tzuriel, the architect heroine of *Snapshots*: "Think about a place that cannot be possessed! And especially in the Land of Israel, Jerusalem, the place that everyone wants to conquer, to possess! Jerusalem, the desired city, the woman, the place of ardor...to know how to let it go..."

In the early 1990s, Ilana Tzuriel, who had left Israel and has now returned to it after a period of several years, is coming to terms with her connection to the country. Her search echoes through her conversations with her Zionist pioneer father during the year following his death, as well as in the split from her anti-Zionist Holocaust survivor husband, in her troubled relationship with her Palestinian lover, in the rift between her and her post-Zionist leftist colleagues, and in her sense of shared destiny with the neighbors in the Jerusalem apartment building where she, together with her two small sons,

---

[19]   "Martyrs or survivors? Thoughts on the Mythical Dimension of the Story War" in *Partisan Review*, 2003 (French version in *Les temps modernes*, mai-juin-juillet 2003; Hebrew version in *Chadarim* [15]).

lives through the first Gulf War. Her response takes shape in the form of a plan for a monument, or, more precisely, an "anti-monument" on a Jerusalem hill overlooking the Temple Mount from the South. The plan calls for a "succah colony" as accommodation for students at the "Sabbatical Year Center" to be established on the site, where they will be taught how to apply the laws of *Shemittah* (the sabbatical year) in agriculture and financial dealings, in a world characterized by global economy and hotbeds of territorial conflict.

But the winds of war disrupt Ilana's plans. Initially, comes the first intifada, and then the Gulf War. Yet, it is precisely in the "plastic succah" of the sealed room that she conceives of a new dimension for her architectural plan. In a gesture of feminine "defiance", she comes up with a plan to renew the flow of water in the ancient aqueduct that carried spring water from Hebron to the Jerusalem Temple.

In an ironic instance of history repeating itself, in the winter of 2001, at the height of the second intifada, I completed the sections that describe Ilana Tzuriel in the winter of 1991, during the first Gulf War. And, as the suicide terror attacks increased in number, so the flow of water — running between the mosque area and the Church of the Holy Sepulcher, into a continuous waterfall near the Western Wall — strengthened its hold on the heroine's imagination, with its symbolic crossing of boundaries of sanctity and hatred, fiction and reality, in an ongoing trickle of life.

5. Conclusion: Responsibility for Otherness

The Scroll of Esther presents us with an analogy between Anti-Semitism (described for the first time) and misogyny. Achashverosh (Ahasuerus), furious with Vashti, succumbs to Memuchan's threats regarding a total war of the sexes: "For this deed of the queen shall come abroad unto *all women*, so that they shall despise their husbands in their eyes" (Esther 1:17). Haman, full of rage against Mordechai, threatens Achashverosh with a global conspiracy of "the others," the Jews: "There is a certain people scattered abroad and dispersed among the people *in all the provinces of thy kingdom; and their laws are diverse from all people*; neither keep they the king's laws: therefore it is not for the king's profit to suffer them" (3:8). In both cases only total annihilation can nullify the threat. When Esther emerges from hiding, both as a woman and a Jew, she is aware of this double threat — the threat that she constitutes, and the threat that confronts her. Yet, even so, she decides to take "responsibility for otherness," in full recognition of the risk incurred: "(...) and if I perish, I perish" (4:16).

Esther's femininity and Jewishness are also her only weapon. After three days of fasting and internal transformation (as in preparation for *ma'amad Har Sinai* — the revelation at Sinai), Esther stands, "in the inner court of the king's house, over against the king's house," face to face with the king who is sitting, "upon his royal throne in the royal house, over against the gate of the house." Everything is decided instantly, at the sight of the woman at the gate. "Esther put on her royal apparel"—so is Esther's appearance described in the text. Rashi (on 5:1) explains that Esther put on *Ruach Hakodesh* (the "Divine Spirit"), and *Gemarah Megillah* (14b) describes this moment of feminine presence, body and soul, as prophecy. Her appearance generates a revolution. She "obtains favor" in the eyes of the king, who at that moment is delivered from his horror of the "otherness" of the "lawless" woman, and from the "subversive" threat of Jewish "otherness." With the skill of an analyst, and with complete command of the ruling regime's intricacies and behavior, Esther brings Achashverosh, step by step, to a state of sobriety. She begins by awakening memory: "On that night the king's sleep was troubled." (6:1). And then, from feast to feast, she steers her course onwards, to the exposure of the utter madness of Haman's passion. Esther does not succeed in entirely reversing the king's decree ("the writing which is written in the king's name, and sealed with the king's ring") or in extinguishing Jew- and woman-hatred from the world. However, she does manage, for a time, to change the story around and to rescue the Jews of the kingdom.

The power of anarchy, of "on the contrary," characterizes the woman's voice in the Jewish myth. It displaces ruling authorities or fossilized truths, thereby awakening rage or mockery. Nonetheless, through the slyness of comedy, the power of passion and eros, or the strength of remonstration, it can be successful in overturning even God's plans. The change in women's status in global society is generating an unprecedented revolution in the place of women in Jewish culture, as it veers between the poles of destruction and renewal. Will the introduction of women's voices into Jewish tradition bring about needed revitalization? Will it change the status of the Jewish people among the nations? And will the strengthening of the feminine attribute in world discourse lead to change in a world that is battling the threat of extremism—an extremism whose first victims are usually women? To quote Mordechai: "*And who knows whether it was for this very moment that you ascended to royalty?*"

For years, a dialogue with the sources has been reverberating in my study. A dialogue of discovery, learning, rebellion, and of innovation. It has transected my life and across historical events, informing my existence and my creative endeavors. In many other studies, in Israel and in other places around the world where Jewish artists are active, ground-breaking dialogues are currently taking place with Jewish heritage. Each of these dialogues, in its own way, is contributing to the contemporary chapter in Jewish creativity, and to the contemporary face of "Jewish Peoplehood."

YOUR PEOPLE SHALL BE MY PEOPLE
Notes on Nurturing Jewish Peoplehood

YONATAN ARIEL

Editor's Summary
While it is difficult to define Peoplehood, the concept is nonetheless salient in the lived experience of many Jews. Until now, however, Peoplehood was invoked in times of crisis that demanded the immediacy and heroism of mass action. Today, when many of the Jewish People's goals *qua* a people appear to have been achieved, a vital sense of Peoplehood can hold sway only if the Jewish people stand for something and work together on a shared project—even if they are doing so in a multitude of ways. This goal—advancing the cause of Peoplehood for Peoplehood's sake—may be propelled by: the pace of globalization, the emergence of an international Jewish culture, the development of pluralogue, the cultivation of an allegiance to Israel as a historical and geographical anchor, the forging of a more sophisticated sense of solidarity, and increased attention to educational curricula. Advancing Peoplehood also requires an integration of Jewish causes, Jewish time, Jewish space, and Jewish texts, in an effort to create a true sense of globalized Jewish community.

Introduction

Jewish Peoplehood strikes me as one of those slippery terms that are a lot easier *done* than *said*. Many of us can readily retrieve moments in which Peoplehood was palpable. One example: in 1991, soon after the First Gulf War and the collapse of the Iron Curtain, I was a British educator working at a Jerusalem institute. I was asked by a Canadian non-profit to travel through Poland, Rumania and Hungary to study both the Jewish communities there and the transit stations for departing Soviet Jews en route to Israel. Our purpose was to learn, so that we could teach Canadian visitors to Eastern Europe and Israel about those places, their history, culture and circumstances. Of course, many of the Canadians had roots in Eastern Europe in the places we were scheduled to visit and there were many poignant moments of visceral experience. The transit stations were staffed by Israelis, mostly immigrants of long-standing from the very countries to which they had now returned on behalf of the Jewish Agency in order to facilitate the smooth passage of Soviet Jews. And some other Israelis on the trips waited their moment and then canvassed the Canadians (who were only too willing) to help fund the entire operation. Try and make sense of that scenario without Jewish Peoplehood!

What characterizes this incident is a number of shared notions: shared genealogy; shared cultural habits; shared memories and nightmares; shared family stories of uprooting and relocation; shared incredulity that this time trains arriving in Poland were bringing Jewish People to start afresh in a new society, rather than to a murderous end; and shared causes to join to achieve something of import based on a strong sense of identification, to name a few. In sum, they each had fragments of a jigsaw that could only be put together collectively.

Thus, whilst Peoplehood is not a word that is common in the lexicon in English or Hebrew, it does have salience in the lived experience of many Jews. If there was a share market for intellectual ideas and you had purchased stock in "social capital" twenty years ago, you would by now have made a handsome profit. If you are smart you will buy Jewish Peoplehood shares now.

As Robert Putnam writes: "Life is easier in a community blessed with a substantial stock of social capital. In the first place, networks of civic engagement foster sturdy norms of generalized reciprocity and encourage the emergence of social trust. Such networks facilitate coordination and communication, amplify reputations, and thus allow dilemmas of collective action to be resolved...Dense networks of interaction probably broaden the participants' sense of self, developing the 'I' into the 'We', enhancing the participants' 'taste' for collective benefits."[1]

A strong hunch says that—even as we know little about it analytically—stay tuned, for the prevailing trends in Jewish identification will require us to be ever more agile at linking our disparate stories one to another, nurturing a sense of Jewish Peoplehood. These notes are a suggestion of what we need to address, so that a renewed sense of Peoplehood comes to pass. I will try and offer some ways of approaching its potential significance for the Jewish People—with an eye more to the future, than the past.

Rhetoric

A rhetorical claim of Peoplehood might well be evidence of its demise. Any time that a group has to keep reminding itself that it has a common language is often testimony to the reality that there is nothing shared. After two generations of intense political, philanthropic and social action, many of the Jewish People's goals as a people seem to have been achieved. The establishment and security of the State of Israel; the freeing of oppressed Jews and their immigration to Israel and elsewhere throughout the free world; the memorialization of the Shoah and the Jewish life that was; and the marginalization of Anti-Semitism

[1]   Bowling Alone: America's Declining Social Capital, Robert D. Putnam in *Journal of Democracy*, 1, Jan 1995, pp. 65–78.

as a potent force in western society and culture—have all been remarkable stories of success.

What shaped this period of vitality in Peoplehood were the pressing circumstances in which one did not really have to ask *why*, or *what*—because the answers were self-evident. This led to both Israeli and Diaspora Jews expending their energies on the *how*, not the *what*. There were numerous other intellectual, cultural and educational achievements during this period that fed some of the more sophisticated responses to the challenges but they were overshadowed in the rhetoric of Jewish public discourse by the immediacy and heroism of mass action.

We need to be very wary of continuing with the vocabulary of previous campaigns (even dressed up in new slogans) because mis-applying crisis de-values our ability to call for support for a genuinely new cause. With a robust Israel and Jews living in freedom everywhere, the language of Jewish Peoplehood itself will have to undergo change.

Errand on Earth

This period of frenetic activity was successful though to the point where people intuitively are now asking—what next? Whereas the aforementioned "causes" to be joined were existentially prominent and lacking in moral ambiguity, one looks around for a similar kind of cause today that has a striking sense of clarity.

The question, ripped free from layers of analysis is this: *what should the Jewish People do next as a People?* That is not meant to be read as a "right to exist" question—that the Jewish People only has a right to exist if it has an "errand on earth," to use Abba Hillel Silver's evocative phrase. Rather it is meant to claim that for a vital sense of Peoplehood to hold sway, the Jewish People as a people have to stand for something and be working on a shared project, even if they are doing so in a multitude of ways.

That is not a simple question and I believe that one of the motors for addressing Peoplehood is that some are unsure whether there is actually something for us as a people to do together, given our tremendous fissures that are well-known and easily articulated. Might it not be that Jewish Peoplehood has been moved front and center during the last two-three generations and that now, given the material successes, it can retreat (honorably) to a more supporting role and let clusters of Jews get on with life? I find this intellectually tempting, but emotionally and culturally vacuous.

The cause of Peoplehood for Peoplehood's sake (i.e. that Peoplehood is constitutive of what it is to be a Jew) will require us to identify some major projects—ones that are mission-based on a prominent Jewish value and market-driven by the interests that we are able to discern across many of the sub-groups that make up the Jewish People. The insight that Jewish civilization contains both religious and ethnic strands that are profoundly intertwined is well known, and I suspect that the many attempts to rebuild Peoplehood will be more successful if they have a profound spiritual resonance. Only if we offer overarching causes that enable many different Jews in many different ways to enter into some practical endeavor, will Peoplehood flourish.

Globalization

Peoplehood can be propelled too by the pace of globalization. Zygmunt Bauman has called this era one of "liquid modernity," in order to capture the overwhelming sense that much of what we thought was steady ground upon which we were building our societies and institutional arrangements has, in fact, turned out to be far more unstable and malleable. We have gustily, and emotionally, sung Hatikvah, with its line *"li'hyot am chofshi be'artzeinu*—to be a free people in our land." Yet, even for those who endorse the Jewish state, we are a measure less sure of what sovereignty can secure in a global village than we were twenty years ago. The movement in the capital and labor markets and the perpetual media spotlight that accompanies so many developments in Israel puts strong restraints on independent moves.

Furthermore, the elites of the Jewish People—the intellectuals, the wealthy, and the community professionals—jump on and off airplanes, work, holiday and surf the internet in all manner of modes. Bauman hints that this lifestyle allows such people to insulate themselves from the world, even as they traverse it. The intimacies and intricacies of local community politics strike many of these people as hopelessly archaic and trivial. They are intuiting that the Jewish People, as the world's first global people, might have a wonderful network to be cultivated.

Yet the very same folks have often undermined this sense of Peoplehood and share some of the blame for the tenuousness of the nation idea. The more Jews around the world, and in Israel, are active partners in the global economy—the more they come to share in terms of lifestyle, habits, and customs—yet the less they have to talk to each other meaningfully as Jews. It becomes a movement of people who have a heightened sense of "me," without a balancing "we," at their core. The service they want must be "now," not "soon," without the patience to allow community processes to mature. The fraying of local community and the decline of our ability to talk in terms of: you "must," you "ought," you "should"—in favor of you "can," places us in a situation where for Peoplehood to succeed it must feed local community ties and bonds and, in turn, be nourished by them. Globalization gives us the technological means to achieve it, while it undermines the social reality that can sustain it.

Thus, one prominent impact of globalization is the undermining of authority. The powerful figures in our societies and cultures are (deliciously) the objects of satire and ridicule. And this becomes a tenable pastime because many of the most important and decisive figures in our lives are not visible. The challenge to authority has been termed "the death of deference" and with it goes much of our ability to say "you ought to..." carry a burden, help a neighbor, or sustain a community.

- Can community flourish only when people want to participate, or must it also have an element of commitment to share tasks even when people don't want to participate?
- Can Peoplehood thrive without local community?
- Can local community come to appear attractive without the lure of globalized community—in Jewish terms, Peoplehood?

The organizational consequence for this is the move from centralized systems to disparate networks. Feeding messages and agendas from the top down will not be a viable strategy. Rather, cultivating the constantly overlapping, multiple frameworks that lurch from one interest to another will need to be the norm. The architects and designers of the linkages and connections will become the new nodal points in a dynamic sense of Peoplehood that stresses not centers of power, but networks of influence.

Culture

One organizational possibility that grows out of globalization stems from another significant feature of modernity: its impact on culture. While we move steadily towards a more homogenized culture which spreads into ever growing corners of our lives, our sense of particularity also rises. A generation ago we had "broadcasting" in the sense that there were limited channels into which to tune. Today we have "narrowcasting," as there is such an abundance of channels and media that only in rare moments of major political crisis or high sporting drama can we assume that a vast majority of the population are involved with the same event. The confluence of technology and globalization allows the fortuitous compilation of a highly personalized culture, drawn from all over the globe. Under these conditions there is an opportunity for Jewish Peoplehood, even as it makes it more unlikely that we will share precisely the same agenda, in the same order.

International Jewish culture is a potentially rich vein for exploration. The multitude of web-based possibilities to share the consumption of books, films and music offer the potential to build shared conversations amongst small clusters of readers and listeners. They can be turned into active interlocutors that spur friends and acquaintances to encounter the same material. Film festivals and book clubs, with their minimal entry requirements and episodic nature, can allow people to share a modicum of identification, even as they disagree on the messages of the cultural products. How new local forms of Jewish expression come to the international Jewish community is a whimsical process at present—is there a way for this distribution to become more fluent, given the technological means at our disposal?

Pluralogue

One of the chief features of the past half century has been the great concentration of Jews into a relatively small number of urban areas. The largest metropolitan communities account for a very high proportion of the entire Jewish world—and we are citizens of a relatively small number of countries. So, whereas Jewish neighborhoods are somewhat less dense than they have been, in terms of cultural homogeneity, the movement to the West, particularly to America and Israel, is marked. Whether the implied downgrading of the current European Jewish population is justified or wise is another matter.

Indeed, Europe is a strange category and, in Jewish terms, it is today a construct of international Jewish organizations, rather than a compelling reality for the Jews that live there. Despite this, given the roots of many in Europe, there might well be a case for cultivating a shared sense of history through enhancing the status and sense of difference-but-sameness with Europe's Jews, if we wish to cultivate Peoplehood. The persistent talk of Israel-American Jewish relations undermines the very ability to pursue Peoplehood: by stressing dialogue, one emphasizes the duality which often leads to frictions and tensions. Yet, were there a third voice in the conversation then a kind of pluralogue could develop that strengthens multiplicity with the capacity to unleash a nuanced sense of unity, without requiring uniformity. What would the Jewish world look like, if every summer camp, Israel experience and synagogue or school retreat made sure to include Israelis, North Americans and Europeans to stimulate each other?

Nationhood

The influence of nationalism and its structural embodiment in the State has self-evidently shaped the world in the last couple of hundred years. The very longevity of the concept of nationhood is probably testimony to its capacity to evolve and emerge anew in various circumstances. The literature speaks of the "primordialists" and the "circumstantialists." The former maintain that there is a deeply grounded complex of cultural components that contribute to a sense of folk. It is robust and attempts to wish it away, or blot it out (that wonderful paradox of remembering to blot out the name of Amalek!), are neither human nor likely to succeed, because nationhood is one of the core human categories. The "circumstantialists," on the other hand, perceive the constructed nature of the nation and look for the pressing and vital circumstances that brought a sense of nationhood to come to prominence at a given time and place. A cursory glance at Jewish history shows both tendencies at play.

The situation is made more problematic by the distinction between civic and ethnic nationalism. "Civic" refers to national communities that are rooted in a shared commitment to a set of political principles and institutions; and "Ethnic" refers to those based on shared ancestry and cultural community. The first enables a multi-cultural, or even a multi-national reality, to develop, as people learn to speak two languages: the language of their own cultural/religious/national group; and the language of the civic community. The second stresses the common bonds and memories and that these should shape the public culture and domain.

As sub-groups continually press for recognition of their cultural rights, and not only their social and political rights, ethnic nations have two options. They may tend to move towards becoming civic nations, i.e. further reduce the frequency, the prominence, and the sanctity of the culturally specific motifs that were inherited from previous eras. Or they may tend to endorse the motifs and continually sharpen their role in the public square, leading to exclusionary tendencies for those who are not part of the cultural lineage.

In our context, while these matters are clearly on Israel's agenda they are not yet part of the global Jewish discussion. Were we to define the Jewish People based on the civic nation, it would require us to build a *voluntary* commitment to abiding by a set of shared principles (that could well end up being tepid, if driven by consensus) and shared global institutions (that are/would be beset by governance issues). The challenges here appear to be insurmountable at this time. On the other hand, if we were defining the Jewish People as an ethnic nation, then we have many of the in-built advantages of the Jewish story, as embodied and embellished by its sanctified festivals and cultural creations. Yet the single biggest challenge here becomes the identification with Israel—ethnic nations are those that are prone to the worst kinds of ethnic supremacy and are identified in so many ways as "un-western," something which the overwhelming majority of Jews could not countenance. Many of Israel's most fundamental challenges come from wrestling with how to be an ethnic nation that plays by civic nation rules.

I cannot see how Peoplehood can thrive without a commitment to an historical and geographic anchor in Israel, and so we are in search of a model of nationhood/peoplehood that is in large measure *sui generis* for the Jews. What might that be and what does it take to earn Jewish allegiance to a unique phenomenon that is painfully difficult to practice?

Solidarity

The intellectual work of Peoplehood can benefit from a more sophisticated exploration of solidarity. If Peoplehood by definition requires a sense of "we" then we ought to have a wee sense of "we." Most western democratic societies are facing enormous questions of social solidarity and the inability of many to provide adequate answers explains, in part, why the welfare state is in such a condition of chaos.

One of the causes of the difficulty is the growing multi-cultural nature of societies which, despite the many blessings they bring, undermine the "there but for the grace of God, go I" sentiment that facilitates a willingness to support those who fall on hard times. I think that the Jewish People is on the verge of finding itself in the same situation. In what meaningful sense can a Haredi Jew extend the warm embrace of social solidarity to a committed Reform Jew? In what sense can a secular-cultural Jew and a national-religious Jew talk to one another, so that a sense of solidarity may develop?

In Jewish terms, we are familiar with countless campaign slogans that rally us to give more, visit more, protest more, and write more. In recent times, the call for solidarity with Israel has often carried with it a stricture to avoid public criticism of Israeli policy and to toe the line in any manner of ways. One of the (unintended) consequences has been that a sizeable number of Jews—how many?—troubled by some of Israel's policies have felt the call to solidarity to be a call for endorsement of more than they can, in good conscience, support. Or, they are asked to support the welfare of groups that deny their legitimacy. This appears to me to be a woefully thin notion of solidarity and it would repay us to deliberate on the concept and its uses. An initial list to "thicken" our sense of what solidarity might be includes:

a) Same Boat Solidarity—think of the shock of recognition caused by some act (usually painful) that generates an immediate sense that, while I was not the victim myself, the event could have been directed at me. Think of the Netanya Park Hotel seder night bombing, or the UN Zionism equals Racism resolution. Jewish nerves were touched. We are in this together. The difficulty here is that constantly stressing how fragile Jewish life is makes it unpalatable. "The psychologist Will Maslow once observed: 'If all you have is a hammer, the whole world looks like nails.' That is a pathological outlook. The whole world is not a bed of nails."[2]

b) Family Resemblance solidarity—think of the ease with which Jews seemingly wherever they are in the world begin playing the age-old game of Jewish geography. The sentiments and sediments of the family gathering mean

---

[2]   From Harold Schulweiss' address, "With What Shall We Enter the New Century?" at the Jewish Council for Public Affairs, 1999.

that we sense there that all Jews are far fewer than six degrees of separation from each other. At worst, it is suffocating. At its best, Elie Wiesel reminds us that:

"My father, an enlightened spirit, believed in man.
My grandfather, a Hasid, believed in God.
The one taught me to speak, the other to sing.
Both loved stories.
And when I tell mine, I hear their voices."[3]

The stories and songs that are mine have their echoes in others. We may well recognize vast differences in outlook and values amongst our family and yet commit to working with each other to enjoin the issues, both those over which we agree and, particularly, those over which we differ (e.g. what should be happening, in my view, in regard to the disengagement from Gaza).

c) Cultural Folk solidarity—here, we Jews possess an expanded set of customs and rituals in which we all participate to celebrate and commemorate good times and bad times. They constitute shared markers and indicate what is worthy enough to fit into these two categories (e.g. Purim, Yom HaShoah), even as we celebrate and commemorate in different ways in various settings. As Robert Bellah commented, "A true community is a community of memory one whose past is retained by retelling the same constitutive narrative, by recalling the people who have always embodied and exemplified its moral values."[4]

d) Particular Obligations solidarity—this is notion that we, the Jewish People, live with a clear sense of obligation. There are things that we **must** do as Jews—individually and collectively, and there are things that we **must not** do. We reach out to support those who are the unfortunate victims of natural disaster (e.g. tsunami), or inhuman acts (e.g., terrorism), actions which result from an unexpected calamity or willful act of destruction. We combine to endorse and realize some thing worthy that we cannot achieve alone and the beauty and dignity of the cause elevates us to do things differently (e.g., the Make Poverty History campaign, protecting the environment, settling the land).

These levels of solidarity increase in strength. What might be the scaffolding that will allow the mass of our people to scale the heights of "obligation"? One needs to maintain the balance between all four levels to ensure that the Jewish People can find their place at different stages of their lives. The rehabilitation of the concept of Jewish social solidarity, alongside a parallel process to develop a more sophisticated understanding of pluralism and a more nuanced understanding of what it means in a global society of Jewish difference, is a task of paramount importance.

3   Elie Wiesel, *Souls on Fire*. New York: Vintage Books, (1972).
4   Robert Bellah, Richard Madsen, William M. Sullivan, Ann Swindler and Steven Tipton, *Habits of the Heart: Individualism and Commitment in American Life*. Berkeley: University of California Press, (1985), p. 333.

Education

The time will soon arrive when educators are asked to devise curricula for Jewish Peoplehood. So it might prove useful to begin creating a list of initial questions that such an undertaking would need to include. Whereas the syllabus of many topics and themes in Jewish civilization is brimming with content that has been elaborated in the yeshivot and/or the academies for generations, the topics of Jewish Peoplehood are far harder to discern.

- Is this a recounting of times when the Jewish People acted in solidarity with each other?
- Is it an exploration of the times when there was "groundless hatred" and the consequences of such actions?
- Is this a Jewish civics curriculum that all Jews study, irrespective of their ideological affiliation and religious commitment?
- Or is this a much expanded notion of Jewish Educational Travel that enables the lived experiences of Jews past and present in far flung places of the world to become the cognitive space in which all Jews encounter strands of their roots, and encounter Jews who ended up doing things differently, by choice or happenstance?
- What are the age-appropriate experiences for varying modes of Jewish Peoplehood?
- Is this in any way something that is educated for, or is it rather the potent outcome of encounters on a range of topics, and value-laden actions that grow out of highly focused particular commitments?

Whilst this listing is by no means exhaustive, it gives a flavor of the issues that will have to be tackled in this regard.

In (temporary) summation, I suggest that there are at least four interwoven strategies for attempting to pursue Jewish Peoplehood:

Jewish Causes

In this era we need ethically constitutive stories to animate Jewish organizational life. The stories I would seek would be ones of trust and worth that address ultimate questions of humanity in general and Jewish life in particular. They should provide compelling narratives that justify involvement and propel engagement with other Jews, including those with whom you have a profound difference, because the Jewish People stand for something. We have a role to play that grows from investigating our heritage through the prism of today. We possess these stories in abundance within our heritage; so much of the work is in locating the resonance that speaks in the cultural idiom of contemporary life, even as it challenges that society and culture. The perennial themes of liberty, justice, solidarity, power and homecoming can thus find their way into our people's life, with a renewed significance.

Jewish Time

We need to mark time, as many of the festivals and lifecycle events do so vividly. Jewish life has excelled at making these occasions significant. Much of life finds its poignancy at those lifecycle moments of birth, bar/bat mitzvah, marriage and death. In those peaks of emotion, one's extended circle gather to mark the passing into a different phase. It does not seem to be stretching it too far to say that these are significant moments for the Jewish People, too.

What would it take to imagine new kinds of supplements (as rituals or customs) to lifecycle events that seek to place Peoplehood (and Israel) at the core of the gathering, so that the personal becomes intimately entwined with the fate of one's people?

Jewish Space

Jewish communities have always managed to build spaces in which they can flourish—the synagogue, the school, the welfare and community center, and now too the sovereign state of Israel. Given globalization, a relatively new mode of Jewish space has become available to us, one that is a cultural expression of this era: travel. Whereas there have been modest attempts made to provide guided tours and educational guide books, the field of Jewish educational travel has much to learn from the accumulated wisdom of the Israel Experience.

For example, if Jewish communities around the world were to train local young Jews to be effective tour educators of their own communities as part of their high-school and Hillel programs, visiting Jews would have an intercultural experience and expand their personal contact books, and the young locals would develop a knowledge and intimacy with their own community's history, culture and narrative. Such a project is based on a profound conception that Zionism as the Jewish Peoplehood project par excellence is about an activist entry into history. Whilst it has succeeded in drawing focus to Israel, it has regrettably undermined the vitality of each community's sense of its own history. A more nuanced exploration of one's own past, situating it in a broader sweep of Jewish history, carries promise for certain, influential, key young people.

Jewish Texts

We can go out of our way to find substantial learning opportunities for Jews from different places to experience and study together. As a rule of thumb, we should move away from dialogue, or *mifgashim*, as they have come to connote the meeting of two sub-groups; instead we should be looking for pluralogue with at least three different cultural groups represented.

A natural laboratory for this is the MASA initiative where young Jews from around the world will come on long-term programs to Israel. This could rapidly become the cauldron for mixing Jews, including Israeli Jews, in a variety of programs, rather than maintaining the "bubble" of segmented populations, as has been the pattern up until now. If the current target is 20,000 young Jews from the Diaspora by 2010, we can match that with 20,000 young Israeli Jews without adding any costs to the public or voluntary purse. Imagine that by 2020 hundreds of thousands of Jews in their twenties and thirties have friends and acquaintances from many parts of the Jewish world, derived from living, learning, celebrating and commemorating together.

Conclusion

Jewish Peoplehood is a shifting, evolving, dynamic sense that the sum total of the different parts is greater than the aggregate of its components. It sees a family resemblance between certain siblings, or cousins, even distant ones, rather than looking all the time for identical twins. It posits that you can make a claim on each other at a time of need, and that you have the potential for a different kind of conversation with each other than you do with non-Jews: one that is at turns warmer, livelier, more heated, more aggressive, and more intimate about Jews, and the meaning of life.

I do not believe that the enterprise of Jewish Peoplehood is an easy thing to accomplish, or teach, or even initiate Jews into, but we have never tried in the modern free world to deliberately intervene to cultivate such a sense, without a sense of crisis.

One of the first references to the *Bnei Yisrael* as a people came from the new Pharoah in Egypt who did not know Joseph, the high-ranking governor. The Pharoah warned that this people was strong and numerous. And, indeed, we do know how to think and act in a peoplehood way when our adversaries are on the march. My sense is that in the last 20 years there have deliberate attempts to re-imagine synagogues, spirituality, education, cultural arts and their respective roles in Jewish life, but not yet a concerted attempt to re-imagine the collective impulse of the Jewish People.

Our challenge today is whether we treasure our sense of the communitarian character of Jewish life enough to try and cultivate it from within our own cultural resources despite the difficulties in so doing. I think we should try.

AFTERWORD

ALAN HOFFMANN

The issues facing the Jewish People today are unprecedented. Barely three generations ago, our great-grandparents—most of whom were new immigrants to North America, Europe, Eretz Yisrael, South America, the U.S.S.R., and Australia—struggled for basic economic and physical security. Less than a century later, we have managed to realize many of our grandparents' dreams of economic prosperity and physical safety.

However, in the wake of this success, and possibly as a result thereof, the survival of the Jewish People has come into question. For the first time in history, the "Chosen People" has the opportunity to *choose* whether or not to be Jewish. The result? Many young Jews have chosen not to affiliate. Along with the shrinking number of Jews worldwide, we are witnessing a growing detachment from the organized Jewish community, especially among young people. Recent studies demonstrate that, although young Jews are often concerned with spirituality and their personal Jewish identities, the modern emphasis on individuality has weakened their interest in participating in organized religion.[1] Whereas their parents and grandparents primarily formed their Jewish identities in the institutional and/or public arena, today's young Jews perceive of their identities as being far more individualized and fluid.

At the very same time, we are also witnessing a marked disconnection between Jews living in Israel and those abroad, particularly among the younger generation. This growing gap exposes the great danger that Jews, who have always held the notion of "One People" to be paramount, will grow into two separate nations—Israeli Jews and Diaspora Jews—possessing little in common.

In the face of this crisis, the concept of Jewish Peoplehood—the sense that a person is a member of one Jewish People around the world, a concept which encompasses all aspects of Jewish culture, including history, homeland, religion, spirituality, etc.,—presents a fresh and exciting entry point for many young people. The notion of belonging to something larger than individual existence offers many Jews a desperately-desired sense of connectedness—something that is sorely lacking, as collective bonds continue to weaken in society at large.

---

1   *OMG! How Generation Y is Redefining Faith in the iPod Era*, a study commissioned by Reboot, 2005.

But danger lurks if Jewish Peoplehood becomes a diluted, lowest common denominator concept, not nearly as powerful or robust as Jewish religious or national identity. Peoplehood, rather than becoming a powerful, overarching, umbrella concept for Jewish life, would become the poor stepchild for those who are not religiously or nationally engaged.

What would it take to make Jewish Peoplehood a meaningful, central, Jewish concept? At least two basic criteria:

1) First, Jewish Peoplehood needs to cross a certain **threshold of intensity**. When Mordechai Kaplan wrote about Judaism as a civilization, in many ways akin to the contemporary use of Peoplehood, he envisioned a text-centered, content-rich Judaism that was so "thick," using Geertz's term, that it could possibly withstand the pressures of a weakened theology. Jewish Peoplehood, therefore, is not just about a shared language and common literacy. It is also about a threshold of intensity, affective or intellectual, absent from most of today's Jewish life. It is about asking the questions:

- What are the minimal conditions of being an active member of this people?
- What contents, acts, or behaviors create the commonalities that give Jewish Peoplehood an active rather than passive meaning?
- What is the level of intensity that needs to be crossed in order for the experience of Jewish Peoplehood to be sustainable in the long-term?

2) Second, Jewish Peoplehood needs to be anchored in a **shared project of the Jewish People**—a collective project with a clear purpose and a clear sense of outcome. In order for the Jewish Peoplehood conversation to have any value, we need to first answer the question, "Jewish Peoplehood—for what?"

With this in mind, the Zionism-Israel project should be viewed as a highly significant "case study" in Jewish Peoplehood. Historically, Zionism owed its immense power precisely to its ability to mobilize the collective energy, its grounding in a shared sense of purpose, as well as its direction towards a set of concrete outcomes and its capacity to provide personal meaning. Even to-day, first-time visitors to Israel are often profoundly affected by exposure to the startling diversity and rich tapestry of Israeli society, the modern Hebrew language, and the use of Jewish time. The visit to Israel thus represents a window into the potential of Jewish Peoplehood and the trip becomes a mini-experience of participating in collective purpose, with some trimmings of language and literacy, at a level of intensity not experienced by many Jews outside Israel.

In addressing the Zionism-Israel "case study," we therefore need to ask ourselves the questions:

- What role can Israel continue to play in building Jewish Peoplehood, now that its swamps have been drained and roads paved?

- How can Israel continue to function as a "shared project" of the Jewish People, now that the State is sixty years old?
- Alternatively, is there a Jewish Peoplehood analogue to the Zionism "case study" that is not intricately linked to Israel?

With this in mind, I was very pleased to have this opportunity to join forces with John Ruskay and the entire UJA Federation of NY, in order to explore the notion of Jewish Peoplehood, as well as its inherent possibilities to provide meaning for Jews in the modern world. The present volume has attempted to present a range of opinions as a means of opening, clarifying and edifying the current Jewish Peoplehood conversation with the goal of developing concrete policy recommendations and a Jewish Peoplehood curriculum. Whether you are a thinker, practitioner, policy-maker, or "simple Jew" committed to ensuring the success of the Jewish future, I trust that this work has informed, inspired, and challenged you. Although this volume has come to a close, our conversation as a global Jewish community has only just begun...

AUTHOR BIOGRAPHIES

Yonatan Ariel

Yonatan Ariel is the Executive Director of MAKOM—the Israel Engagement Network and adjunct faculty at the Hebrew University's Melton Centre for Jewish Education. He lectures widely in his fields of interest and research—Contemporary Jewry and Experiential Education.

Yonatan Ariel has taught in academia, public school, adult education, and in educational travel settings, and has accumulated leadership experience as the Deputy Director of the Mandel Leadership Institute, Executive Director for Program of the United Jewish Israel Appeal, Director of Melitz's International Department and Education Director of the Israel Experience. He has published monographs, essays and articles in various journals that explore aspects of the linkages between liberal ethnicity, education and leadership.

Dr. Ami Bouganim

Dr. Ami Bouganim is currently Strategic Consultant for the Department of Jewish Zionist Education of the Jewish Agency and Director of its Research and Development Unit. He has served as strategic planner to the Mandel School for Educational Leadership, as the Director of the Jerusalem Fellows and as Educational Director of the Alliance Israélite Universelle in charge of its schools in France, Morocco, Israel and in Europe. He has extensive research and consultancy experience in professional development projects, in the Jewish Agency, as well as the French and Israeli Education systems.

Dr. Bouganim has written extensively on issues of Jewish education and identity. His recent publications include: *Sites & Sources—The Book of Israel*, and *Sites & Sources—The Book of Jerusalem,* he edited the bilingual publication, *Minds Across Israel* and contributed to *Levinas and Education: At the Intersection of Faith and Reason.*

Prof. Arnold Eisen

Arnold M. Eisen is the current Chancellor of the Jewish Theological Seminary of America (2007) and was previously Professor of Religious Studies at Stanford University. He is a frequent speaker before lay and scholarly audiences throughout North America on issues related to contemporary Jewish life, and an active participant in communal discussions addressing the future of American Judaism. His research and teaching focus on the transformation of Judaism in the modern West, against the backdrop of secularization and modernization.

Professor Eisen is the author of *The Chosen People in America; Galut: Modern Jewish Reflection on Homelessness and Homecoming; Rethinking Modern Judaism: Ritual, Commandment, Community;* and co-author of *The Jew Within: Self, Family and Community in America.*

Rabbi Laura Geller

Rabbi Laura Geller is Senior Rabbi of Temple Emanuel in Beverly Hills, California and the first woman to lead a major metropolitan synagogue since 1994. She is a Trustee on the Board of Brown University, on the Board of Governors of the Hebrew Union College, and the founding chair of the Beverly Hills Human Relations Commission.

Rabbi Geller has taught at the University of Judaism, the University of Southern California, the Wexner Fellows Program, and the Wexner Heritage Foundation. She has served as scholar-in-residence for many synagogues, federations, and Jewish Community Centers around the country.

She has received many distinguished honors for cultural harmony, professional achievement, and Women's recognition awards. Her articles on Jewish feminism have appeared in Tikkun, Sh'ma, Reform Judaism, and other journals. She has contributed to several books, including *Beginning Anew, Four Centuries of Jewish Women's Spirituality; On Being a Jewish Feminist; The Jewish Woman; Spinning a Sacred Yarn; and Gender and Judaism*, and has written Torah commentaries for Torah Aura and Torat Haim. Rabbi Geller graduated from Brown University in 1971; in 1976, she became the third woman rabbi to be ordained, at Hebrew Union College.

Dr. Michal Govrin

Michal Govrin is a writer, poet and theater director, and lectures at The School of Visual Theater in Jerusalem. She has published eight works of poetry and fiction, including, *The Name (HaShem*, 1995), the novel for which she was awarded the Kugel Literary prize in Israel; the English translation (1998) was nominated for the Koret Jewish Book Award. Govrin's other books include *Hold on to the Sun, Stories and Legends* (1984), three books of poetry, *That Very Hour* (1981), *That Night's Seder* (1989), and *Words' Bodies* (1991), all largely anthologized in Hebrew and several other languages. Michal Govrin's most recent novel, *Hevzekim [Snapshots]* (2002), was the recipient of the 2003 Akum Prize for the Book of the Year, and has been published in English translation (2007).

Her prose poetry, *The Making of the Sea: a Chronicle of Interpretation* (2000), was published with original etchings of the great Israeli painter, Liliane Klapish. *Body of Prayer*, by David Shapiro, Michal Govrin and Jacques Derrida, was published recently at The Cooper Union School of Architecture in New York. Among her internationally published essays are *The Journey to Poland; The Case of the Jewish Biography; Martyrs or Survivors—Thoughts on the Mythic Dimension of the Story War*. In April and May 2002, an exhibit of etchings, drawings, drafts and the final lay-out was held in Jerusalem's prestigious artists' center, Mishkenot Sha'ananim.

Michal Govrin holds a Ph.D. in Jewish Ritual and Theater from the University of Paris.

Prof. Moshe Halbertal

Prof. Moshe Halbertal teaches Philosophy and Jewish Thought at the Hebrew University of Jerusalem. He was visiting professor at Harvard Law School and a Fellow at the Society of Fellows, Harvard University.

His publications in English include *Idolatry* (co-authored by Prof. Avishai Margalit) and most recently, *People of the Book* (Harvard University Press). In 1999, Prof. Halbertal was the first recipient of the newly instituted Bruno Prize, established by the Rothschild Foundation. Parallel to the highly coveted MacArthur prize in the United States, it enables promising scholars to dedicate three years to their research.

163

Alan Hoffmann

Alan Hoffman is the current Director General of the Jewish Agency's Department for Jewish Zionist Education. Since his aliyah from South Africa in 1967, Alan Hoffmann has dedicated his professional life to promoting Jewish Education, initially as the director of *Hadassah Youth Activities in Israel*. Following three years of graduate study at the Harvard School of Education, he spent 13 years at the *Melton Centre for Jewish Education in the Diaspora* at the Hebrew University, including six years as its Director. More recently, Mr Hoffmann served as the Executive Director of the *Council for Initiatives in Jewish Education* (CIJE) in New York; in 1997, he was appointed the head of the *Mandel Center for Jewish Continuity* at the Hebrew University.

In February 2000, Alan Hoffmann assumed his current position as Director General of the Education Department. Under his leadership, the Education Department is playing a critical role in developing and launching new initiatives to intensify the unique and multi-dimensional significance of Israel in connecting the next generation of Jews to their heritage, people and homeland. Through these initiatives, the Department is identifying and meeting local educational needs in the Former Soviet Union, Latin America, North America, Europe and many other communities around the world.

Dr. Ezra Kopelowitz

Ezra Kopelowitz is a sociologist specializing in Israel-Diaspora relations and issues of Jewish identity, education and religion in Israel and the United States. He is the founder and CEO of Research Success Technologies Ltd. (http://www.researchsuccess.com), a Jerusalem venture specializing in Internet systems for data management, communication and evaluation. He also acts as consultant to the Research and Development Unit of the Department of Jewish Zionist Education of the Jewish Agency.

Ezra Kopelowitz lectures on issues addressing Jewish community, education and strategic thinking at the Mandel Institute for Educational Leadership, in Jerusalem. From 2000–2003, Dr. Kopelowitz served as Director of the Research Activities of the Department of Jewish Education of the Jewish Agency for Israel and as a Fellow at the Institute for Advanced Studies at the Hebrew University, in 2004.

Prof. Riv-Ellen Prell

Riv-Ellen Prell, an anthropologist, is Professor and Chairperson of American Studies at the University of Minnesota and teaches in the Department of Women's Studies and at the Center for Judaic Studies. She is the editor of Perspectives: the newsletter of the Association for Jewish Studies, serves on the Board of Directors of the Association for Jewish Studies, and is founder and co-curator of the Counter Cultural archive of the American Jewish Historical Society. She is also on the academic advisory boards of: the Center for Jewish History; the American Jewish Historical Society; the Jewish Women's Archive; the Brandeis-Hadassah Center, and others. She has also taught about American Jewish life in Jewish communities throughout North America and consulted for a variety of Jewish organizations, museums and filmmakers.

Professor Prell has conducted both historical and ethnographic research and writes about twentieth and twenty-first century American Jewish culture. She is the author of: *Fighting to Become Americans: Jews, Gender and the Anxiety of Assimilation; and Prayer and Community: the Havurah in American Judaism*. She is editor of the forthcoming *Women Transforming American Jewish Life*, and the co-editor of *Interpreting Women's*

Lives: Personal Narratives and Feminist Theory. She has written more than sixty articles, essays and reviews. She is currently working on a book about American Jewish youth culture in the decades immediately following World War II.

Menachem Revivi

For the past twenty-five years, Menachem Revivi has been a leader in Israeli and Jewish Communal affairs and is recognized for his expertise in the areas of Jewish education and Israel-Diaspora relations. Most recently, he was the Director of the North American Region Mission for the Jewish Agency and Education Delegate to North America. Prior to his shlichut to New York, Mr. Revivi was Founding Director of the United Israel Office of the UJC, a position he held for eight years.

Menachem Revivi served as a community shaliach in Bergen County, and later became the Youth and Hechalutz Department Representative (World Zionist Organization / Jewish Agency) to the United Kingdom. Mr. Revivi was subsequently appointed Director General of the Youth and Hechalutz Department, a position he held for eight years. Mr. Revivi has held the positions of Director of the Division of Human Resource Development for the senior civil service in Israel, under the aegis of the American Jewish Joint Distribution Committee (JDC) and Executive Director for the World Confederation of Jewish Communities.

Menachem Revivi received his BA in psychology and sociology from Bar Ilan University in Israel and his master's degree in educational psychology from New York University.

Prof. Michael Rosenak

Michael Rosenak's field is the Philosophy of Jewish Education. He is Mandel Professor (emeritus) at the Melton Center for Jewish Education of the Hebrew University,and is resident scholar at the Jerusalem Fellows program at the Mandel School for Educational Leadership. He has lectured widely on issues in Jewish education, thought and identity. Professor Rosenak has been associated with Melitz (Centers for Jewish Zionist education) and The Pardes Institute from their inception, and serves on the boards of both the Lifshitz and the Ephrata Academic Colleges Teachers.

Professor Rosenak has written numerous articles on issues in Jewish education; his books include: *Commandments and Concerns* (1987), *Roads to the Palace* (1995), *Tzarich Iyyun (On Second Thought)* (5763), and *Tree of Knowledge, Tree of Life* (2003).

Professor Rosenak came on aliyah in 1957 and lives in Jerusalem.

Prof. Shmuel Trigano

Shmuel Trigano is Professor of Sociology of Politics and Religion at Paris Nanterre University, founding Director of the College des Etudes Juives (Paris) and of the European Journal of Jewish Studies, *Pardès*.

He also writes extensively on the subject of Jewish Peoplehood. Titles include:

Books: *Philosophie de la Loi, l'origine de la politique dans la Tora,* Paris, Le Cerf, 1992; *La demeure oubliée, Genèse religieuse du politique* (1982, 1994); *La République et les Juifs* (1982); *L'idéal démocratique à l'épreuve de la Shoa* (1999); *L'ébranlement d'Israël; Philosophie de l'histoire juive* (2002); *Les frontières d'Auschwitz* (2004).

Articles: "La fonction lévitique," in Frank Alvarez-Péreyre (ed.), *Le politique et le religieux* (1995); "The French Revolution and the Jews," in *Modern Judaism* 10 (1990); "From Individual to Collectivity: the Rebirth of the 'Jewish Nation in France'," in F. Malino et B. Wasserstein (ed.), *The Jews in Modern France*, (1985); "Le concept de communauté comme catégorie de définition du judaïsme français," in *Archives Européennes de Sociologie* (XXXV—1994).

Prof. Michael Walzer

Michael Walzer is a philosopher of Society, Politics, and Ethics currently holding the position of Professor at the Institute for Advanced Study in Princeton, New Jersey. He has written on a wide range of topics, including social criticism, toleration, political obligation, and most recently, the Jewish political tradition.

Beyond his academic work, Professor Walzer acts as editor-in-chief of *Dissent*, an American left-wing magazine and is a contributing editor to *The New Republic*. He is also on the Editorial Board of the academic journal *Philosophy & Public Affairs*. To date, he has published over thirty five articles in scholarly journals. He is a member of several philosophical organizations, including the American Philosophical Society.

INDEX

Printed in the United States
204823BV00002B/28-30/P